GW00726941

Legacies of our fathers

EDITED BY CAROLYN NEWMAN

World War II prisoners of the Japanese —
their sons and daughters tell their stories

For
Joan Kwek
(1952–1998)

and

all former prisoners of the Japanese
and their families

Lothian Books
An imprint of Time Warner Book Group Australia
132 Albert Road, South Melbourne, Victoria 3205
www.lothian.com.au

Copyright © Carolyn Newman 2005

First published 2005
Reprinted 2006

All rights reserved. No part of this publication may be reproduced, stored in a
retrieval system or transmitted in any form by any means without the prior
permission of the copyright owner. Enquiries should be made to the publisher.

National Library of Australia
Cataloguing-in-Publication data:

Newman, Carolyn.
  Legacies of our fathers.

  ISBN 0 7344 0877 3.

  1. World War, 1939–1945 – Prisoners and prisons, Japanese.
  2. Prisoners of war – Australia – Family relationships. 3.
  Prisoners of war – Asia, Southeastern – Family
  relationships. 4. Families of prisoners of war – Australia.
  5. World War, 1939-1945 - Psychological aspects. I.
  Title.

940.547252

Cover and text design by Leonie Stott
Typeset by Leonie Stott in 11.5/14 pt Granjon Roman
Cover image courtesy the O'Brien family
Map by Keith Mitchell
Printed in Australia by Griffin Press

Contents

Our Stories

Acknowledgements

First and foremost, my thanks to everyone who has shared their story: Robyn Arvier, Suzette Boddington, Ethnee Brooks, Sue Byrne, Carol Cooper, Fran de Groen, Di Elliott, Margaret Gee, Ron Gilchrist, Angie Gunn, Jacqui Hickson, Joan Kwek, David Matthews, Elizabeth Moore, Pauline Morgan (who wrote two stories), Kerin Mosiere, Paddy O'Brien, Peter O'Donnell, Peter Sinfield, Diana Vallance, Jack Waterford and Claire Woods.

My thanks also to the 8th Division Signals veterans who welcomed me so warmly into their 'family' after my meeting at the Australian War Memorial and who were so keen to help me with my own research. Russ Ewin and Harry Fletcher have both been particularly generous with their time and others from the Sigs family have sent me their autobiographies, letters and memorabilia — all of which have helped to 'fill in the gaps'.

Most importantly, the Kweks — Hong, Ellen, Perrin and Leon — have permitted me to publish Joan's wonderful essay, the basis for this collection. Joan's parents, Hugh and Del Waring, have provided not only numerous meals and valuable support but much food for thought. Diana and Ray Vallance, Joan's sister and brother-in-law, have also expended considerable time and energy on my behalf.

Doug and Yvonne Phillips generously invited me to stay in their home and Doug's widow, Yvonne, has permitted me to quote from her father-in-law's diary.

Robyn Arvier, Russ Ewin, Dr Eric Fisk, Margaret Gee and Professor Hank Nelson, have all permitted me to reproduce extracts from their published work.

I am most grateful to the Australian War Memorial for providing the location for so many of my most fruitful meetings and also for permission to reproduce images from the Memorial collection.

Dr Fran de Groen, Di Elliott and Dr John Moremon have provided both practical and moral support throughout the project.

Lastly, my thanks to John and Michael, who have always encouraged me and who have left me to work in peace while they go off to sea.

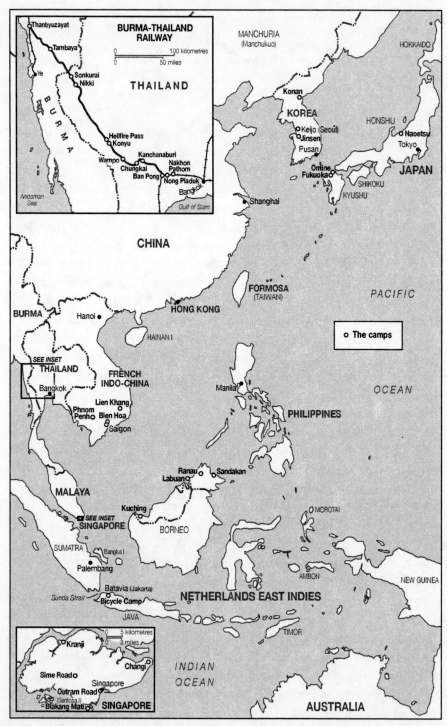

* The spellings used on this map have been standardised throughout the stories.

The Beginnings

In March 1996 I was at the Australian War Memorial in Canberra when, quite by chance, I met some veterans from my father's wartime unit, 8th Division Signals. Here were men — just a few — who had known my father more than fifty years ago and who, quite possibly, had known him better than I did.

My father was one of the thousands of Australians imprisoned by the Japanese during World War II. After he returned to Australia, he met and married my mother and together they settled down to renovate an old house in the Adelaide foothills. My father survived his incarceration but not his liberation. Nine years after he returned from the war, he was killed in a traffic accident in Adelaide.

I had always known that he had been a prisoner of war, but as I grew up he and his experiences became so remote that it was not something I dwelt on. My chance meeting with the veterans from his unit prompted me to look for him again.

During my search for information about my father's war years, I met numerous other sons and daughters of former prisoners. They all had their own stories to tell and some of them have been prepared to share those stories.

These are the experiences of the sons and daughters of just a handful of the men who were incarcerated by the Japanese during World War II. They reveal the diversity of our fathers' experiences and of our own lives.

These are the legacies of our fathers.

Carolyn Newman

The Camps

After the wave of Japanese victories during the early months of 1942, thousands of Allied prisoners of war (POWs) were placed in camps around South-East Asia. Having realised the huge potential of their captive 'workforce', and the potential danger of having such a large group of prisoners together in one camp, the Japanese soon began to transport the men to different areas in their newly captured territories. Large numbers of POWs were sent off in work parties to Borneo, Burma, Thailand, Korea, Japan and Vietnam, where they built airfields and railways and worked in coalmines and in shipyards.

Many of the POWs were transported by rail and sea in appalling conditions, with scant supplies of food and water. Crude toilet facilities exacerbated their already rampant bowel diseases. A significant factor in the high casualty rate of Australian prisoners was the number who died as a result of Allied submarine attacks on the unmarked Japanese convoys in which they were transported.

In the work camps the sick and malnourished POWs were forced into hard labour for long hours. Thousands of the starving, exhausted men died of malaria, beri-beri, dysentery, meningitis, tropical ulcers and cholera, and in the colder camps, pneumonia and other cold-climate diseases. Some were executed after trying to escape; many others died as a result of the brutality of the camp guards. Only two-thirds of more than 22,000 Australian POWs survived to return to Australia.

Three and a half years after the Allied surrender in Singapore, the Japanese capitulated to the Allies on 15 August 1945. Naval vessels poised ready to collect the POWs at points around South-East Asia were ordered to stay put. There were to be no local surrenders or liberation of POWs until after General Douglas MacArthur, Supreme Commander of the Allied forces in the South-West Pacific, had presided at the official surrender ceremony on board USS *Missouri* in Tokyo Bay on 2 September.

Thus, many POWs and civilian internees remained in their camps awaiting liberation for up to a month after the August surrender, albeit sustained by airdrops of medical supplies and food into their camps. Once rescued, they were moved to specially organised reception centres to recover their health, to be 'fattened up' and to be prepared for their return to Australia.

Changi, Singapore

The largest group of Allied POWs was captured when the Allies surrendered in Singapore on 15 February 1942. Thousands of POWs, including about 15,000 Australians, almost all from the 8th Division Australian Imperial Force (AIF), were taken to Changi, the former British garrison in the north-east of the island. Once in Changi the Australians occupied Selarang Barracks and settled into a routine. In contrast to many of the other camps, most of the prisoners at Changi were able to avoid regular contact with the Japanese. Although subjected to the already well-documented deprivations of POWs, the men at Changi nevertheless managed to develop a workable infrastructure for day-to-day life: a prison hospital, vegetable gardens, a poultry farm, a yeast factory (for the manufacture of vitamin B), educational and hobby classes, and medical and dental facilities.

AWM 116541

RECENTLY LIBERATED AUSTRALIAN POWs WITH THEIR HOMEMADE COOKING POTS OUTSIDE THE COOKHOUSE, CHANGI, SEPTEMBER 1945

In May 1942, the Japanese started to disperse the prisoners. A Force was sent to Burma and then in July B Force left for Sandakan in Borneo. Later in August 1942, the POWs in Japan Parties A and B were dispatched to camps in Korea, Japan and Manchuria. More work parties left Changi in 1943 and other groups were transported back and forth between camps during the next three and a half years. Some POWs, like Captain George McLoughlin (2/18th Battalion) and Sergeant Jack O'Donnell (2/10th Australian General Hospital), spent much or all of their POW years in Changi.

Burma-Thailand Railway

The 3000 Australians of A Force left Singapore for Burma on 15 May 1942, under the command of Brigadier Arthur Varley. Among the 8th Division POWs were Lance Corporal Bob Gilchrist (2/10th Ordnance Field Park), Sergeant Fred Howe (2/19th Battalion) and Major Charles O'Brien (2/18th Battalion). The men were crammed into the holds of two transport ships. They suffered from seasickness, diarrhoea and dysentery, and if they could make it to the deck, they may have defecated or vomited into the rough, wooden box toilets hung over the sides of the transports. They arrived in southern Burma some days later and were put to work building roads and an airfield.

In October 1942, after the airfield was completed, the officers and men in A Force were moved again. They were taken by ship, rail and road to Thanbyuzayat in the north to start work on the railway, which, when completed, would enable the Japanese to transport men and supplies more than 400 kilometres from Thanbyuzayat in Burma to Nong Pladuk in Thailand.

Also in October, Black Force and Williams Force arrived from Java. Among the POWs seconded to Williams Force to work on the railway was Able Seaman Allan Gee, one of the men who survived the sinking of HMAS *Perth* in the Sunda Strait early in the morning of 1 March 1942. Able Seaman Gee with other *Perth* survivors had spent seven months imprisoned in the Bicycle Camp in Batavia (Jakarta). Various other groups of POWs were transported from Singapore to Thailand. In April 1943, British POW Lance Corporal William Smith (Royal Norfolk Regiment) and Captain Colin Juttner (2/9th Field Ambulance) came by rail from Singapore with F Force. These 7000 men (including more than 3500 Australians) were dispersed

AWM P00406.034

<small>AUSTRALIAN AND BRITISH POWs IN 'A' FORCE LAY SECTIONS
OF THE RAILWAY AT RONSI, BURMA, 1943</small>

and marched from Ban Pong, hundreds of kilometres, to the work camps
in the centre of the railway line. In May 1943, Private John Waterford
(2/18th Battalion) joined more than 650 other Australians in H Force who
were sent by rail to Thailand.

There are many published accounts that document the appalling
conditions on the Burma-Thailand Railway. By the middle of 1943,
Australians were the third largest group of POWs, with more than 13,000
in work camps in Burma and Thailand. By the time the railway was
completed on 16 October 1943, nearly 3000 of them had died. Most of the
survivors were returned to Changi but some hundreds remained working
at the railway and, like Able Seaman Allan Gee and Sergeant Fred Howe,
were liberated from there at the end of the war.

As with all the camps, many variables affected the POWs' chances of
survival: the conditions in the different camps, the personalities of their
captors, the work they were forced to do. Officers were not expected to
work on the railway and POW statistics reveal the imbalance between the
death rates of the officers and the men.

Despite the differences in their fathers' experiences, the accounts of
these 'railway' sons and daughters are linked with the common thread of
their fathers' ill health and, for Carol Cooper, her father's (Lance Corporal
William Smith) death.

Sandakan camp and Lintang Barracks, Borneo

On 7 July 1942, the first of more than 2500 British and Australian POWs left Singapore for Sandakan on the north-east coast of Borneo. The first group, B Force, was crammed into the hold of an ancient tramp steamer, the *Ube Maru*, arriving at Sandakan eleven days later. The next group, E Force, joined them during early 1943. Some prisoners also arrived from Java. The men had no idea that they were going to build an airfield for the Japanese. They had been promised 'a land of milk and honey with plenty of food' and many of them had volunteered to join the first party.

At Sandakan, officers were also sent out on work parties to the airfield. During the remainder of 1942, life was 'bearable' but in 1943, there was a change in the prisoners' conditions when new Formosan guards arrived at the camp. Then on 17 July 1943, the Allied underground network was betrayed. The consequences were shocking. Captain Lionel Matthews, MC (8th Division Signals), was executed for his role in establishing and directing the network. Dr James Taylor, the principal medical officer in British North Borneo, and his wife Celia were also involved. Together with a group of other Sandakan residents, they had also taken enormous risks smuggling valuable information, medical supplies, radio parts and money through the underground to the POW camp. Those implicated in the movement, both POWs and local men, including Dr Taylor, were subjected to horrific torture, moved to Kuching and put on trial. Captain Matthews and some of the local residents were sentenced to death. Dr Taylor and the other men involved in the underground were moved to the infamous Outram Road gaol in Singapore to serve their sentences. His wife Celia was sent to Kuching, where she spent the remainder of the war in the Lintang camp.

Determined to squash any future resistance the Japanese tightened their security and discipline at the Sandakan camp. In October 1943, they suddenly removed all but eight of the officers from the camp and transported them hundreds of kilometres to Kuching, on the south-west coast of Borneo. The officers were not allowed any farewells and they heard nothing more of the men left at Sandakan until after the Japanese surrender in August 1945.

The POWs who remained at Sandakan after the discovery of the underground network were subjected to ever-harsher conditions. Their health and diet deteriorated and in January 1945 their Japanese rice issue stopped altogether. After that they were forced to rely on stores they had

AWM 118601

Inside one of the POW quarters at Lintang Barracks, Kuching, Borneo, 1945

accumulated. Fearing an Allied invasion in Borneo, their captors moved groups of the 'fittest' POWs further west to Ranau on the infamous 'death marches'. In May, the Japanese evacuated the Sandakan camp and incinerated the buildings. Those prisoners who were not fit enough to march were left to die in the burnt-out ruins. Only six Australians who escaped from the marches or from Ranau survived to return to Australia.[1] Without them we may never have known the fate of the more than 1700 Australian POWs who died in Borneo.

Among the officers who were moved to Kuching were Captain Maurie Arvier (2/10th Field Regiment); Lieutenant Russ Ewin (8th Division Signals); Captain Ken Mosher (2/18th Battalion); Lieutenant Victor Sinfield (2/18th Battalion); Lieutenant Hugh Waring (8th Division Headquarters) and Captain Stanley Woods MC (2/10th Ordnance Field Park). Ironically, following their liberation, their departure from Kuching on 15 September 1945 was also the date of their scheduled execution. The Kuching camp commandant, Colonel Suga, had received orders to dispose of all his prisoners — men, women and children. Instead, the newly liberated POWs were taken from Kuching to the 2/5th Australian General Hospital on Morotai in the Netherlands East Indies, (now Indonesia), for assessment and treatment. One month later they arrived in Australia in the hospital ship *Wanganella*.

9

Keijo, Jinsen and Konan camps, Korea

On 18 August 1942, Japan Party B with some 900 British POWs and about 90 Australians left Singapore in a small tramp steamer, the *Fukai Maru*. The men were part of a party of around 1300 British and Australian POWs that had originally all been loaded onto the same steamer. However, the more than 300 senior Allied officers also loaded into the vessel complained of the congestion on board and the Japanese removed them (Japan Party A) to another vessel. These senior officers were eventually imprisoned in Manchuria where they remained until their liberation.

By the time the *Fukai Maru* reached Formosa (Taiwan) on 29 August, 40 per cent of the men were sick and one POW was suffering from diphtheria. They remained in Formosa until 15 September and finally arrived at Pusan in South Korea seven days later. In Pusan the POWs were paraded through streets lined with Koreans, carrying their kits in the hot sun to the station. From there they travelled by train to Keijo (Seoul). On 25 September 1942, 400 British and about 60 Australian POWs, including Captain Wilf Fawcett (8th Division Signals) and Sergeant Geoff de Groen (2/19th Battalion) were marched into Keijo camp, a propaganda camp used to demonstrate POW conditions to visiting International Red Cross representatives. The remainder of the Australians including Corporal Alex

COURTESY CAROLYN NEWMAN

POWs LOADING CARROTS IN THE OFFICERS' VEGETABLE GARDEN AT KEIJO, 15 JULY 1944.
WILF FAWCETT CAN BE SEEN ON THE FAR RIGHT OF THE PHOTOGRAPH.

Johnstone (2/18th Battalion) were sent to Jinsen. Some of the men from the *Fukai Maru* were dispersed to Konan, Manchuria and Japan during the final two and a half years of their imprisonment.

POWs in Keijo and Jinsen camps spent their first six weeks learning Japanese military drill. Having transported them from Changi, it seems that their captors were unsure how best to use them for propaganda purposes. Eventually various tasks were found for them but as well as excavating roads and railway embankments, some of the men were put to work unpicking knots in ropes or repairing Japanese uniforms.[2] Despite their constant hunger and the below freezing winters in these camps, many of the POWs felt that their trip from Singapore on the *Fukai Maru* had been the worst part of their ordeal in Japan Party B.[3]

In September 1945, American troops liberated POWs in the Keijo and Jinsen camps, while Russian troops liberated the men at Konan.

Naoetsu, Omine and Fukuoka camps, Japan

A number of parties of POWs were transported to Japan between 1942 and 1945. Some went straight from Changi or Java but many others were transported during 1944, after they had worked on the Burma-Thailand Railway or in other camps. A number of the 10,000 Allied POWs who died

AWM P00142.001

CHRISTMAS IN NAOETSU POW CAMP, 25 DECEMBER 1944.
HENRY SWEET'S SLEEPING QUARTERS WERE IN THE HUT AT THE REAR.

when their unmarked transports were sunk by Allied attacks, died during these voyages. In Japan the POWs worked in coalmines, copper mines, factories, shipyards, unloading coal ships and any other menial jobs the Japanese could use them to do.

Conditions in the Japanese camps varied — some were also propaganda camps with slightly 'better' conditions — but the bitter winter cold put further pressure on the malnourished bodies of the POWs. More than 3000 Australian POWs were in Japan by 1945,[4] among them, Signalmen Henry Sweet and Hilton Morgan (both from 8th Division Signals).

Coming home

All but two of the POWs whose stories are told here survived the Japanese prison camps. They returned from camp experiences that were as diverse as their post-war lives would become. Some returned to their pre-war homes, wives and children, while others started completely new lives and families. Now, their sons and daughters continue their fathers' stories.

COURTESY ROBYN ARVIER

RECENTLY LIBERATED POWs LINE THE RAILS OF THE *WANGANELLA* AT THE NEW FARM WHARF IN BRISBANE, 11 OCTOBER 1945

Our Stories

—

My Father's Diary

CAROL COOPER

Lance Corporal William Smith (5777563)
6th Battalion, Royal Norfolk Regiment
POW: Changi; Burma-Thailand Railway

In October 1941, William Smith left his wife and two young daughters in Great Yarmouth on the most easterly point of East Anglia in England and sailed with his regiment to defend the British Empire in the Far East. Less than four months later he was a POW, captured during the Allied surrender of Singapore on 15 February 1942. In April 1943 William Smith was one of approximately 3300 British prisoners sent with F Force to work on the Burma-Thailand Railway. The conditions were shocking and by April 1944 more than 2000 of the British prisoners were dead, including Carol's father. William Smith died on 17 December 1943.[1]

Carol Cooper was two years old when her 26-year-old father left home to fight in World War II. Although she never 'knew' her father, the extraordinary discovery of his diary and her own journey prompted her, in 1997, to set up the organisation, Children and Families of the Far East Prisoners of War (COFEPOW). Since the discovery of her father's diary, Carol has made several trips to Thailand and the Far East. She has visited her father's grave in the war cemetery at Thanbyuzayat in Burma during two of those trips.

Carol has been tireless in her efforts to pursue the story of the POW experience. The COFEPOW membership continues to grow and its website provides a forum for sons and daughters of Allied POWs around the world. Despite the British government's consistent refusal to help with funding, Carol's own fund-raising, donations from COFEPOW members, and a grant from Lottery Funds have raised nearly £450,000 for the new Far East Prisoners of War Memorial Building in Shropshire.

Carol is also writing about her father's experiences but her energetic commitment to completing the FEPOW Memorial Building has meant that her own book has been put on hold. Not only has she made a huge personal journey, but, through her efforts, she has enabled many others to do the same.

Friday, 16 December 1994, began as any other day. However, it was to be a day that was to completely alter my life in so many ways that it is difficult now to imagine what it would be like to revert back to 'the days before the diary'. It was the day that my husband discovered an article in our local paper about a diary that had just been auctioned in Hull, a diary written by a local soldier during his two and a half years in a Japanese prison camp. My husband passed the paper to me.

I read the name and address of the soldier and realised, with a tremendous shock, that I was reading about my father. He had gone away

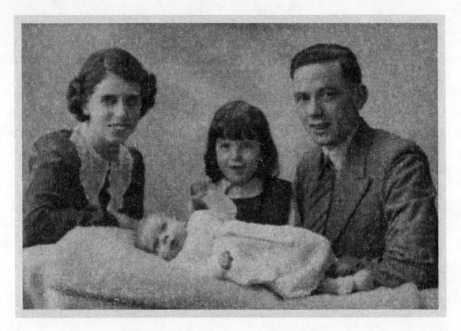

IDA, OLIVE, WILLIAM AND BABY CAROL, 1939

when I was two years old and had never returned. The article gave his name: Lance Corporal William Smith, and the address where I was born in 1939: No. 13, Row 11, Great Yarmouth. The article mentioned my mother and sister who were both dead, but I knew neither of them ever knew the diary existed. All they had known was that he died in a Japanese prison camp and was buried in Burma.

My first thought was that this diary should have been returned to my mother. Then it would now be mine. None of Father's personal belongings had been returned to her and I had nothing tangible of his — until now. I set about making phone calls, the first of many in my efforts to gain possession of my father's diary. Even then I had no idea of the tremendous impact all of this was to have on my future.

I traced the new owner of the diary, but he refused to sell it, choosing instead to hand it over to the Royal Norfolk Regimental Museum. I didn't even see it. I sought legal advice, but was told that my father's diary had been bought legally at an auction and there was nothing I could do about it.

Thus began a two-year battle to gain ownership of something I truly believed should be mine. Fortunately the Regimental Museum staff were very sympathetic and sent me a transcribed copy of what my father had written. Reading this copy was a traumatic experience. He and my mother shared the same birthday and he had started the diary on 28 October 1941, their twenty-sixth birthdays. It was the day he had left England. The whole diary was written as a letter to my mother, with many moving and loving poems. Despite what he was going through, he always remembered our birthdays with a loving word and prayed and dreamed of coming home.

But he never came home. I wept when I read of his determination to stay alive. To the very end he was so sure that, although so many were dying all around him, *he* was going to make it, *he* was going to come back. He was starving, he was very ill, his few clothes were filthy, but he still managed to write in the diary: 'Don't worry Ida darling, I'm coming back to you one day'. The last entry in the diary was 8 December 1943, when he wrote, 'having another bad attack of malaria'. He was then in a camp called Tambaya in Burma. He died nine days later on 17 December. I was to learn later that he had died of malaria, malnutrition, diphtheria and cardiac beri-beri.

My early childhood memories are of nights spent in air raid shelters, as German planes bombed the eastern regions very heavily on their way towards London. On one such night, the small house where my mother and father lived was completely demolished. My mother lost everything except for a few personal belongings she had with her. We were then forced to live in a house that had been partly bombed — the roof was missing, but we lived in the two lower rooms. In spite of this I can only remember a happy childhood. We were very poor, but so was everyone else. I had no father, but then most fathers were away and we did not ask why. My mother was the youngest of a large family and I had many aunts and a dear Uncle Wally, her brother, who brought us small gifts, including a pair of white rabbit skin mittens which I have never forgotten. My mother had been a machinist before her marriage and now my aunts would give her the odd cast-off dress and she would take it to pieces and make us a pinafore dress. I do not recall my father being spoken about very much, although later I found my mother had received two cards from him, much the same as every prisoner had sent, stating he was well.

But in October 1945 my mother discovered she was a widow. I remember the day very well. I was at school when the headmistress came in and said I was to go with her. I was terrified — what had I done wrong? Outside in the hall, one of my aunts was waiting and, standing me on a nearby large trunk, she put my coat on. I asked where I was going and remember her reply: 'Your mummy needs you'. I recall entering our house and seeing my mother sitting on the old wooden chair in front of the cooking range; she was crying. My grandmother and another aunt were there and one of them lifted me up onto her lap. My grandmother told me, 'Mummy is crying because your daddy will not be coming home any more'. The enormity of her words was lost on a five-year-old, who didn't know who or what 'daddy' was.

My mother cried a lot after that day. She became very ill and, although she was already a petite person, her weight dropped and she became extremely thin. Looking back we were terribly poor but I can never remember ever being cold or hungry: I think my mother went without food so we could eat. She also became very superstitious. She said it had been a tradition in her family that when a man went off to war they always said their goodbyes at home, never at the station where it was considered bad luck. My mother had taken no notice of this 'rubbish' and went with my father when he left. Out of all her brothers and brothers-in-law (thirteen in total) who went to the war, my father was the only one who never returned. She never forgot that.

I have no memories of my father. I wish I had. Most of all I wish I could remember the sound of his voice. In retrospect there is so much I should have asked my mother, but I learned at an early age that any reminder of him used to upset her very much. Vera Lynn singing 'We'll meet again' would cause my mother to leave the room in tears. Birthdays and Christmas were usually difficult times, when she would lock herself in her room. I didn't understand and asked her once why she did this. She just replied: 'When you grow up and meet someone you love, you will understand'.

I am ashamed to say that I grew up without thinking too much about my father: I never grieved for someone I never knew. Later in life when the subject ever came up, I would say quite casually, 'My father died during the war'. There was no sadness or sorrow, the words meant very little.

It was not until after my mother's death in 1993, when I was sorting through her personal effects, that it really came home to me how very little I knew of the man who had fathered me. I came across a box containing letters, photographs, poems and the documentation she had received from the War Office. There were two letters from my father after he left home for the last time, one from Bombay and the last from Malaya, written just a few days before his capture. At the bottom he had written, 'Give my love to my Olive and my baby Carol'. I wept. These words were from a father I didn't know and it was now too late. It may sound strange, but I think I was meant to discover the diary and through my father's words find out what kind of person he was.

Reading the copy of the diary in 1996 I was able, finally, to answer a question that had puzzled my mother until the day she died. In 1943 she had received notification that he was a prisoner in Singapore and she believed that was where he remained. In 1945 she learned of his death and that he was buried in Burma. But believing him to still be in Singapore, she could not understand why he had been buried a thousand miles away in Burma. She always thought that it was a mistake and that one day he would come home. The diary would have told her so much she never knew or understood: that he was sent from Singapore in April 1943 with the ill-fated F Force into Burma. She would also have had the comfort of his loving poems and it is tragic that she never saw the diary.

Now knowing so much more about my father strengthened my resolve to one day gain possession of the original diary. About eighteen months later, I had a stroke of luck that was to set off another series of remarkable events. My endless letter-writing had brought the conflict of the diary to the attention of a BBC producer, Dick Meadows. He rang me and asked if he could come over and talk about the diary. I was so excited, I thought that if I could get a little bit of media attention then someone out there might have the answer to this endless task of trying to obtain the diary.

He spent the whole afternoon asking questions about me and my parents, looking at the copy of the diary, old photographs and letters. I was speechless when he said he wanted to make a documentary about my father. And not only that. He wanted to take me to Thailand and Burma to retrace his steps as a POW and to visit his grave. All I had wanted was my father's diary and now I was going to visit his grave.

We commenced filming the documentary in August 1996, dramatising my struggle to gain ownership of the diary. In due course, Dick Meadows went to interview the person who had bought it and shortly after that he relented. I paid him £300 for my father's diary and it was worth every penny. Just prior to leaving for Thailand on 8 November 1996, Dick Meadows brought the diary to my house and later millions of BBC viewers were to see a very tearful me receiving and holding my father's diary for the first time.

Filming in Thailand along the route of the infamous 'Death Railway' was to prove an emotional and unforgettable experience. Standing in Hell-fire Pass where 700 men died of brutality in a few short weeks, brought choking tears. There were more tears again when early one day, I climbed into one of the original metal trucks which had transported hundreds of prisoners from Singapore to Ban Pong in Thailand.

My father had written in the diary of travelling in these trucks for five days: thirty men to a truck and going for thirty-six hours without food or water. But at 8.30 in the morning, the sides and roof were already very hot to touch and it was not hard to imagine what it must have been like at midday.

By chance we met an Australian, Doug Ogden, who like myself, was also retracing his father's footsteps. By an amazing coincidence his father had been in the same camps as mine. He had died at Sonkurai near the Burma border and was buried in the same cemetery as my father. Dick invited him to join us and we were filmed talking together, sitting on a bench near Hellfire Pass. As we talked, Doug was overcome with emotion and started to cry. I put my arms around him and we just sat and hugged each other. Viewers around the world witnessed that moment. It brought tears to everyone's eyes and forged a special bond between the two of us.

AWM NEG. 157866

THE BADLY VENTILATED RAILWAY WAGONS IN WHICH POWS WERE TRANSPORTED FROM SINGAPORE TO THE BURMA–THAILAND RAILWAY, C. 1945

But the whole journey from Kanchanaburi to the Three Pagoda Pass, on the Burma border, was one of emotion, passing through camps like Nikki where my father wrote: 'It seems like it will never end, but one must keep smiling and eating the rice. I pray to God that it won't be long now, over 2000 have died so far since we left Changi'.

One of the most moving occasions during my trip was visiting the Chungkai and Kanchanaburi Commonwealth War cemeteries. Walking through the larger Kanchanaburi cemetery under a scorching sun and weaving between thousands of small, neat headstones brought home to me the whole dreadful fate of the Far East POWs. They had all been so young, mostly between twenty and twenty-eight years of age. But for me the real tragedy lay in the knowledge that not one of the 7000 men lying here had died in a battle. Not one had been given the chance to fight for his life. They had been ordered to surrender and all died in captivity — prisoners, dying of starvation, brutality, slavery, dreadful tropical diseases, malaria, diphtheria, dysentery, cholera, beri-beri and terrible leg ulcers.

Standing in the hot sun, I cried for their suffering. I felt a dreadful injustice when I realised that nowhere along the length of the railway had I seen a memorial, a plaque or a stone from the British government, honouring the thousands of British servicemen who had died there. The cemeteries were beautifully kept, but I felt that my father and all those who suffered deserved a more fitting tribute.

The saddest moment of the whole journey was when we tried to enter Burma: the BBC was refused entry. Because of a flare-up of internal political problems, and even though the BBC only wanted to film in the Thanbyuzayat War Cemetery, the Burmese government refused to allow any foreign media into their country. This was a bitter blow and a huge disappointment for both Dick Meadows and myself and we had no option but to turn back. But Doug was an Australian travelling alone and he was allowed to enter Burma and visit the cemetery, although still at some risk to his personal safety. We were all terribly worried about him, but some two or three weeks later I received some beautiful photographs of my father's grave and one of Doug placing some flowers on it. Bless him.

The documentary *The Diary* was first shown in the Eastern Regions and then on national TV on 12 August 1997. After it was shown, I received many kind letters from people, from children and families who had also lost someone in the Far East. I also received many books: books written by the ex-POWs themselves, books on their experiences, their suffering and their three and a half years of hell. These books endorsed all that I had learnt in Thailand and more.

After the visit to Thailand and the broadcast of the documentary I expected my life to return to normal, to go back to being an ordinary working housewife with a husband, three grown-up children, a house and a garden. But not so. I could not forget the experiences of Thailand and the knowledge of so much misery. Nor could I forget the deep sense of injustice I felt. The uncaring attitude of all British governments, past and present, kept nagging away at me. Why have they refused to acknowledge the suffering and ill treatment of their own servicemen by the Japanese Army?

The formation of COFEPOW

Until the discovery of my father's diary and the visit to Thailand, I am ashamed to admit that I had known only that the Far East prisoners were not treated very well and were poorly fed. The true extent of the treatment of these British men was completely unknown to me and it would appear unknown to many others as well. Why, I often wondered, does everyone know what happened to the Jews in Germany, but so few know of the similar suffering of the Far East POWs?

I started writing letters to the government: 'Why has the government never honoured or paid tribute to the Far East Prisoners of War, servicemen who died for their country?' I went to see my own MP who eventually brought the matter up in the Houses of Parliament. The reply I received was that: 'It is not the policy of the government to erect memorials to servicemen. Any memorials have to come from private fund raising'.

I realised then that there is nowhere in England where one can go to see and learn the story of the Far East POWs. So in August 1997 I put an advertisement in the local newspapers calling for the children and families of Far East Prisoners of War to join me in asking the British government to pay these men the honour they truly deserved.

In November 1997 we formed The Children and Families of the Far East Prisoners of War (COFEPOW) with twenty-five members. Seven years later we had 700 members from all over England, Australia, New Zealand, America, Canada, Borneo, Spain, Taiwan, Switzerland and Norway. A year after being formed, six charity trustees were appointed and COFEPOW became a registered charity. We have the support of many MPs and the help and friendship of the FEPOW associations. We have planted two Trees of Remembrance to our fathers and we have three patrons, Terry Waite,[2] Sir John Baird, a former surgeon general to the Queen and Lieutenant Colonel C.G. Stallard, RA, whose father was a FEPOW padre.

Our ultimate aim is to create a permanent place that will tell the visiting public the full story of this unprecedented chapter in British history. We want future generations to see, learn and never forget. We hope to record the names and ranks of all those sent out there, together with their regiments, battalions, insignias, dates, places, maps, photographs, names of ships, details of the capitulation, prison camps and statistics. We want to embrace the story of their treatment and the thousands who died as a result. We have members whose fathers died on the Burma railway, on the Sandakan death marches in Borneo, in the copper mines in Formosa and in Japan. Other fathers died in Ambon, Haruku,[3] Java, New Guinea and in torpedoed, unmarked ships where survival was impossible because the holds were battened down. We would like to display information panels with an illuminated map of the specific areas in the Far East where the prisoners were held. The Far East Prisoners of War Memorial Building is in oak-framed timber, built off the ground on stilts and with a pitched roof. It has been designed to create the look of a prisoners' long hut. It is set among the trees at the National Memorial Aboretum in Staffordshire and was officially dedicated on 15 August 2005, the sixtieth anniversary of the end of the war in the Far East.

We have never sought compensation or an apology from the Japanese. We simply wanted the British government to acknowledge the suffering of the FEPOWs by helping us to build a lasting memorial in their name. British governments have had sixty years to build a barricade against questions about the Far East: it is a subject they would prefer to forget, but the debt they owe will never go away.

The FEPOWs and other organisations have erected many memorials over the years, but these do not say *why* they have been dedicated to the Far East POWs, nor do they tell their story.

In February 2000, we established an extensive COFEPOW website with many links to other organisations, both here and abroad: <www.cofepow.org.uk>.

Each month the site registers thousands of hits. I spend a great deal of my time now writing and answering letters. People are still searching for the smallest detail of what happened to their fathers or other relations and we try and help in any way we can. Twenty thousand names appear on the Kranji Memorial in Singapore, 20,000 men who have no known grave, and people are still searching for clues as to what became of them.

I work hard and I work long hours for what I believe in. I will always feel guilty that I lived most of my life not knowing how my father suffered and died and never really giving him too much thought. Now he is so often in my thoughts and always in my heart. If I ever have doubts about what I am trying to achieve, I look at his photograph. Then I read the motto on a small bookmark that I took from the hotel near Hellfire Pass and the 'Death Railway'. It says quite simply: 'One step at a time you may walk over the highest mountain'.

COFEPOW took those first steps and now we are almost at the top of the mountain.

My father's grave

On 10 April 2001, I took a group of more than thirty people on a pilgrimage to visit the graves of our POWs in the Far East. We visited Singapore, Borneo and Thailand. There we went to Kanchanaburi where we visited the sites of the POW camps and inched our way over the Wampo viaduct. It is still standing there more than fifty years after the prisoners built it. We held candles at the dawn service on the Australian and New Zealand Anzac Day and we listened to the Last Post. Later that day, in the scorching sun, we attended the remembrance service in the much larger Kanchanaburi cemetery. But on 27 April, when most of our group went home to the UK, five of us flew to Burma, now known as Myanmar. This time, arrangements had been made to take us south to the war cemetery at Thanbyuzayat where my father is buried.

The very rough and bumpy journey took about ten hours over almost non-existent roads. We had to stop at many checkpoints to have our passports inspected, but finally we reached Thanbyuzayat. I stopped at the local market and purchased armfuls of fresh flowers for both my father's grave and others. They probably didn't last long because the heat was intense but it was the first time in my life that I was able to buy something for my father. Only the children of POWs buried in the Far East can understand and feel the pain caused by the knowledge that the fathers that most of them never knew died agonising deaths, all alone, thousands of miles from their families.

Postscript

I found this lovely poem among my mother's papers after her death. My father wrote it to her just after he joined the Army, before he left for overseas. It was written on a very small piece of paper and was in a tiny envelope addressed to his 'Darling Ida'. It reflects what a truly wonderful person he was. My life would have been far, far richer had he lived.

There is no hour that passes by
But some sweet thought of you
Shines like a lamp on high
To light my whole life through.

There is no day, but at its end
My prayers for you I say
That God will guard and keep you
Forever Mine Alone, Darling Ida May.

Caesar's Ghost

ROBYN ARVIER

Captain Astley Chavard (Maurie) Arvier (QX6328)
2/10th Field Regiment, AIF
POW: Changi; Sandakan/Kuching

Maurie Arvier acquired the nickname 'Caesar's Ghost' while he was in the Army. It was the expression he always used when exasperated or annoyed and the nickname stayed with him throughout his life. So it was natural when she published her father's memoirs in 2001 for his daughter Robyn to use that phrase as the book's title: *'Caesar's Ghost!'*.

Maurie was born in Brisbane on 30 May 1919. He first developed an interest in artillery when he joined the Brisbane Grammar School cadet corps. He was a champion rifle-shooter, winning numerous awards with his school rifle club and later with the Brisbane Rifle Club when he represented Queensland in Commonwealth matches. It was not surprising then that, when the 2/10th Field Regiment was formed in July 1940, Maurie eagerly left both the Militia and his clerical position with the AMP Society to become a recruit.

In February 1941, 21-year-old Maurie farewelled his parents and older sister Gabrielle and sailed with the first contingent of 8th Division troops to Malaya on the *Queen Mary*. His regiment's first action against the enemy occurred during the night of 26/27 January 1942 in the Nithsdale rubber plantation, where they supported the 2/18th Battalion in a successful ambush that slowed the Japanese offensive in eastern Malaya.

After the Allied surrender in Singapore on 15 February 1942, Maurie spent four months as a POW in Changi, until he left with B Force for Borneo. At Sandakan, he and the other officers were sent out on work parties and Maurie worked on the construction of the Sandakan airfield. In July 1943, after the Japanese discovered evidence that an underground network was operating, they separated the officers from the men. By the end of October 1943, Maurie and almost all the other officers at Sandakan had been moved to Kuching on the south-west coast of Borneo.

Confined in the barracks at Kuching, the bored and starving men concentrated on surviving — often by developing new or existing skills.[1] Maurie had always had an amateur interest in plants and nature and according to Robyn, 'His little notebooks from his POW days are crammed with details of nutritional values on kang kong, Chekur Manis[2], sweet potato leaf etc ... all plants they grew in Kuching to counter the effects of slow starvation on a diet of polished rice'. Kuching was liberated on 11 September 1945 and a 'very thin and malnourished Maurie' arrived home in Brisbane on board the hospital ship *Wanganella* on 11 October 1945.

Maurie left the AIF, studied agriculture at Queensland University under the Commonwealth Reconstruction Training Scheme and went on to a successful career in agricultural science.[3] He was a new graduate working for the Department of Agriculture and Stock (now the Department of Primary Industries) at Kingaroy in Queensland when he met his wife Alison, a high school teacher in the town. Alison remembers that when she met Maurie he had 'a number of plots laid out in his yard and amongst other things, he was trying to grow rice'.[4] They were married in Brisbane in 1951 and their first son John was born in 1953. Peter arrived in 1954 and Robyn, their daughter, in 1960. According to Robyn, Maurie rarely talked about anything other than the amusing incidents of POW life with his family. He died in 1996, at the age of seventy-seven.

'*Here, taste this,*' *Dad said.*
I took the leaf and chewed hesitantly.
'*It just tastes like leaf,*' *I replied.*
'*That's not just any leaf. That's kang kong.*'[4]
'*What's kang kong?*'
'*It's what kept me alive in Kuching.*'

That conversation with my father, which took place some time during the 1980s, has always stuck in my mind. It was the closest Dad ever came to talking about how desperate the conditions were in Kuching POW camp. Until then, I hadn't realised his chances of survival had been so slim.

As a young child, there were some objects in our house that I didn't really understand and simply took for granted. For instance, there was an old shoebox in a cupboard, labelled 'Letters from Malaya'. For a long time I had no idea where Malaya was, nor was I curious about the contents. And then there was a musty book with an old-fashioned cloth cover — *Borneo Burlesque* — where I could find a sketch of my father looking youthful and serious in a gallery of simple portraits. The other faces were complete strangers.

Dad had some slightly odd habits that my brothers and I accepted without question: for example, he never threw anything out. In his 'workshop' under the house, he had an array of rusty tins, which contained things like mismatched nuts and bolts and little pieces of wire he'd salvaged from

The Arviers, December 1961 (left to right):
Peter, Robyn, Maurie, Alison and John

various places. We used to buy apples by the crate and, after the contents were eaten, Dad would methodically take the wooden crate to pieces, then carefully straighten the used nails, and stack the flat pieces of timber. There was always the explanation: 'You never know when these things might come in handy'.

Any kind of loud noise always made him jump, even if he could see the cause of the commotion — perhaps as trivial as a door about to slam in the wind, or a car backfiring in the street. At teatime, it almost became a joke as we waited for the inevitable scraping of his plate, an action that always drew the comment from Mum, 'You're not in a prisoner of war camp now'. I can remember feeling ashamed that Dad had been in some sort of prison. The 'of war' part of the expression meant nothing to a child who had never known war.

Years later, I began to see the connection between Dad's peculiar habits and his POW experiences. Unlike the small comfortable world I knew, I realised he had once lived under conditions where material resources were virtually non-existent and where every grain of rice counted. No wonder his habit of scraping his plate was entrenched.

Some time in my thirties, I eventually opened the 'Letters from Malaya' shoebox to discover one hundred airmail envelopes containing Dad's correspondence to his parents. They were accounts of his experiences during the twelve months before the catastrophic fall of Singapore. There was also a handful of letters he'd written as a newly liberated POW in Kuching camp and from on board the hospital ship *Wanganella*. It was a box of living history that, needless to say, is now one of my treasured possessions.

Dad was supremely content with the simple pleasures of family life. I never saw him lose his temper. For my brothers and me it was marvellous to have a patient father who could build us cubbyhouses and elaborate sandcastles, and one who also took a keen interest in both our schooling and our schools. There are, for instance, numerous trees he planted that are still growing in the grounds of various kindergartens and schools in Brisbane. He gladly assumed the role of personal debating coach and willingly attended countless sporting and school events.

Dad was an agricultural scientist, so my brothers and I had the benefits of our own personal science teacher during our school years. Dad was genuinely interested in our homework, and never lacked suggestions for school science projects. Studying how quickly a colony of weevils could eat a quantity of rice was one I remember well!

Dad always seemed able to locate technical information for us from his own collection of texts, and every so often he would bring out a battered and well-thumbed book, Lowry and Cavell's *Intermediate Chemistry*, to supplement our more modern school chemistry books. It contained some puzzling loose pages that had columns of oriental characters going one way and, at right angles, miniscule pencilled notes in Dad's handwriting. Only in the last decade did I learn that Dad had brought this book home from the Kuching POW camp 'library'. It was a volume that had provided him with many hours of welcome distraction from his dreary surroundings so, at the time, its value to him was priceless.

He was a knowledgeable and patient teacher on family holidays; my brothers and I learned elementary astronomy at Tugun beach at night. During rainforest walks in Lamington National Park on the Queensland–New South Wales border, we inevitably absorbed a good deal of botanical knowledge from Dad.

Like most young children, we didn't fully appreciate our father's generous help and his caring nature. Only much later did we understand something of the impact of those years of deprivation — why he was always trying to calculate the time from the position of the Southern Cross, and why he was so satisfied with his efforts to grow kang kong in our front garden!

Dad's resourcefulness is a characteristic that I remember well. He could always make do with the most basic of implements and equipment — a knife blade could be an effective screwdriver, a shoe could function as a hammer, and our family well remembers the time Dad made us raincoats from blue banana bunch covers one very wet holiday! I recently came across a photo of Dad on a family picnic where there were obviously more people than folding chairs. He's perched on a little seat that is simply a stout piece of timber placed across two rocks — a typical Maurie Arvier construction!

Dad truly appreciated living in a country that was at peace, a country where we live under our own flag. In his retirement, he installed a flag pole at home and regularly flew the Australian flag. Over time, he gathered a sizeable collection of international flags that he hoisted on relevant national days. A notable omission from his collection was the red and white Japanese 'poached egg' — after three and a half years living under that hated symbol, he clearly had no desire to see it flying outside his own home.

Despite a busy family life, Dad made a point of staying in touch with his Army friends, especially those who had shared his POW experiences. Marching in the Anzac Day parade was important for him, as was attending the Singapore Day Memorial Service in Brisbane each year. He travelled to Sydney as often as possible for the reunions of Old Sandakians — those officers who were moved from Sandakan to Kuching POW camp in 1943, and met regularly to commemorate the momentous day when, as free men, they 'sailed down the river to the sea'. He would usually come home chuckling over the funny anecdotes of Army and POW life that seemed to be the principal topics of conversation at those events.

Although I'll never fully comprehend the profound effect those POW years had on Dad's life, I'm happy to think that he left me with some positive and lasting legacies from his experiences. I know that he unconsciously taught me to better appreciate those things so often taken for granted, food on the table and a roof over my head.

But perhaps best of all, he gave me the foundations and material for an entire book. He had started a memoir, and didn't begrudge me gathering up his notes when he couldn't continue the work himself. 'Caesar's Ghost!' Maurie Arvier's Story of War, Captivity and Survival is Dad's own story, told in his words, for the generations of Arviers to come.

If Only I Had Understood

DI ELLIOTT

Sergeant Frederick (Fred) Howe (NX35481)
2/19th Battalion, AIF
POW: Changi; Burma-Thailand Railway

When he enlisted for service at Boorowa on 1 June 1940, Fred Howe was working as a telephone linesman. He and his wife Elsie had four children, aged between one and eleven years, two children having predeceased him. He joined the 2/19th Battalion and was posted to their Signals platoon.

Fred's battalion was one of the first to engage with the Japanese in the famous battle of Muar on 18–22 January 1942 at

Bakri, Muar and Parit Sulong, on the Malay Peninsula. The battle almost decimated the unit and ended even more tragically when they were unable to carry their wounded with them. Forced to make a rapid retreat, they left behind 110 wounded Australians and 35 wounded Indians at Parit Sulong. The Japanese massacred all but two of the men left behind.

Fred Howe and the other 2/19th Battalion survivors became POWs after the Allied surrender in Singapore. On 15 October 1942 he sailed on the *Celebes Maru* with A Force to Burma, where he worked on many projects for the Japanese, but in particular, on the Burma-Thailand Railway. He remained there on maintenance gangs until the end of the war. After he was liberated he recuperated in both Thailand and Singapore. He arrived back in Australia on 20 October 1945 on board the New Zealand hospital ship *Tamaroa*. Di, his seventh child, was born after his return.

I first met Di Elliott in January 1999 in the new Second World War Gallery at the Australian War Memorial (AWM). It was only at a second meeting, some months later, that I realised why her name seemed so familiar to me. In 1997 she had written to *Vic Eddy*, the official journal of the 8th Division Signals Association (NSW), requesting donations of books she could take with her to Thailand to donate to the new Hellfire Pass museum. She and her husband Paul were going to visit their daughter Meredith who was working at the Australian Embassy in Bangkok. While they were there they planned to attend the Anzac Day dawn service in Hellfire Pass and to visit many of the places which had become familiar to Di through her own research. Unfortunately Di, Paul and Meredith were involved in a serious traffic accident during that visit and both Di and Paul had to undergo surgery necessitated by the accident for some time afterwards. Di continued with her research projects despite her injuries.

Di Elliott's interest in her father's war service and imprisonment has dominated her life since 1995. Recently she has been instrumental in researching and editing the 2/19th Battalion's unit history for republication. Her absorption in the unit's history has made her an important resource for many 2/19th families and she has spent incalculable hours in the Research Centre at the War Memorial researching details for them. Di doesn't receive a cent for this; all her work is voluntary. She is also a volunteer in the Memorials Research Centre, helping people to locate service records on the public databases. She has become a focus and source of support for many of the offspring of POWs, some of whom have been desperate to discuss their own experiences with someone who understands. Di regularly visits 2/19th veterans either in hospital or at home, sometimes travelling hundreds of kilometres to do so. Her enthusiasm and energy for her projects are daunting.

DI WITH HER FATHER ON HER WEDDING DAY IN BOOROWA, JANUARY 1970

My father died in 1975, aged sixty-nine, but it was not until 1995, the year in which the Australian government commemorated the fiftieth anniversary of the end of World War II with 'Australia Remembers', a program of commemorative events and services both in Australia and overseas, that I really began to understand him. I attended two memorial services in Thailand on Anzac Day that year: the dawn service in Hellfire Pass and the main Anzac Day service in the Kanchanaburi War Cemetery.

I cannot recall exactly when I had first learned where Dad had been during the war but I do know it was many years after his death. As a child I remember him marching on Anzac Day and getting drunk afterwards, so I knew he had been to the war. I also knew it had something to do with Japan because Mum would not allow anything 'Made in Japan' into our home. Dad had also taught me to count in Japanese but that was about the extent of my knowledge. In 1994 I made my mind up to learn all I could about this part of his life and I hoped that the information would help me to understand aspects of my own life.

My very early memories of my dad are of his heated arguments with my mother. I do not recall any physical violence but the raised voices were certainly very threatening to a young girl. I also recall his heavy drinking which, in most instances, led to the arguments. I then recall him not drinking at all and being very irate with anyone who did drink. This in turn caused a lot of friction with my brother who was drinking heavily at this stage. He, unfortunately, was violent and this was very traumatic for me. Dad blamed himself for my brother's problems. I recall him saying that it was all because he was not there for my brother at a crucial time in his life: he was at the war. My brother's problems never resolved themselves and he eventually committed suicide.

Dad mostly went to work, as he wasn't the sort of person to easily take a 'sickie' but I do remember him being always very ill and moody. There were many times when he would lock himself in his bedroom and I was forbidden to go near him. Mum told me that it was his malaria back again. You would not know from one day to the next how to approach him. What you would say one day would be fine but say it the next day and all hell would break loose. He never wanted us to have people around the house when he was there. He wanted his home, and us, all to himself. If anyone called in unexpectedly he would disappear to the shed. When his mood was at its worst, he would take the fishing line and disappear until well after dark.

His health problems mostly seemed to be intestinal conditions. He had a couple of operations for this but it always seemed to be there. I recall how ill he was about a year before he died and the look of embarrassment on his face when my mother used to try and care for him. He suffered from horrendous haemorrhoids and the doctors didn't seem to be of any help in this matter. He always had diarrhoea and on a lot of occasions he didn't make it out of his bed to the toilet. This was when my mum took over. I never once recall her complaining about the work she had to do and a lot of it was not pleasant. As a matter of fact, I don't ever recall her complaining, no matter what he did. I guess she understood it all.

This is where my pain comes in, if only I had understood. Since late 1994, the things I have learnt and the people to whom I have spoken have helped me get to know my dad as a completely different person from the one I thought I had known. To me he was just a cranky old bastard who, for some reason, was always sick and miserable. Our lives seemed to be disrupted so often because of him and I always wondered why I had to be the only one with a miserable old father.

For the last three years that I lived at home, I worked for our local doctor. I do not remember my dad coming to the doctor very often in those days and I often wonder if it was because he didn't want me knowing what his problems were. It is most likely that he visited the doctor in Crookwell where he worked for those three years. Maybe this had an effect on Dad not getting a better pension from what was then the Repatriation Department. Not having continuity with one doctor may have made a difference. I always thought the doctor I worked for was to blame for Dad's poor treatment from the Department but maybe it was my fault that Dad didn't open up to the doctor who could have helped him.

In recent years, the men who worked for him have told me of their utmost respect for him and how they appreciated being able to work with him. They have also told me that at times he would be so sick at work that he would have to spend some time lying down in the lunchroom. We knew none of this at home: Dad lived away from home for the last few years of his working life and only returned at the weekend. He wanted to retire on a higher superannuation so he and Mum could do a lot of the things they had not had the chance to do. Sadly he was forced to retire early because of his ill health and they were unable to do those things anyway.

I have met and talked with the men he served with in the gallant 2/19th Battalion, AIF, and one actually wrote a book a few years back in which he mentions my dad on several occasions. What a treasure that book is to me. I have spent ten years reading all I can about POWs of the Japanese, in particular, those who slaved on the Burma-Thai Railway, and I have met and now claim many of these men as my very special friends. These men have a quality not found in others.

I will admit that when thinking back to my dad, at times I can recall this quality in him too, but I was too focused those days on his moods and illnesses. I can recall an amazing gentleness and a faraway look in his pale blue eyes and this I have seen in other ex-POWs. They have an understanding of themselves, of life and of priorities that none of us will ever have. They have a unique understanding of each other and they share a very special bond: they have been to hell and back together.

When I first began to realise what my dad had been through as a POW working on the Burma-Thai 'Death Railway', I knew this was something so enormous that I would probably spend the rest of my life learning about it. Back in 1948 Dad had written twenty-seven weekly articles for our home-town country newspaper and my sister obtained copies of them from the Mitchell Library in Sydney.[1] They were the beginning of my search but even reading his articles didn't really help me to comprehend what it was all about.

In 1994 I read my first book about the Burma-Thailand Railway, Hugh Clarke's *A Life for Every Sleeper*. My journey began through this book. From this book and my dad's articles, I worked out that he must have been on what was called A Force. The book mentioned Tom Morris from Canberra, also a member of A Force. Would I be able to find him? Would he want to meet with me? Would he want to talk about his ordeal? Well, I made one phone call and all the answers were 'Yes'.

I arrived on Tom's doorstep with a bunch of flowers and a million questions. I was shaking so much it is a wonder the flowers had any heads left on them. Tom was so generous and actually lent me a copy of his personal story about his time as a soldier and as a POW. (Since then, Tom and his family have been very special to me and I was devastated when Tom died on 25 June 2003, having rung me that very night to say goodbye.) He suggested books to read and that was the beginning of my personal library, a library that now has over 300 books about the war in the Pacific and in particular, prisoners of war. I've made three trips to the Burma-Thailand Railway and am about to make a fourth, and so far I have walked about 12 kilometres of the old trace. I've also spent two weeks in Singapore, tracing the battle areas there, mostly on foot. I also plan to visit the site of the Battle of Muar on the mainland of Malaya (now Malaysia) when a proposed memorial is dedicated at Parit Sulong in memory of those who died there in the massacre.

I have met dozens of former POWs and their families, not all are ex-railway. They include men who were POWs in Japan, Singapore, Borneo and Indochina (now Vietnam). They have related their experiences to me, both good and bad. They do not elaborate too much on the bad.

Walking the areas of the railway has been a very emotional experience for me. I have been in the company of the men who worked there during those walks and I have found myself imagining that it is my dad talking to me of his experiences. How I envied my friends whose dads were relating their experiences. If only it could have been my dad telling me. How I wish we could go back and I could tell my dad that now I understand. I was not always the daughter my dear old dad deserved. I could have been more patient with him and forgiven all the things about him that I didn't like much. I could have even loved him more — if only I had understood.

Why was it, and in some cases is it, that we were not told their story? Did they want to protect us or was it their way of protecting themselves? We hear now that they were told to come home and forget what happened to them and their mates and get on with their lives. Their families were told when they did come home not to ask them any questions about what might have happened to them.

What I also don't understand is why my brothers and sisters, who were all born before the war, didn't talk to me about that time in their lives either. I was not born until three years after Dad came home so I was totally in the dark. Did my brothers and sisters not know much either or did they block that part of their lives out? In recent years when I have thought I had found something out about Dad and related it to my sister I have been told, 'Yes, I knew that'. Well, why didn't you tell me? I guess I didn't ask.

My brother who was only one year of age when Dad went to war has recently spoken to me of his memories of Dad's return home. Then aged seven, he was terrified of this 'person' who was coming into his life for what felt like the first time. When he saw him alight from the train he was most relived to see he just looked like any other man.

I came upon a stumbling block at the very beginning of my search to learn about my father. When I talked about going to Thailand for the first time, my brother-in-law was most upset.[2] He phoned me one day and abused and accused me for half an hour. He had also been a POW in Changi and then in Japan. He said I was only going to Thailand for a holiday, it would mean absolutely nothing to me, and that I would come home from there and in two weeks time, forget what I had seen and not understand what it was all about anyway.

I was devastated. I seriously considered not going at all, mainly for the sake of peace in the family. Then I thought 'No'. I know why I am doing this; he is quite wrong. Damn it, I was going, even if it meant he never spoke to me again. Well he almost didn't speak to me again. The silent treatment lasted for about twelve months until he learned that we were then going to Singapore to trace some more of the story. To my surprise he rang me and said, 'You are serious about learning about your father aren't you?' My answer was a positive 'Yes'.

From that day in 1995 until my brother-in-law died in 1999, every time I spoke to him I was told more of his wartime history, which also included stories about my dad, as at times they had worked closely together during the battle. He also related things to me about my father after the war and the effect being a POW had had on both of them. He especially felt sorry for Dad following their return to Australia. My brother-in-law was living in Sydney where there was a facility for ex-POWs to visit during times of difficulties in coping with being back home. There they could meet men in the same situation and talk. But for Dad, living in a very small country town, this facility didn't exist and it is felt this was the reason he tried to solve his problems with alcohol.

I went to Thailand twice in 1997. On the second trip in April we witnessed the turning of a sod to mark the commencement of the building of a memorial museum at Hellfire Pass. It was built to commemorate all POWs and native labourers who worked on the Burma-Thailand Railway. In 1987 a memorial plaque was unveiled in the cutting. This was mainly due to the efforts of Tom Morris who had been to Thailand in both 1983 and 1984 searching for this area of the railway. He had remembered it vividly when the war had ended and he had come through it on the way out of the jungle. After locating this area Tom came home to Australia and lobbied the government for funds to ensure this area would be preserved as a memorial. Tom's original idea was a most significant one as the area is now recognised as a focal point for survivors, their families and friends. This then prompted the Australian government to make it more prominent by erecting a museum there.

My chance to do something in memory of my dad and all those who worked there came when it was proposed to include a library in the museum. I already knew all the good secondhand bookshops that stocked relevant titles and I also contacted newspapers throughout Australia, who helped by publishing articles about my search for books. I managed to get approximately a hundred books for the library and it is pleasing to know that others, including many people from the UK, have donated about 200 more.

Sadly I did not get back there for Anzac Day 1998 when our prime minister officially opened the museum. While still in Thailand in 1997, my husband, daughter and I sustained serious injuries in a motor vehicle accident. We spent two weeks in hospital in Kanchanaburi undergoing the first of several surgeries. I spent two weeks there in Intensive Care and experienced some incredible things. The hospital is close to what remains in operation of the Burma-Thailand Railway. On many occasions I lay in that bed drawing from the strength of my dad and those other incredible POWs who had toiled there fifty-four years previously. As I struggled to survive myself, I concluded many of them had come home after suffering far more horrendous conditions than I was suffering.

I was in a modern hospital with modern drugs, plenty of food and the most caring doctors and nursing staff one could wish for. The only thing that I and the POWs had in common was the care we received. They too had amazing doctors and medical orderlies who took such care with their patients when practically all they had to offer were their healing hands. I am convinced to this day that when I was at my lowest point I received assistance from some forces more powerful than any medicine. I certainly felt a presence there that helped get me back to Australia. After many more weeks in hospital in Canberra and five more operations between us, we still have problems but our spirits are higher than ever.

During all our trials and tribulations you can guess who gave us all the words of encouragement and strength we needed to see us through the rough times, those wonderful caring and compassionate ex-POWs. I could repeat many stories they wrote or told me about different POW mates with conditions similar to ours who came out the other side of it all. On many occasions these men gave me a reason to get myself out of bed. I had so many letters and cards to reply to — they never let me slacken off and give up.

I would do anything I can to thank these men, not just for their help to me when I needed it, but for the life we are all privileged to live today. We live in freedom and we live in the best country in the world. We can be proud that here in Australia, unlike in Britain, our ex-POWs have been well cared for in recent years. Before that though, help for ex-POWs and families was also poor here.

I have often wondered why, in later years, Dad didn't go to the Anzac Day service and dinner. Maybe he didn't want to remember or have anyone remind him of that time in his life. Maybe he was afraid he might start drinking again. Maybe he just felt too ill. I do remember the last Anzac Day that he was alive. He got out of his sick bed, went to the march and the dinner and got drunk. When he got home he went straight to his bedroom and we didn't see him until next morning. Could he have realised it would be his last Anzac Day and so went all out for his finale?

Mum always worked hard on Anzac Day. She was a member of the Boorowa RSL Ladies Auxiliary and they always catered for the dinner. Those veterans who were too ill to attend the dinner always had their dinner delivered to them and once I had my driving licence, I would take Mum to deliver these meals around the town. I felt very proud doing this for my mum and the men. Mum worked for the RSL Auxiliary for many years and always held one or other of the committee positions. She would go off to each annual meeting saying this was her last year and she would not be taking on any more official positions but she would always come home wearing either the secretary or president's badge. Dad would always give her a ribbing about this. After decades of this work Mum was awarded life membership of the RSL and she was extremely proud of the honour.

Dad was also honoured when he retired in 1971 from the PMG (Postmaster General's) Department. He was awarded the Imperial Service Medal for his faithful service to the Commonwealth. It was a proud day when we went to Government House for his investiture.

There are things I can remember about my father that I do not want to write about. Maybe like the men, I feel that some things are best left in the past. Like them too, I try not to dwell on the bad, just skim over it and instead try to remember some of the nicer or funnier things that happened. I prefer to remember with pride what my dad did for his country and at the same time, remember and honour all his fellow countrymen who did the same. Let us never forget these men who became prisoners of the Japanese for they have shown us what true mateship, spirit and courage are all about. God rest the souls of those who didn't come home and of those who have died since. Let's show all those who are still with us that we will make sure, even after they have gone, that 'We Will Remember Them'.

The Burden at the Other End

PAULINE MORGAN

Sergeant Frederick Howe (NX35481)
2/19th Battalion, AIF
POW: Changi; Burma-Thailand Railway

Pauline Morgan was nine years old when her father sailed to Singapore with the 8th Division, and already a teenager by the time her father returned from the war. In contrast, her younger sister Di grew up with a father who was a returned POW. Thus, Pauline Morgan's and Di Elliott's stories reflect their different memories of life with Fred, their father. In 1950, Pauline married a former POW she had first met when she was fourteen years old — her father's close friend, Hilton Morgan.

We were very proud when Dad joined the Army but of course we did not foresee the possibility of being without a father for almost five years. I was a child when World War II began and I did not understand the seriousness of it — the other side of the world was so far away. I can vaguely remember Mum being very worried when Japan attacked Malaya and everyone was told of all sorts of rumours.

Although Singapore had fallen on 15 February 1942, it was a long time before information became available. It was not until 11 October 1943 that Mum was informed that Dad was confirmed as a POW. We received only three letters from Dad between 1943 and 1945.

We had plenty of family support in Dad's absence: we lived next door to my grandmother and aunt and saw our uncle regularly. As we grew older we became more aware of the uncertainties, even though we were still too young to understand the terrible burden our mother was carrying on her own. With four children to feed and clothe, she struggled to make ends meet, not knowing whether her husband was dead or alive. She would also have known how he was suffering as he worried about us. In 1941 he had sent her this poem he had written for her in Malaya:

> *As we progress along the weary way*
> *Which duty calls upon us to defend*
> *Our thoughts will ever of you fondly stray*
> *Who face the burden at the other end.*
> *And smiling bravely await the news each day*
> *For little crumbs of comfort God may send.*
> *With a smile you cover all your hopes and fears*
> *And children's needs will occupy your mind*
> *Although your eyes will often fill with tears*
> *For the one who heard the call to all mankind*
> *To oust the foe who would your freedom take*
> *We had to leave you for the future's sake*
> *When the last great battle has been won*
> *And peace forever has been nobly earned*
> *His thoughts will end just where his life began*
> *At home with you where faith in him has burned*
> *And each night he repeats this little prayer*
> *That God will keep you in his tender care.*

Little did he know when he wrote that poem that his great battle for survival would be against the conditions on the 'Death Railway'.

Sometime during these war years the Army arrived in town to conduct a mock war against the local Volunteer Defence Corps (VDC), using flour bombs. I can remember a lot of white dustings. And, as children, we were always aware when the military police were in town chasing Army deserters. I also remember that when I was about twelve I was ejected from the local picture theatre for booing the Japanese emperor in a newsreel. My uncle sorted that one out with the theatre manager.

Finally came 15 August 1945 and the war was over. There was great jubilation and expectation of hearing about our father but it wasn't until 13 September that Mum was informed that Dad was alive. With hindsight I realise that those twenty-nine days must have seemed like years for Mum and everyone else who was waiting for news. I remember the local telegram boy, a friend, delayed the delivery of the telegram for a few minutes so he could bring it to Mum in his lunch hour and share the good news with her.

Dad arrived at Ingleburn on 19 October 1945 after travelling from Singapore on the ship *Tamaroa*.[1] Mum travelled to Sydney to meet him. When they came home, he seemed like a stranger to us and we had to get to know him again. I guess he also had to make many adjustments to family life after living like a slave for three and a half years.

During the next six months before his discharge from the Army, Dad travelled back and forth for health checks at Concord Hospital, then known as Yaralla. His sight had suffered while he was a POW and I can still remember the boxes of Vegemite/Marmite he brought home. If he had consumed all he was given he would have spent all day eating it, so we were given the task of helping him. After Dad was discharged from the Army he went back to his pre-war employment as a telephone linesman with the Postmaster General's Department (now Telstra).

I left home five years later but between 1945 and 1950 I witnessed many incidents with Dad's drinking bouts and the arguments they caused with Mum. However, there was only one occasion when I saw him push Mum away. Dad did not share his trauma and I realised in later years that the drinking probably dulled his memories of all those dreadful days and atrocities. There was no counselling for these men and women and certainly no preparation for what the families could expect. No one but a POW can express the feelings bottled up inside and it took many years before they could express them. This made it very hard for us — one day our behaviour would be accepted and the next day we would be in trouble for being too cheeky.

Dad's ill health never really left him and in 1960 he was admitted to St Vincent's Hospital in Sydney to have portions of his badly ulcerated stomach removed. The surgeons who operated suggested that he should claim some benefit from the Repatriation Department, as it was obviously a result of his time as a POW. He wouldn't do it as he had just had a long battle with Repat over them paying for his glasses. I guess he felt he didn't have the strength for another fight with them.

(LEFT TO RIGHT) ELSIE AND FRED HOWE WITH ELSIE'S SISTER DORIS RILES ON THE DAY OF
FRED'S RETURN TO BOOROWA IN OCTOBER 1945. THE 'WELCOME HOME' FLAGS ON THE
ARCH OVER THE GATE HAD BEEN MADE BY HIS CHILDREN PAULINE, JOAN, JOHN AND NICKY.

I do remember one incident that reignited his hatred of the Japanese.
His home town held an annual Gaytime festival (not to be confused with
the gay Mardi Gras) which raised money for charity. Each year they invited
a dignitary to open the festival and this particular year the Japanese ambas-
sador was coming from Canberra. The committee decided it would be a
'nice touch' to fly the Japanese flag at the local hall. To Dad that was intoler-
able and he threatened to tear it down. He said that he didn't suffer three
and a half years of incarceration to have the Japanese flag flown in his home
town. When he was threatened with police action he replied, 'Go ahead, it
will make nice reading in the *Truth* newspaper on Sunday when I report it'.
Needless to say, the flag wasn't flown. If Dad believed he was right, he
never backed down.

Eventually his ill health forced him to retire. When he was well
enough, he loved to visit members of the family. By now we had scattered

to various parts of the state and my brother was in Queensland. Dad would also indulge himself by spending hours in his beloved garden. He grew the most wonderful flowers and bulbs, as well as a large vegetable garden.

He was a tolerant grandfather, always willing to listen. My youngest daughter was very talkative and she used to sit with him and chatter away. In his later years he seemed to have put his demons to rest and to be at peace with himself. I don't think anyone who has not undergone this ordeal can understand the torture inflicted on minds and bodies. Dad described it this way in one of his stories:

To bring this story to a conclusion, I would like to add a word about the unbreakable bond of fellowship, which exists whenever one meets one of his fellow-prisoners. To have been comrades in adversity the like of which, unless experienced personally, is beyond most people's understanding. It has so linked us together that one would go far out of his way to help another who showed any signs of being in distress.

My dad died on 7 August 1975. Colonel Anderson, who had been the commanding officer of the 2/19th Battalion, gave the valedictory at his funeral. I can always remember the haunting notes of the Last Post at the cemetery and the bugler, a friend of Dad's, with tears running down his face.

A Blessing and a Burden

MARGARET GEE

Able Seaman Allan Howard Gee (21440)
HMAS Perth
POW: Bicycle Camp, Java; Burma-Thailand Railway

Allan Gee was born on 10 October 1919 at Beechworth in northern Victoria.

During World War II he served in the RAN in HMAS
Perth and first saw action in the Mediterranean. HMAS *Perth*
returned to convoy escort duties in local waters in August 1941
and was sunk in the Sunda Strait on the night of 28 February–
1 March 1942. Of *Perth's* complement of almost 700 personnel,
more than half (including her captain, Hec Waller) were lost in

action. Most of the men who survived the action were picked up by the Japanese or managed to make their own way ashore. All, including Allan Gee, became POWs. Of these survivors, more than 100 died during captivity from illness, ill treatment or as a result of Allied action.

Allan Gee, with some of the other *Perth* survivors, was picked up from the water by a Japanese destroyer, transferred to a Japanese transport ship, the *Somedong Maru*, and landed by barges onto a Javanese beach ringed by heavily armed Japanese soldiers. The men spent their first days as POWs in a cinema at Serang before being moved to the Bicycle Camp in Batavia (now Jakarta), the former quarters of the 10th Battalion Bicycle Force of the Netherlands East Indies Army in Java. In October 1942 they were shipped as part of Black Force to Burma via Singapore. Once in Burma, Black Force, which included approximately 1500 Australians, was split into two forces and Allan became part of Williams Force under the command of Lieutenant Colonel Williams, 2/2nd Pioneers.[1] The two groups immediately began working on the Burma-Thailand Railway.

Allan remained in Burma working on various work parties for just under two more years. After his liberation he was flown to Rangoon where he and his friend Able Seaman Percy Partington, two of the fittest of the POWs, waited about three weeks for their turn to be evacuated by the Americans. According to Percy, 'We were among the last of the *Perth* guys to leave. I was alright, and Allan was in reasonably good shape, except for his eyes. I think Allan's bugling and haircutting helped to save his life. He was also young, strong and had a good attitude.'[2] From Rangoon they were flown to Singapore and from there returned to Australia on the Dutch ship *Circassia*, arriving in Melbourne in November 1945.

On 18 March 1946, Allan Gee was discharged from the RAN as medically unfit. He had only 10 per cent of his eyesight and was technically blind. He spent almost six months in Heidelberg Repatriation Hospital in Melbourne where he was 'pumped full of vitamins and food'.[3] According to his family, Allan would have loved to remain in the Navy — it was all he had ever wanted to do and after his treatment he tried again to pass the RAN medical. He was unsuccessful, so instead of the sea he turned to the land.

On 7 September 1946, Allan married Kath at St Matthew's Anglican Cathedral in Albury. Their son Bruce was born in 1947 and, seven years later, Margaret and her twin sister Christine. In 2000, Margaret published her father's story as *A Long Way from Silver Creek*.

Margaret has known her father's ex-POW friends throughout her childhood and, more recently, has become involved with the HMAS *Perth* Association. In 2004 she was invited to be the 'launch lady' for the tenth Anzac frigate *Perth* at Tenix Dockyard in Melbourne. On 20 March 2004, fifty-eight years and two days after her father left the RAN, Margaret Gee launched *Perth*. Both Margaret and her father have travelled *A Long Way from Silver Creek*.

I have an identical twin sister and I am often asked what it is like to be a twin. When considering what it is like being the daughter of a prisoner of war, I realised I faced the same dilemma. 'It is all I know. What would seem stranger is not being one — a twin or the daughter of a POW.' My blunt assessment of both of these *conditions* is that it is a blessing and a burden, bittersweet at worst, and at best, a rare and wondrous privilege.

As I have written in my family memoir, *A Long Way from Silver Creek*, we grew up spending long winters in north-eastern Victoria, crowded around the open fire, with the misty Ray Parkin watercolour of my father's ship HMAS *Perth* in pride of place above the mantlepiece. As a young child I had an even fuzzier view of Dad's wartime experiences. In fact, I was more concerned about the fate of the ship's company's beloved and doomed cat Redlead, than the fate of the crew. I was alerted to Dad's maritime skills when he tied a perfect reef knot to secure a gate on our farm, or if there was a news item about Greece, he would mutter something about the time they were in the Mediterranean slugging it out with the Germans.

However, the references were fairly oblique and totally removed from our day-to-day existence. What was glaringly apparent was that my dad was not like the other kids' fathers, pleasant enough, but rather parochial rural men. Dad used to say about himself, 'I'm a bit odd'. Allan Gee had a worldliness about him, an unspoken something which left us in no doubt that we were being shielded from a much darker story.

That story unravelled as I grew older, and was not fully apparent to me until after his death in 1992. Then I learned of the full extent of his experience of the sinking of *Perth* in Java's Sunda Strait, in late February 1942, and his horrendous years on the infamous Burma-Thailand Railway. Almost half the ship's complement was drowned. My brother Bruce, who is seven years older than my sister and I, had a much broader and more intimate knowledge of Dad's war history.

Allan Gee was also technically blind. When he was discharged from the Navy in 1946 as medically unfit, he had less than 10 per cent of his eyesight, caused by severe dietary deprivation during his time as a POW. His blindness was a dominant factor in our lives. It dictated many aspects of my parents' domestic and farming life. For instance, my mother had to do virtually all the driving, read aloud much of their correspondence, and assisted him with myriad tasks where normal vision was required. But, when she 'dressed up' to go out, he would always tell her how nice she looked.

In spite of his blindness Dad had tenacity and a fierce independence which everyone who knew him admired. He charged around the property on his old Massey Harris tractor, missing gateposts by inches and rattling down hillsides at a frightening pace, virtually without incident. His early farming life and great knowledge of raising animals served him in good stead for his new life after the rigours of war. As he used to say: 'I either had to go onto the land or it would have been digging ditches for the town council for the rest of my life'.

His temperament was another matter. The intense frustration he experienced from his poor sight, and doubtless some demons from the war, sometimes welled up inside him like a simmering volcano until he blew up. The simplest tasks a sighted person could do — hammering in a nail, for instance — would result in Dad exploding. Not averse to a good burst of expletives, he would curse and rage, never at us, usually at the dog or the task at hand. Nevertheless, being around these verbal eruptions was not a pleasant experience.

Dad's saving grace was that he was inevitably filled with remorse about these incidents and would later be gruff and apologetic: 'I'm sorry about this morning, lovey. I get a bit cranky sometimes.'

One thing was certain though, we were never struck. In fact, he sometimes said that the reason we were such wilful children and adults was that we hadn't been belted! He had a volatile temper but he hated the idea of children being beaten, a common enough occurrence in those days. 'I've seen enough bashing by the Japs to last me a lifetime,' he'd say. Apart from a few chooks in an enclosure, he loathed anything being kept in a cage, and had a great love of soaring birds, perhaps a symbol of the freedom once lost.

We felt enormous compassion for him, although at times I'd think, 'Oh dear, he's gone off his rocker again'. When as an adult I bothered to sit down and read more about the true history of the sinking of *Perth*, and his incarceration and ill treatment by the Japanese, I was surprised that he was as sane as he was. I was stunned by the horrific facts as most people are. The squalor, the cruelty, the relentless heat and sickness, and unremitting deaths of their comrades in jungle slave-labour camps. Dad was a bugler in *Perth* and played the Last Post to fallen mates in the camp. Shortly before he died he told me that he buried more than 1500 men during the time he was a POW.

BRUCE, CHRISTINE AND MARGARET GEE WITH THEIR FATHER AT 'LYNDALE', 1958

One significant fact about other POWs' families I have talked with is that they invariably say their father or husband didn't say much about the war. Clichéd as it sounds, the expression I have often heard is, 'No one would ever know what they went through'.

As a youthful sailor I thought my father had film-star looks, and I feel very sad that this gorgeous young man, brimming with life and dreams, was trapped in those hell-holes for over three years.

No wonder that he sometimes blew his top, and looked anguished and desperate. As children my sister and I shared a bedroom opposite my parents and I remember hearing him groaning in his sleep, and moving around during the night. He hardly had a good night's sleep for the balance of his life, except when he was bombed out on sleeping tablets and tranquillisers. As is now routinely acknowledged, the side-effects of these addictive medications caused a whole other dimension to their mental stability.

When they emerged from the Japanese camps as he said, as 'broken men' in their mid-twenties, the expression post-traumatic shock disorder was not in popular usage. 'Shell-shocked', derived from the experience of dealing with survivors of World War I, was usually how their ordeal was summed up. They had fairly minimal psychiatric counselling when they arrived home, were given a swag of pills, and told to get on with their lives. The Repatriation Department and other POW associations were as supportive as they knew how to be, but their knowledge was limited about how to deal with these traumatised young men.

My mother knew from the outset that the man she had fallen in love with at the age of fifteen, and who had unexpectedly returned — he was presumed lost after *Perth* was sunk — in his twenties was a different person to the carefree, fun-loving man she had first known. She was a loving and devoted wife for forty-six years, but there were undeniably some tough times. Dad was riddled with anxiety and the smallest thing — a door slammed or loud music on the radio — would cause him to erupt. She said when they first married he would often walk out of a cinema or an event with no explanation other than 'I want to go'.

My mother Kath died in 1999, but I recall her difficulties dealing with his impatience and perennial anxiety with enormous understanding and forbearance. The wives of other POWs I have spoken to have also described what it was like living with these 'wrecks of men' after the war. But the love and loyalty of these exceptional women kept their, at times, strained marriages intact.

As my mother always said, 'He was different'. Although he had been physically and mentally stretched beyond most normal people's level of endurance, the positive side was that he was very open-minded and accepting of life's challenges and quirks. He had a fantastic and irreverent sense of humour that added considerable joy to our lives, and incensed many of his detractors.

Dad's experience in the Navy and as a POW had certainly catapulted him out of the bucolic but very narrow upbringing he had with his Salvation Army parents and five siblings in Silver Creek. At twenty, he was sailing for London, then off to exotic destinations such as New York, Cape Town and Jamaica. He had a battered photograph album with shots he'd taken on his world travels, and as a little girl I marvelled at these images of natives riding rickshaws, elephants and camels, the Acropolis and the Statue of Liberty. Always a great reader, he was suddenly living out many of his boyhood fantasies of seeing the world, meeting an astonishing mix of people, and enjoying a high level of pleasure and responsibility, a far cry from tending cows and dogs on his parents' small holding.

If I could summarise what he was like as a man I would say he was like someone who had been turned inside out. With my father you were never in any doubt about the way he felt. If he was angry he'd shout and curse. If he was happy he'd beam and laugh and light up the room. His responses were fairly extreme, so he was either marvellous to be around or impossibly difficult. The only time he looked completely peaceful was when he was strolling around their picturesque property Lyndale at Wooragee, or half-asleep in his armchair listening to Nat King Cole or Frank Sinatra.

If I was sick as a child he was spectacularly loving. He'd fling his arms around me, sing songs, bring me boiled eggs and toast in bed, and say something I cherish to this day. 'Lovey, if I could I'd be sick in your place, then you wouldn't have to feel so rotten.' When he lay dying of cancer in the early 1990s, I said the same thing to him.

When I was seven I was yelling out in a dentist's chair and he barged into the surgery, swept me up in his arms and took me home. As an adult if I ever complained about a relationship problem, he'd say, 'If anyone ever hurts you I'll kill them'. I thanked him but said I didn't think he needed to take such drastic action! None of us were ever in any doubt that we were completely loved, and that he would never let us down, and he never did.

Because he had lived out many of his youthful dreams, in spite of the advent of war, he was tremendously encouraging to me, my sister Christine and brother Bruce. He urged us to make something of our lives, to see the world, and 'get away from here' — away from what he regarded as the conservatism and insular aspects of rural life. As a young man prior to the start of the war he hung around with a pretty bohemian crowd of writers, artists and intellectuals, so as a role model for country kids he was very special.

With hindsight I am always surprised at the lack of bitterness and resentment he felt towards the Japanese. If I had been through what he had, I don't know if I would have been as magnanimous as he was: 'Hating never did anything for anybody. No one likes war, killing only leads to more killing.'

He once said he thought that the Japanese were very cruel people, and he added 'to animals as well', but he didn't labour the point. Who can blame him for saying that after his treatment at their hands? Years later when my sister and I went on a cycling holiday to Japan he was delighted. He was extremely warm and hospitable to a Japanese Rotary exchange student who was being hosted by some of our relatives and I recall him saying, 'Yoko's a real sweetheart'.

However, I think the most salient fact about my father is that for the entire time I knew him he was always in *survival* mode. He ate each meal as if it was his last, worried about financial security, and was fearful of many things — mainly due to his lack of sight. He was terrified of snakes because it was difficult for him to see them, was an anxious traveller and had a totally defensive outlook on life. His elder brother Napier's wife, my Auntie Vera, once said to me, 'Allan had a haunted look about him when he came home from the war'. His ebullient smile eclipsed that haunted gaze; at other times he looked as if he had turned to stone.

I always regarded my father as a remarkably brave man, and he subsequently fought the ravages of cancer in his early seventies with great courage and dignity, as did my mother when its evil tentacles enveloped her seven years after his death.

I have covered many of these issues in my own book, but perhaps what is a more problematic question is how did having an ex-POW as a father impact on my life, and my siblings? Were any of his personality traits, his 'baggage' from the war passed on to us, and if so at what cost? The shrinks will say there is no definitive answer to the nature/nurture question in regard to child rearing. I think it is undeniable that he had a significant impact on us, and that as children of a long-term POW we are different too.

Without boring everyone with the flotsam and jetsam of my personal life, or my siblings', I think it would be fair to say that we all inherited a restlessness from him, a quest for inner peace we are probably still striving for. As a young adult I had a relationship with the firstborn son of two Holocaust survivors, and although we didn't discuss being the offspring of POWs in any great detail, I always felt we shared some mutual issues.

My sister and I, in particular, have been almost perversely compulsive travellers and have only in our mid-forties established calmer, more stable personal lives. My brother Bruce roamed the South Pacific for more than a decade, and has had a similar peripatetic private life.

Despite these ups and downs we have always prided ourselves on our unusually close bond to our parents and to each other. There is intensity, an intimacy and loyalty, and yes, like Allan Howard Gee, a fierce sense of independence about us. Indeed, we are very much our father's daughters and son — consummate survivors.

Everyone Was on Their Own

ELIZABETH MOORE

Dr James Taylor, OBE, and Mrs Celia Taylor
Principal Medical Officer, British North Borneo
Civilian internees: Sandakan/Kuching; Outram Road gaol, Singapore

Elizabeth's story is special. Her parents lived at Sandakan in North Borneo where her father was a medical practitioner employed by the British government.[1] Elizabeth lived with them there until early in 1939 when her mother brought her back to Sydney to start her schooling. Her mother stayed with her in Sydney until early in 1941. Despite her husband's plea for her to remain safely in Sydney, Celia Taylor was determined to rejoin her husband and they were together in Sandakan when the Japanese landed there early on the morning of 19 January 1942.

Life for the European residents continued much as usual until May, when most of them were interned in the quarantine station at Berhala Island. Dr and Mrs Taylor, together with the rest of the medical staff, were moved into the hospital grounds but were permitted to continue to work at the hospital. It was during this time that Dr Taylor, with some of the local Chinese, European, Indian and Malay residents, began to smuggle messages, food and medical supplies to the internees at the quarantine station. They also made contact with Filipino guerillas operating under the Americans in the Philippines and so were able to set up the beginnings of the underground movement at Sandakan.[2] Once the Allied troops in B Force arrived from Changi in July 1942, the pace changed and Dr Taylor and his wife ran even greater risks. During the next year they, like others involved in the network, risked their lives by passing messages and supplies back and forth to the POWs. On

17 July 1943, the underground network was betrayed. The Taylors were among the many conspirators rounded up by the Japanese and imprisoned at the local police station in Sandakan. Dr Taylor was subjected to horrific torture and interrogated by the Kempei Tei for three months.[3] After this period Celia Taylor was sent to Kuching camp in south-western Borneo and imprisoned with other civilian internees. Her husband was less fortunate. In October 1943 he and fellow conspirators were handcuffed to the rails of a small coastal steamer, the SS *Subuk*, and transported to Kuching for their trial. The 'mock' trial was held in February 1944. Dr Taylor was sentenced to serve fifteen years and in March 1944 he and a group of the conspirators were sent to the harsh Kempei Tei gaol at Outram Road in Singapore to begin their imprisonment.[4]

Servicemen must inevitably enter a war zone with a certain expectation of hardship, possible death or capture. But what about civilians who have been caught up in the maelstrom of war? Untrained for the rigours of Kempei Tei torture, Dr Taylor, who was not a young man, also had to cope with his separation from his wife. Neither knew where the other had been sent. One imagines that it was at least some small comfort for both of them to know that their precious young daughter was safe in Australia.

How did Elizabeth cope for nearly five years without either of her parents? Josephine Metcalf, an old friend from her schooldays, recently reminded Elizabeth that she remembered her 'as a kid — worried — when I suppose most of us were carefree'.[5] Fortunately Elizabeth was unaware of her parents' circumstances and that they had been separated. She was being well cared for by the staff at the Convent of the Sacred Heart in Rose Bay, as well as spending holidays and weekends with her much-loved aunties Wag and Ange. Elizabeth's friend Josephine also recalled them both sitting in their dressing gowns listening to radio journalist Colin Simpson interviewing her father in Labuan in September 1945: 'I remember his voice as matter-of-fact and flat — not excited at all ... I was just impatient for him to talk to *you*.'[6]

Elizabeth's father had been released from Outram Road

gaol on 19 August and transferred to the Sime Road Internment Camp in Singapore. He was kept in hospital there for nearly a month after the end of the war. Having failed to get news of his wife, Dr Taylor managed to organise a flight to Labuan. He arrived there on 16 September 1945 and Celia arrived from Kuching the next day. The Taylors remained together in Labuan until early November when they sailed for home on the *Merkur*, a Burns Philp vessel.

During the five years they were separated, Elizabeth and her parents were all forced to concentrate on their own survival.

I suppose my life before the war in British North Borneo could be described as idyllic. Some of my most vivid memories at the age of about six were the medical trips into the interior, which my father undertook to see the native population. My mother and I would quite often accompany him on the trips in the government launch up the beautiful Kinabatunga River, stopping at the many villages or travelling out to some of the islands off the coast. When the launch pulled into the sandy beaches on these tropical islands the crew would often catch a turtle and my father would put me on its back. The turtle would waddle back to the water and dive with me astride until finally I slid off. My life was one long adventure.

My father, James Taylor, an Australian medical practitioner, had worked in Borneo since 1922 on rubber plantations and then in government service. In 1930 he came home to Australia on leave, when as fate would have it, he accidentally met up with my mother, who had been his sweetheart in his teenage and university days. After a whirlwind romance they married in Sydney on 1 July 1930 and sailed on their honeymoon back to Borneo on the Burns Philp steamer, SS *Marella*. My father resumed his medical duties in Jesselton, where I was born in April 1931. And so it was that I came to live this idyllic life in a close-knit community of approximately 500 Europeans in a British colonial outpost in the early thirties. I can recall the many French doors opening onto wide, covered verandahs on three sides of our large two-storey house, which was perched on top of a hill over-looking Jesselton harbour. I understand that my mother ran her house with five servants, one of whom was a Chinese *amah*, who was my nurse in my first year or two of life. She was followed by a *dusan babu* (nurse). My every need was catered for. There were other European children to play with in the cool of the late afternoons and birthday parties and fancy dress parties.

In 1935, when I was four, my father took leave. We returned to Australia and I was introduced to relatives I had never seen before. My father bought a Ford car and we did a lot of travelling out to country areas as he was looking for a racehorse to buy for someone back in Borneo. At the end of this leave we, the car and the racehorse were shipped back to Borneo and I resumed my carefree, happy lifestyle.

On our return to Borneo my father became district surgeon and we were relocated to Sandakan, where I was sent to the local Catholic mission school. I don't think I attended too often as my mother and I shared an unspoken conspiracy that life was all too good to be interrupted. Secretly I think my mother was quite happy to have me at home, probably because she knew that in the not too distant future, like all European children living in the colonies, I would have to return to Australia for my education. It was a custom that was traumatic for both children and parents.

In March 1939, when I was eight years old, my mother and I left Borneo and returned to Australia so that she could settle me into the Australian way of life and supervise the commencement of my schooling. Within two years she would return to Borneo to my father.

My mother and I took a flat in Strathfield in New South Wales and I commenced school at Santa Sabina Convent. In September of that year war was declared in Europe and I can remember Mummy and I hearing this dramatic announcement on the radio. I was terrified that this might put Daddy in danger but was reassured that the war was a long way from Borneo and Australia.

It was about this time that my mother decided to look at other boarding schools for me and during her search she came to Rose Bay convent to speak to Mother Macrae. My mother had an instant rapport with Mother Macrae and so she and my father decided that I should start at Rose Bay in 1940, first as a day girl, and by mid-1940 as a weekly boarder. In late 1939 my father returned to Australia on leave and in February 1940 I commenced a memorable nine years at the Convent of the Sacred Heart, Rose Bay. During this time, while on leave, my father offered himself to the Australian Army but was told that his services would be better utilised by remaining with the colonial service in Borneo.

ELIZABETH WITH HER PARENTS, JAMES AND CELIA TAYLOR, IN PITT STREET, SYDNEY, 1940

Before returning to Borneo my father bought a pair of semi-detached cottages in Coogee as an investment. This purchase proved to be one of great foresight because as time progressed the war forced our family to be separated and these cottages provided for my education and other material needs.

My father returned to Sandakan in mid-1940 to take up his position as principal medical officer for the whole of British North Borneo and my mother and I moved to Cremorne to live with my mother's cousin. It was now time for my mother to make arrangements for her return to Borneo. She chose my Auntie Wag and her greatest friend, Ange Hickey, to be my surrogate mothers and guardians and what a wise choice she made. They were wonderful women, who proved their true friendship during an unforeseen period of prolonged darkness between 1942 and 1945. They took it in turns to have me for weekends and school holidays, making sure I was kept busy and entertained, attending at the same time to my material needs. I really depended on them, as a child does, for advice, love and support. They attended school functions and had my friends to stay over at weekends and during holidays. In other words, they completely fulfilled a parent's role.

My mother decided to return to Borneo in March 1941, despite the fact that my father did not encourage it because he 'could see the Japanese menace getting worse'. Although I had been well prepared for this moment, it was with deep sadness that I watched Mummy pulling away from the shore in a small boat to go out to the flying boat at Rose Bay. Little did I realise that I would not see her again until November 1945, by which time I would have grown from a child to an adolescent.

The nuns at Rose Bay, particularly Mother Macrae, were always there for me and perhaps even more so for my mother. After my mother's return to Borneo Mother Macrae wrote to my parents fortnightly over the next nine months, relaying all those little things that parents love to hear:

I wonder if you will be able to read Elizabeth's faint pencil letter! We really must get a black pencil or promote her to using ink. You know, I am sure, what a labour a letter is to a small person ... Elizabeth is looking so well — her cheeks are pink and she is all smiles. At the moment she is turning up her plaits with bows just at her neck, and she looks perfectly sweet.[7]

Just nine months after my mother left Sydney, all communication with Borneo ceased. The Japanese landed unopposed in January 1942 and Sandakan fell before Singapore in February.

During the latter part of 1941 I had tried to persuade my father to allow me to return to Borneo for the long summer holidays. He refused my pleas and of course he was quite right to do so, realising that the threat of war was very real. But I was not happy about his refusal. In retrospect how different my life may have been if he had granted me my wish!

During the early days of the war in the Pacific, I didn't fully appreciate the significance of the situation. At the age of ten years I was protected from the seriousness of the conflict and, of course, no one realised that it would continue for another three years.

The Japanese posed a real threat to Australia as well. Fearing for the safety of the children at Rose Bay on the harbour foreshore, the nuns decided to evacuate two-thirds of the school to Bowral in the Southern Highlands of New South Wales. We in the junior school went to the Rift, an established boarding house that the nuns took over for the duration of 1942 and 1943. These years at the Rift proved to be a great adventure, where we sampled the delights of country life without too many of the rigid restrictions of boarding school.

It was at this time in May 1942 that most European civilians in Borneo were interned on Berhala Island. My parents, however, were moved by the Japanese from their home into a cottage on the hospital grounds. My father and his staff were to keep the hospital and all medical facilities running, but they were restricted to the confines of the hospital.

The first stirrings of the passive underground movement began during these early months of occupation, when the poor diet of the civilian internees was secretly supplemented, along with much-needed medical supplies and money. In July 1942, Australian POWs captured in Singapore arrived in Sandakan to build an airfield. My father established contact with the Australians, in particular with Captain Matthews, and so the underground movement was expanded into other areas.

However, by mid-1943 the underground movement in Borneo was being betrayed. I was eleven years old, still at school in the Southern Highlands and totally unaware of the tragic circumstances in which my parents found themselves.

Although I was, to a certain extent, cocooned by all my relatives, nuns and close friends, the war was never very far away. I remember one evening, while on May holidays in Sydney, staying with my Aunt Wag at Cremorne Point, huge explosions erupted which seemed to last a long time. I was terrified, as Wag turned all the lights off and huddled with me under the kitchen table. It was not until the next day we learned that Japanese midget submarines had come into the harbour in an attempt to destroy Allied naval vessels anchored there. For me, war was a reality that night.

Wag's sons were both in the armed services and her life seemed to be spent writing letters, knitting articles of clothing for the comfort fund, or making fruit cakes to send to 'the boys'. Tragically, one of her sons was killed in New Guinea. As I had been taken into the family, as one of their own, this was a harsh reality for me as I saw Wag grieve for her son.

During these years from 1942 to 1945, I wrote to my parents every two weeks via the Red Cross. I look at these letters now and they seem so poignant. I remember at the time how hard it was to compose them, bearing in mind the restriction of only twenty-five words.

I received just one letter from my mother throughout the four years, and it was twelve months old when it arrived. She received two cards and one letter from me. Many of my letters came back from Japan after the war.

Mrs C G Taylor.
   Sandakan
 British North Borneo
  British Civilian Internee
c/o Japanese Red Cross Society
     Tokyo Japan

Miss E Taylor .
   Convent of Sacred Heart
   Rose Bay,
   Sydney,
   May 20ᵗʰ 1945.

Dearest Mummy ,
       Well and happy at Strathfield For
some holiday. Don't give up I love you dears
never out of my thoughts Praying , cannot be long,
           Loving,
           Elizabeth .

ELIZABETH'S CAREFULLY COMPOSED LETTER TO HER PARENTS, MAY 1945

Many people tried to obtain news of my parents. My aunts and friends tried every means through the Red Cross to somehow learn of my parents' whereabouts. The nuns, too, through their contacts, tried to get information through the Vatican radio. All to no avail.

After junior school in Bowral I returned to Rose Bay to commence senior school in 1944. I was twelve years old, an adolescent and feeling deeply the separation from my parents. The lack of communication and the years away from them brought about a greater awareness that the invasion of Borneo had changed everything that I remembered and that it would never be quite the same again.

In February/March 1944 my father and all his co-conspirators in the underground movement underwent a mock trial which took place in Kuching. Captain Matthews, six local citizens and two of the constabulary members were sentenced to death. My father and twenty others received prison sentences of varying lengths, to be served in Outram Road gaol in Singapore. My mother was sent to the civilian internment camp at Kuching and from then on there was no contact between either my mother and father, or between my parents and myself. Everyone was on their own.

As 1944 progressed into 1945, I longed for my parents. Although outwardly my life progressed relatively normally, there was a great void inside me. My faith in God was most important to me during this period, and I prayed in the chapel, most earnestly, to the Blessed Virgin for the safe return of my parents.

Peace was declared in Europe in May 1945, bringing jubilation and much relief. It also provided some hope for a quick end to the war in the Pacific. The end of the war in Europe allowed the major powers to concentrate their energies in the Pacific. Both nuns and girls watched the increased naval activity in Sydney Harbour from the school windows.

I was on school holidays when peace was declared on 15 August 1945. I spent the day in bed being violently ill, a severe reaction to years of pent-up emotions. Fortunately I spent the next two weeks with the Flynn family at their holiday house in Cronulla where I was entertained and surrounded by lots of young people my own age. This helped to minimise my anxiety while awaiting news of my parents' whereabouts and safety.

Two weeks after peace was declared, when we were back at school, I received a telegram from the Red Cross to say that my father was alive and in Singapore, but no word of my mother! This was my first inkling of my parents' separation during the war! Soon after my father's release, Colin Simpson, an ABC correspondent interviewed him. Mother Macrae had been notified of the broadcast and she and I and my best friend Josephine Lentaigne went around to the parlour to listen to the only wireless in the convent. It was 9 p.m. and with great anticipation we three sat close to the wireless listening to the broadcast. This interview was most revealing as it described my father's involvement in the Sandakan underground move-ment and the subsequent interrogation, torture and trial of all those in-volved. This was the first indication I had that my parents had suffered so badly at the hands of the Japanese. With these revelations I was, of course, very proud of my father's bravery and I realised how fortunate I was that my father had survived those years of Japanese occupation and cruelty and that he at least would return to me.

Meantime, there was still no word of my mother's whereabouts. It was not until 11 September that the 9th Division reached Kuching. It was with enormous relief that I again received a Red Cross Telegram on about 15 September, telling me of my mother's safe release from the Kuching camp. I also heard a recorded message from her on the wireless and it was wonder-ful to hear her voice again after so long. They were both coming home!

It was two months before my parents actually returned to Australia.

This allowed them time to recuperate at the convalescent camp in Labuan and it also gave my father the opportunity to return to Sandakan to assist in identifying the Japanese military police and to help with the interrogation which followed.

During this period we wrote many letters to each other:

Daddy and I are just longing for our reunion with you darling but I am afraid we must have patience a few weeks longer as Daddy has urgent business to complete before returning home.
… we shall try to make up to you for all your worries on our behalf… However my darling we shall try to forget all that and think only or our future happy lives together.[9]

There were also letters from my aunts to my mother, preparing her for the changes that had come about. I had grown into a 'charming young lady' or 'Elizabeth is splendid and prepare yourself to see a grown up young lady'.

As the *Merkur* sailed down the Queensland coast towards Brisbane, I wrote to my parents. I think this extract from that letter before our long awaited reunion vividly describes my feelings:

I am getting terribly excited, only three more days till you reach Brisbane, and then oh it will be wonderful to see you both again and also to hear you speak and oh so many wonderful things which I have missed for so long, but I will try and make up for all you have both had to suffer.[10]

The *Merkur* berthed in Brisbane on 25 November 1945. My mother and father flew to Sydney in an Army Dakota and landed at Mascot some time that afternoon. It had been raining before they landed and I remember waiting anxiously on the wet tarmac with my aunts, cousins and other relatives. I approached my parents with some caution as they stepped down from the plane onto the tarmac. It was hard to realise that the thin, weathered couple was my mother and father. We recognised and embraced one another and everyone present shed tears of joy and relief.

My Auntie Wag offered shelter at her home in Cremorne and we all went back there after our reunion at the airport. My parents stayed with her for the next twelve months and I joined them there for school holidays. They regained their health in the warmth of Wag's home and from there the post-war adjustments evolved.

My father decided not to return to Borneo to work. My mother's health was a deciding factor. She was also quite adamant that she did not want to return to Borneo. I suspect another reason was that she did not want to leave me again. My father joined the Repatriation Department and in 1946 he started work with tuberculosis patients at Lady Davidson in Turramurra. He eventually became the medical superintendent of Concord Hospital in 1962.

Although I was aware of their suffering at the hands of the Japanese, my parents spoke very little about their experiences during those early years after the war. It was not until later in my life that I learned more of the hardships and the dangers they had endured. I know that they were grateful to have survived and they just wanted to resume their lives as best they could here in Australia. They eventually bought 14 acres of land at West Pennant Hills, where my father bred sheep in his spare time and my mother kept her new home and 'replaced possessions' in beautiful order. She spent a great deal of her spare time creating lovely meals, bottling fruit and making jams. Emphasis was placed on good food, plenty of it, and nothing was ever wasted. This preoccupation with food was, I feel, a result of the severe privations they suffered during the war in the POW camps. It was only natural that after all their ordeals, my parents were most happy in one another's company and they retreated into a peaceful life together at West Pennant Hills.

I suppose that I felt most vulnerable during the war years when I was separated from my parents and didn't know where they were. But it was not easy to adjust after the war either. When my parents returned from Borneo I suspect they expected me to be the same little girl that they had left behind. Not only had I grown into an adolescent, I had also become self-reliant and independent and had developed certain survival skills to cope with the long years of separation from my mother and father. Getting to know each other again was difficult. I continued to go to boarding school and then went nursing, which also required living away from home. I loved my parents very much but the close, pre-war, family unit that I remembered as a child was never really the same. Fortunately, as the years passed, we did recover our close relationship, particularly after I married and had children myself.

A Special Contribution

PETER SINFIELD

Lieutenant Victor (Vic) Alfred Sinfield (NX56209)
2/18th Battalion, AIF
POW: Changi; Sandakan/Kuching

Born in Ryde, New South Wales, on 29 December 1919, Vic joined Texaco/Caltex Oil Company when he was sixteen, and, apart from his five years in the Army, spent his working life with Texaco. In 1940 he left the company to enlist in the AIF and six months later, in February 1941 he sailed with the 2/18th Battalion to Malaya. In July 1942 Vic was shipped with B Force from Changi to Sandakan in Borneo. After the betrayal of the underground network at Sandakan in 1943, he was moved with most of the officers to Kuching, remaining there until Kuching

68

was liberated on 11 September 1945. He returned to Australia on the *Wanganella* in October 1945, rejoined Texaco and married Gladys Dean. Two years later they moved to Melbourne with the company. They lived there for more than forty years.

Vic Sinfield died of a heart attack on 2 February 1992 in the Heidelberg Repatriation Hospital in Melbourne.

My parents knew each other before the war, and were married in November 1945, little more than a month after my father returned to Australia. My brother was born some two years later, and I arrived in early 1950. The fact that Dad had been a prisoner of the Japanese for three and a half years did not affect my early family life in any physical way. He wasn't violent, he did not (as far as I know) suffer from nightmares or depression, or display any of the other symptoms of trauma that have been recorded for these survivors. In fact, he always appeared to be one of the most balanced and well-adjusted men I've ever met — slow to anger and without any obvious bitterness towards his former captors, either individually or collectively. The only signs I can remember that it affected him deeply, were his declining an opportunity to visit Japan and his refusal to buy a Japanese car.

He seldom mentioned his Army service or time as a POW, there was little family discussion, and he didn't attend Anzac Day parades (perhaps because we lived in Melbourne and his unit was raised in northern New South Wales as much as anything else). Nevertheless, I grew up with exotic-sounding place names such as Jemaluang, Borneo, Mersing, Sandakan, Kuching and Singapore, and was familiar with them long before I knew with any certainty where they were.

The main way my father's internment has affected me is the development of my abiding interest in Australian prisoners of the Japanese, particularly in Borneo. This initially arose from family history research (at that time, the only comprehensive narrative was Peter Firkin's *From Hell to Eternity*), but the more I read, the more interested I became and the more I was inspired to find out still more. The official and available unit histories have since been 'devoured' with avidity, as well as countless articles and the well-known books by Hal Richardson, Don Wall, Athol Moffitt, Sheila Ross, Lynette Ramsay Silver, Kevin Smith and Janet Uhr. I continue to read everything I can find on the subject, and coming across the now-familiar names is like meeting old friends. Since the mid-1980s, I've also been undertaking research using the original records held by the Australian War Memorial, helping to flesh out the story and fill in many obscure details.

I learned that my father had gone to Malaya with the rest of Elbow Force aboard the *Queen Mary* in February 1941. Captured when Singapore fell twelve months later, he was initially imprisoned at Changi on Singapore Island. In July 1942 he was shipped with 1500 others to Sandakan, where the prisoners of B Force were used to build an airstrip. Unlike other camps, at Sandakan the officers were required to do the same work as the men, and Dad would have shared the gruelling physical labour of carting wood and clearing the land. After the Sandakan underground was discovered in mid-1943, most of the remaining officers (two earlier parties had already gone) were transferred to the Batu Lintang camp at Kuching. Although I have found no evidence, I assume he was in this last group and, although one can never tell about these things, I've always felt this move saved his life.

The more I learn, the greater my admiration for these men. I feel they endured — and overcame — not only the terrors and danger of battle, but even greater hardships in captivity: the brutal treatment, malnourishment and disease highlighted in all the narratives, the insidious psychological effects of helplessness, Japanese propaganda and — for the officers at Changi and Kuching — boredom. Although 'heroes' is a much-overused word today, to me they are true Australian heroes.

All this led me to make a pilgrimage to Malaysia in 1995, undertaken with the son of another ex-POW, captured in Johore, imprisoned in Changi and subsequently sent to Japan. Our object was to be in Kuching on the fiftieth anniversary of my father's release (which we were). We also visited the Sandakan and Batu Lintang POW camp sites, as well as Labuan War Cemetery (where Allied POWs who died in Borneo are interred or commemorated). This was followed by a car trip around the southern half of Malay Peninsula, visiting many of the places we'd heard or read about — Mersing, Jemaluang, Parit Sulong and Muar, among others. My mate was also able to find sites significant to his father's story in Malacca, so the whole trip was a very emotional but rewarding experience for both of us.

GLADYS, PETER AND VIC, C. 1950

My conviction that ex-prisoners of the Japanese made a special contribution to Australian military history has led to a desire to help others to understand. In particular, I feel the story of the Kuching camp has not been adequately told and I've given a number of presentations to various groups including the War Memorial's volunteer guides. I was also asked to contribute an entry on Charles Wagner of the 2/18th to the *Australian Dictionary of Biography*.[1] More recently I have reviewed David Milne's bibliography 'POWs in Japanese Camps' for *Sabretache*, the journal of the Military Historical Society of Australia.

It is obvious that my father's incarceration as a POW has had a marked effect on my feelings, as well as on what I've chosen to do in my leisure time. I'm immensely proud of him, and would refute any suggestion that he (and other POWs) somehow did less for their country — in fact, I think in many ways they gave more, and their story is a marvellous tribute to the human spirit. It deserves to be more widely known.

The Other Years Between

SUZETTE BODDINGTON

Corporal Alexander (Alex) Roland Campbell Johnstone (NX20572)
2/15th Field Regiment, AIF
POW: Changi; Jinsen, Keijo and Konan

Alex Johnstone was born in Willoughby in New South Wales on 5 January 1911 and died in 1967, when he was only fifty-six years old. He had started to study accountancy but before he finished his studies, he enlisted in the AIF and sailed to Singapore with the 27th Brigade in August 1941. Alex managed to keep a diary between February 1942 and January 1944, much of it written in the form of notes to his new bride Peg. They had been married only three months before he left for overseas and he couldn't wait to return to her and start their life together.

Suzette's husband John spent three years transcribing her father's diary by holding a magnifying glass over the pages of his beautiful, tiny copperplate handwriting.[1]

After the Allied surrender in Singapore, Alex went to Changi with everyone else and then in August 1942 he was transported to Korea as part of Japan Party B. In Korea the Japanese split the party into two groups and Alex was sent in a group of mixed British and AIF personnel to the Jinsen camp on the south-west coast of Korea. In Jinsen the men were put to work excavating a graving dock, bagging salt and reclaiming land.[2] Like most POWs, Alex thought constantly of food and while he was in Jinsen camp he managed to compile a wonderful collection of his 'dream' recipes. They range from such delicacies as Arabian coffee cake and coconut tarts to peanut butter cookies, all carefully indexed in his neat handwriting. Unlike many of the other camps, the POWs in Korea received some Red Cross parcels. Many of the items in the International Red Cross parcels were wrapped in pages from newspapers and magazines. Alex carefully copied more than 500 recipes from the pages in the parcels during his imprisonment at Jinsen.

In 1944, he was transferred to Keijo camp where there was still a small group of Australians, including Wilf Fawcett. Unfortunately his diary ends in 1944, but according to his Army service record he was liberated from Konan camp on 15 September 1945. He was taken to No. 8 Prisoner of War Reception camp in the Philippines and returned to Australia on 17 October 1945.[3]

My dad gave his war diary a title: 'The Years Between'. Between what? One life and another? Or simply between the years of his imprisonment — 1942 to 1944? I never did get to ask him. He died when I was twenty. He was fifty-six, not very old at all. That was during the 1960s and he was, I think, disappointed and confused by the seeming recalcitrance of his then teenage daughter. We didn't talk much. We argued a lot. I was daring to question the established and proper conventions. My parents, especially my mother, knew without a shadow of a doubt what was 'right and proper'. The code of 'acceptable' behaviour had been instilled in her from her childhood. My father naturally supported her views, but I sometimes wondered if, perhaps, he might not have wanted to push those boundaries just a little himself. I'm not sure why I thought this — just a sense, occasionally, that he was living a life not always quite to his liking. I wonder what his hopes and expectations were after his wartime experiences? I certainly never knew. It was never discussed, at least in front of the children.

I think of the many conversations about life that I've had with my own three children. We have shared at least some of our hopes and dreams. We know each other a little. I never really *knew* my parents. Especially my dad. He was just a dad like most others. Special to me, but not *known*. I have come to know my mother better over the years and to understand a little of who she is and why. That has taken fifty-five years and a good deal of life experience. I assume that it would have happened with Dad too. I hope that we would have begun to talk, eventually. Probably. I have been told that I am very like him, but I'm not sure that I know exactly what that means. Except that I'm a 'people person'. I get on well with people, like most of them, talk easily as Dad did, apparently. Mum told me that Dad could talk to anyone, anywhere, anytime. I think that that was a bit of a backhander actually.

In the 1960s I had heard him say that he didn't hold with conscription. I was at uni by then, caught up, at least peripherally, with the anti-Vietnam demonstrations. A few of my friends lost out to the dreaded Birthday Ballot Box. One, the boy who took me to my end-of-school formal, went off to that terrible war and returned, lost to its horror, to his earlier innocent self. I heard from another friend that he was 'committed' soon after his return. Life moved on, as it does. I don't know what happened to him in the long term. I have often wondered as I have listened over the intervening years to the stories of other traumatised Vietnam vets. A very different war from my dad's. But how does one compare? My dad, who didn't believe in conscription, who enlisted with his mates to 'fight for king and country', who had returned from his terrible war and resumed an apparently normal life, never said much about Vietnam. At least that I can remember. I don't think that he thought that we should have been there, but at the same time he seemed baffled and angry, very angry, by the anti-war sentiments of most of my generation. It was another time, another place and not to be countenanced. It certainly did not warrant discussion with his daughter who knew nothing about anything. What might have been discussed over the bar at the Balgowlah RSL on his occasional forays out with a couple of mates is another thing. Secret Men's Business, obviously.

One of the few times my dad ever hit me was during this difficult, non-communicative time. It was at the tea table. I was seventeen. I was sitting on his right. He had been reading the evening newspaper as usual and made some comment, I can't remember exactly, about the long-haired louts in one of the demo marches. I hadn't been involved much in the street marches but felt the need to defend my peers. I muttered something about him stupidly believing everything he read in the newspapers. He knocked me off my chair. To this day I'm not sure why. Perhaps it was simply because he was tired and I'd presumed to question his views and those of the *Evening Sun*. He never offered an explanation. I'll never know. That's the saddest part. When one is a self-interested, self-absorbed seventeen-year-old, struggling with the monumental imperatives of the mid-sixties, one is not the slightest bit interested in who one's father really is and why. What a pity. We lost the chance. He died before we could even attempt to reconcile our differences.

My dad was not a hero. He was an ordinary bloke. He was not a Desert Rat or a Burma Railway survivor. He hadn't seen action in Europe or on the muddy Kokoda Trail. My dad was a corporal, 2/15th Field Regiment, 8th Division, AIF abroad. Captured Singapore 15 February 1942. He didn't get a chance to be a hero. He was, forever, simply a POW. He returned to Australia in October 1945 — an ex-POW. No great fanfare. No ticker tape. (Nor for the Vietnam vets years later.) Dad never went to the Anzac Day march. He couldn't, because his damaged legs wouldn't allow him to walk that far. By the time the march came to be televised, he would watch quietly with a few beers and not say much. Mum, on the other hand, would mutter about 'the bloody 9th, that's all we ever hear about'. *They* were obviously the 'heroes'. There never seemed to be as many men marching under the banner of the 8th. But that was the Sydney march and a lot of the 8th Div. lads were country boys, so perhaps they were marching elsewhere. My mum's bitterness always seemed to far outweigh my dad's. I often wondered why. Surely it should be the other way around? Somehow, Dad must have managed to make his peace with his war but my mother never did. Ever.

When my dad returned and my mum first saw him at the Sydney Showground where the men were demobbed, he weighed in at about 8 stone (50 kilograms), and was all but eclipsed by his huge American-issue kit. He had a barely healed leg ulcer and within a very short space of time not one of his own teeth left in his head. All the rotted top ones, the result of near-starvation rations in the camps, were whipped out in one go and a week later all the bottom ones as well. When his gums healed, he was fitted with full dentures, and told to go away and take it easy. Somewhere else. Somewhere warm. Recuperate, he was told. The temperatures in Keijo camp in Korea had been very bloody cold.

Reveille 0700 roll call 0701. All taps frozen (not withstanding straw). Temperature 12 degrees, 20 degrees of frost (−11 deg. c.)…0830 working party to docks… 11.1.43 will live in my memory for ever; it was so bitterly cold that at 1200 we knocked off, had dinner, rice, gravy and roll and returned to camp petrified, frozen and chilled to the bone. 11/1/43 – 330th day POW

My dad was just an ordinary bloke, like my friend the bank clerk, the one who took me to the formal. Blokes who were supposed to come home and 'get on with life'. How did one get on with life after experiences such as theirs? How did Dad return to his bride of three months, his almost unknown wife of three and a half years? To begin again. Familiar yet strange. Known yet changed. A sense of humour was paramount. It had been in the camps, it was now. My dad had always been 'a bit of a lad' according to Mum. 'A bit of a card'. A tease with a ready grin. We gathered over the years that in the camps a sense of humour was what kept the Aussies alive, well, some of them. That and mateship and God and the memories of girls like Peg. Like his wife. The Aussies were known for their 'larks', said Dad. The Pommies not as much. The Aussies were 'larrikins' and had great officers, Dad said. It was these officers and the general morale of the blokes that kept the Aussies going.

At least as much as the near-miraculous efforts of their extraordinary medical officers. When I was fourteen, I was operated on by a leading Macquarie Street surgeon, Dr Kevin Fagan. I met one of the 'saints' of the Burma rail.[4] One of my dad's heroes. I met the doctor who had 'looked after the lads', who had amputated limbs and performed other dreadful doctoring feats with inadequate medical supplies. He operated on me. When my parents took me to his surgery, the 'saint' and Dad shook hands. I don't remember what they might have said to each other, but the look of reverence on my father's face is memorable to this day.

We never heard much about the gruesome stuff afterwards, just the funny stories. Not much was ever said about holding blokes down while their limbs were taken off, the dengue fever and malaria, the tropical ulcers which wouldn't heal and had to be scooped out with metal spoons. The beri-beri and the malnutrition. Dad never said much about all of this. I'm not even quite sure how I know at all. I suppose a sort of osmosis from adult conversations. Perhaps from Mum, partly from The Diary and from things I've read since. Dad mostly told the funny stories. Funny? After the event, possibly a panacea for the horror. The ones I remember best were mostly from the end of the war. How the liberation army from across the Manchurian border was made up largely of Russian women troops who drank avgas (aviation fuel) in lieu of vodka and went berserk through the camp. How the US Air Force dropped supplies in 40-gallon petrol drums from cargo planes flying just a few hundred feet up and nearly demolished most of the camp, including the hospital tent where Dad was being treated. Ironically, the supplies were next to useless, except for the ubiquitous cigarettes. Chocolate and heaps of canned sweet food weren't much use to shrunken stomachs. All a bit of a joke really.

What the men longed for were the apples growing in an old orchard outside the camp. It had been forbidden fruit for so long. Food. It's what The Diary is mostly about.

Dinner 1200 rice and gravy plus a curried soya bean cake stew from Capt. Sinclair (he made it) 7/2/43

Food and the obsessive daily record of survival. Their preoccupation with food was a given constant: what one actually ate, recorded meticulously to the last grain of rice; what one dreamed about eating; what food and supplies were swapped for what food and supplies; what recipes could be remembered or collected; how to make a chocolate pie with meagre supplies — rice, cocoa, marg and sugar etc, etc. The Diary is about the minutiae of life and about Peg and poetry and mates.

*Reveille 0800. Showered and then breakfast at 0900
consisting of rice meal, pea meal and tea. We added grated
coconut. Dengue is very prevalent – several of our chaps have
contracted it. Finished what I hope is my last job of army
auditing this morning and read till dinner time. 24/7/42.*

As a girl growing up, I could never understand how my dad could
eat bread slathered with dripping. I understand now. He also loved tripe in
white parsley sauce, steak and kidney pudding with suet crust, lamb's fry
and bacon and pale Irish stew. Mum obviously felt the continuing need to
nourish both his body and his soul with these 'treats' as the years went by.
He obviously relished the richness and fattiness. Whenever these dishes
appeared on the table, I gagged and choked and got into trouble for not
eating what was put in front of me. In the end I think that my mother gave
up and cooked a separate meal for my sister and me. To this day I cannot
cook or eat any of Dad's 'favourites'.

I always knew that The Diary existed. Mum kept it carefully stashed
away with other bits and pieces of memorabilia. I looked at it sometimes,
but I could barely read it. It was full of pressed frangipanis, desiccated and
brown with age, but with Peg's name and a date clearly visible on their
tissue thin petals.

*Our prison camp has hundreds of frangipani trees and they
are in bloom. I have picked a frangipani flower and am
pressing it here. I can just see you in your glory with them, they
smell very strongly… 6/5/42.*

There were some small sepia photos and the tattered 'Papers of
Instructions' issued to all prisoners in Chosen (Korean) camps in September
1942 at the beginning of their incarceration — 'Firm and unshakeable is
our national resolve that we should crush our enemy, the U.S.A. and the
Britain. Heaven is always on the side of justice.' I remember thinking at the
time that this was interesting. Heaven was on their side too? Was the
Japanese heaven the same as ours? Was the God that my dad held continual
conversation with during his imprisonment the same God who smiled on
the warriors of the Rising Sun? A weighty imponderable for one so young,
who wasn't too sure about God anyway. I don't remember Dad ever
mentioning him again after the war. We went to church, of course, but I

never remember Dad talking about God. As far as I could tell we went to church because that's what one did. To the Kirk. In a hat and white gloves and came home to Sunday baked dinner afterwards. Perhaps Dad was silently very thankful for just that. Perhaps God wasn't just for 'in extremis'. Perhaps his conversations continued unbeknown to us all.

Mum was occasionally heard to mutter 'bloody Japs', but little else. She was very bitter. Hated the 'bloody Japs' with a vengeance. I don't remember Dad ever saying that. I do remember him saying that the Korean guards were much worse than the Japs. Very cruel. Perhaps that was their revenge for being a conquered people, not an intrinsic trait. The other thing that I remember quite clearly was Mum's ability to quote Dad's service number — NX20572 — at the drop of a hat. It's on her Gold Card today. She can't remember telephone numbers very well now but she can rattle that number off in her sleep. 'Daddy's number.' I never took much notice of his number but I could count to ten in Japanese and bow and say *How konichi wa* when I was very small. People thought that was cute, I guess. Perhaps it said something more about my father's liberality.

Excellent day today. Early breakfast, went ashore in a lighter launch to the oil dump. 100 of us. 50 A.I.F. and 50 British. Loaded, unloaded and stacked oil drums. An excellent Jap guard party were over us. Had a great chat with one. I taught him a few English words and he taught me a few Japanese words. At dinner time he gave me a plate of Jap delicacies, cigarettes, bananas and toffee. We left the ship at 0800 and returned at 1630. Said goodbye to the Jap guard, shook hands and can honestly say he was a little gentleman. 4/9/42 – 201st day POW

There were other bits of yellowed paper with The Diary — recipes and drawings, badges and service medals. All kept safely in the bottom drawer. I wonder how often Dad looked at them. He did say once that he thought he might write a book, hence the title, 'The Years Between'. He never got around to it. I think that in some perverse sort of way, Mum hated these mementoes, even as she preserved them. I was really only interested in the pictures. There was a pencil sketch of Dad but I couldn't see the resemblance. It was, possibly, a very good likeness of him when it was done — gaunt and cold-looking. There were beautiful coloured-ink drawings for Christmas Day lunch menus and Aussie-style Christmas cards. All these assorted bits and pieces had been carefully hoarded and had survived the camps, the ubiquitous Japanese spot searches, and surreptitious burial under the camp latrines. Dad never said quite how this was accomplished but it was done and most successfully. Aussie ingenuity without doubt. Paper of any kind was especially prized and the wrappings from Red Cross supply parcels (when allowed — the Japanese were not always strict adherents to the Geneva Convention) assiduously saved. I don't know how my father would have coped had he not had access to pencil and paper.

At breakfast time out of the blue J.P. Mewies comes along with an eversharp pencil and a very nice note. He is a great scout, can you beat it – a birthday present in Jinsen Prison camp! 5/1/43

Dad had been a trainee accountant at McCarthy's in Yass in the late 1930s. He hadn't quite completed his training when he enlisted. He never did quite complete it. But he obviously knew enough and employers made allowances I guess. He was, apparently, an excellent accountant, for the firms he worked for at any rate but, as I was later to learn, not for himself. He struggled and juggled all his life to balance his own books, without success. When he died, his affairs were a mess and Mum was left almost penniless. Legacy stepped in to help and without their expertise and generosity Mum and my sister would have been near destitute. No house, no car, no nothing! Perhaps The Diary with its tiny, meticulous, copperplate script, its columns of bridge scores, books read, temperature graphs and camp plans was evidence of his excellence in bookkeeping. He organised bookkeeping classes in the camps off his own bat, as well as his work auditing with the officers. Figures came naturally. Years later he could envisage no better career for his eldest daughter than that of a comptometrist in a big bank. Unfortunately, I did not inherit his love of and aptitude for columns of figures, and had my rebellious heart set on an Art course at East Sydney Tech. This was not going to be allowed. No way. I had proved myself to be a fairly able student at high school and Dad seemed proud of my achievements. But I did lean towards the Arts and excelled in English, French, Ancient History and Art. Biology was fascinating too and entailed a multitude of carefully labelled specimen drawings. Dad really appreciated those. I was made a prefect in 5th year and won one of only twenty-five Art

Teacher's Scholarships awarded in New South Wales that year. Dad did *not* appreciate this. I envisaged myself as a total reincarnation in black stockings, velvety eyeshadows and long, long hair, lugging a heavy art portfolio around the corridors of East Sydney Tech. Dad would fight this ambition every inch of the way. He could not countenance his daughter as some sort of bohemian rebel. Why couldn't I be a nurse or an ordinary teacher? Something 'respectable', something 'safe'.

My parents tried hard to 'do the best' by their two girls. Dad had struggled for the final five years of my education to pay fees, uniform costs and assorted sundry extras at the private girls school they had chosen for us. My parents hoped that I would meet 'nice' girls from 'good' families. I did. We had very little in common. They came mostly from comfortable, established families with big old homes who had lived forever on the lower North Shore. Their fathers were mostly professionals and seemed not to have been to the war, or, if they had, they had returned directly to the secure tenure of a previous life. We had just arrived, lived in a rented half-house, didn't have a lot of money and, sometimes, not even a car. But the girls must go to a good school. Meet nice people. It was an extraordinarily difficult and confusing time for me on the whole. I should have been grateful and happy for this wonderful opportunity. I'm not sure that I was. Dad had to take out yet another loan, it was whispered, to pay the bills. My little sister, six years younger, had started in the junior school as well, so Dad must have been hard pressed.

Things had to be 'nice' at home too. My Mum strove always to have the house 'just so'. The best Sanderson linen on the lounge suite and the Queen Anne furniture polished to perfection. The ubiquitous china cabinet displayed the precious pieces that were so important to her. She worked hard to keep house for her family. That's what most mums did then. Two of my friends had divorced parents and the mums worked. This was unusual — not quite 'the done thing'. I thought it was very interesting and admired their independence. Their homes were different too, easier and more comfortable somehow.

My art teacher, the widow of a well-known playwright and my much-loved and admired mentor, also lived by herself in a wonderful little pink cottage near the beach. Sometimes, a few of the 'art girls' would be invited to visit for a cosy afternoon tea. I felt as if I was in another world. I was. Surrounded by a colourful, eclectic clutter of beautiful things. I seemed irresistibly drawn to rooms that were diametrically opposed to the pretty neatness and order of home. A little later, I would be similarly bemused by the noise, laughter, music and clutter of my boyfriend's family home. Everyone talked incessantly, played music constantly. Books and conversation were all-important. Adults and young people discussed and argued, shared opinions. How extraordinary. I was so taken aback when asked for an opinion on something, I could barely get a word out. My opinion wasn't asked for at home. I was told, not asked. Adults had their conversations, children had theirs. I wish we'd talked more. I wish my home had been more of a 'drop in' kind of place, instead of a 'come by invitation only' place. I think that Dad might have liked it to be too. He was more easygoing in a lot of ways than my mum. Perhaps 'standards' weren't all that important after life in the camps. But my mother's needs were always paramount to him.

I have always wondered about my parents' constant moving — our oddly peripatetic life. They never lived in one place for more than three years. A 'home' never really had a chance to develop into a place of easy and comfortable familiarity. Most of my friends had had an uninterrupted growing up. They were settled. Their lives had a centredness that mine didn't. Their homes were an accretion of lives lived in some sort of easy continuum. Or that's how I saw it. My parents' life seemed an endless struggle. To put my sister and me into that expensive girls school was admirable in intent but rather cruel in fact. Why? Because most of the girls had more and better and I was very aware of it. I wanted more too! I was confused and unhappy most of the time. I can remember having to have an expensive art text for 5th year, Helen Gardener's *Art Through the Ages*. I was given it as a birthday present. A little thing, I know, but it didn't seem fair. I'm very grateful for the education my parents strove to give me, grateful for the opportunity it afforded me to go to university, but I wonder if I wouldn't have been happier and just as much of an achiever in my own right at the local high school. Who knows? And yes, I lost that desperate battle with my father to go to East Sydney Tech. I mustn't have been quite enough of a rebel after all! I was only sixteen. My Art Teacher's Scholarship was, with great difficulty, converted to a Commonwealth Teacher's Scholarship and I went to Sydney University to major in English, History and Archaeology, my second great love.

Also, my boyfriend was there studying second-year Medicine so I comforted myself with that. I did an Art option in my DipEd year and found myself with six periods of Art on my timetable in my very first teaching position at an all boys high school in the western suburbs. I graduated as an English/History teacher, but it was thought that I could manage the Art, given my background. Dad wasn't there to share the irony.

Had there been no war my parents would probably have married and settled in Yass — friends, tennis, golf — a pleasant country lifestyle. A settled life. Perhaps. As it was, they became itinerants. When Dad was told to go 'somewhere warm', they went north to Hayman Island in 1946.[5] Dad took on the bookkeeping for the small guesthouse there. There was a good deal of blue sky and sunshine, tennis, fishing and reef-walking. Time to recover and reorder a life. I arrived in 1947. Born in Sydney but soon to spend the first eighteen months of my life in a clothesbasket on an isolated Whitsunday island. Idyllic, one assumes. Perhaps, especially for Dad. But Mum? I'm not so sure. Such isolation with a new, fretful baby cannot have been easy. She had apparently one kerosene tin of fresh water a day for my entire baby needs. There was no doctor or nurse on the island. Cairns was a long sea-plane flight away. Mum missed her family and friends down south. Then to Cairns. I have been told that Dad loved the North and would have been more than happy to stay there, perhaps on a small cane farm.

At this stage I feel Peg that I want to take you away all to myself perhaps to some new state – Queensland or Western Australia – where we can settle down and live for one another and our happiness and contentment alone, together with our kiddies. 7/6/42

Mum couldn't cope with the heat and humidity and was not happy. Dad did the right thing by his wife and little daughter. They came back to New South Wales, where Dad got a job and tried to settle.

.. Peg, when I get back I am getting a job that will enable me to spend a tremendous amount of my time with you. I have one or two in mind... 30/4/42

But somehow, no matter where they went, roots didn't go down. They were to move constantly, on average about every two years, for the rest of their life together: Sydney, Canberra, the Blue Mountains, Sydney, Canberra again. We even lived for a while with my grandmother in Homebush. She'd come down from Yass to nurse her dying mother and we all

ALEX AND PEG WITH SUZETTE AND HER YOUNGER SISTER JANETTE
AT CURRUMBIN BIRD PARK, QUEENSLAND, 1961

shared the house. Then my parents built a small house at Springwood in
the Blue Mountains, the only house they ever owned. My dad commuted to
Sydney on the 'Fish and Chips'[6] and played golf on the weekends. I pretty
much ran wild in the bush — no one worried overmuch then about kids
disappearing for a day to play. I don't know what happened when they sold
that little house but from then on they had to rent. What happened to the
money? Once we rented three different places in the same street in
Mosman. Very strange. Two didn't even have our own furniture. Sometimes Dad had a car, sometimes he didn't. Money always seemed to be an
issue. The furniture was arranged and rearranged in yet another house.
Mum packed and unpacked. I made a few friends here, a few friends there.
Then we'd move again. Nobody else seemed to move like we did. Even
during my five years of high school we moved twice. People have often
commented over the years that I have a real flair for decorating and creating interesting personal spaces. It doesn't seem so surprising really when I
think about it. Whatever small space was allocated to me as a kid, I would
try to make it my own, if only for a little while. Then off we'd go again.

Did my dad's wartime experiences make a settled life impossible?
The Diary suggests that all he ever wanted was to come home to Peg,

married life and all that it entailed. I think that his POW experiences had changed his expectations of life and that he would have liked to walk bare-foot in the sand, holding Mum's hand, forever.[7] But that's not how it panned out. He did not seem to be able to reconcile the reality with the dream; his needs and wants with what he saw as his duty to my mother and to us, his daughters. His and Mum's expectations of life must have been so disparate as to make their partnership fraught with conflicting needs and wants. I think that Dad yearned for a simple life and wished that he had stayed on that little sugar cane farm in Queensland.

I wish that I had known him, really known him. I wish that we could have had more time. I wish that he could have known his grandchildren. I wish that he could have known me, the person I grew into. I wish that he himself could have told me the truth about 'The Years Between'. He died in Canberra in 1967. He was going to pick my sister up from a friend's place in the early evening. He had a massive heart attack as he was starting the car. He fell onto the horn, which alerted the neighbours. It was the May holidays and my mum was in Sydney visiting me. I hadn't gone home be-cause I was working. I hadn't seen Dad since the Christmas holidays and we were still arguing. Mum and I flew home to Canberra the next day and I found myself unexpectedly in charge. Mum couldn't cope. She wasn't there when he died. She was completely lost. I don't really remember much about it all except that someone took me to the hospital that afternoon to collect his things. They handed me his sportscoat and grey trousers, his wallet, watch and pipe. They all smelt like Dad. It wasn't fair.

My dad was just an ordinary bloke. At least I think he was.

I will record what I can of all my doings, but once freedom is gained I desire to forget the period, as it has cost me dear but brought home to me what my love for you has been, a love which has not altered except that of an intense yearning at all times to have you with me; with me never to be parted again — that is my wish each and every day, with the hope that soon all earth's wars may cease and the voice of Christ will again say peace

Alex
Jinsen Prison Camp, Chosen
Sunday 10th. October 1943.

In the Footsteps of a Hero

DAVID MATTHEWS

AWM NEG. 059358

Captain Lionel Matthews, GC, MC (VX24597)
8th Division Signals, AIF
POW: Changi; Sandakan/Kuching

Lionel Matthews was twenty-eight years old when he left his wife Lorna and two-year-old son David in Melbourne to sail with 8th Division Signals to Malaya. His Signals colleagues nicknamed him 'the Duke' because of his resemblance to the Duke of Gloucester, a former governor-general to Australia. Even today, years after his death, they refer to him by this nickname.

Lionel was recommended twice for a Military Cross during the fighting against the Japanese in early 1942: first for his actions during the operations against the Japanese at Gemas in Malaya, and then again for operations on Singapore Island before the Allied surrender. He did not survive to receive his award at the end of the war, but at a ceremony in Changi after the surrender, General Percival, the senior Allied officer on Singapore, presented him with a spare ribbon provided by Captain Stan Woods MC.[1]

On 7 July 1942, the Japanese transported approximately 1500 British and Australian POWs in B force from Changi to Borneo to build an airfield. Captain Matthews, with nine other officers and thirty-five of the troops from 8th Division Signals, went with them.

In Sandakan Matthews, who had started learning the Malay language while he was in Malaya, directed the underground movement. A group of local residents, including Dr and Mrs Taylor, ran enormous risks assisting both the Sandakan civilian internees and the POWs. They smuggled in messages, money, radio parts, food and medical supplies, and even helped with some of the escapes from the POW camp. In the middle of 1943, the underground network was betrayed. Those implicated were rounded up and a group of more than fifty civilians and Australian POWs was shipped to Kuching to be put on trial. Most of the conspirators, including Dr Taylor, received prison sentences, but Lionel Matthews and eight others were sentenced to death and executed on 2 March 1944. 'The Duke' was buried in a grave at Kuching and at the end of the war his body was re-interred in Labuan cemetery. In 1999, David visited his father there.

While David Matthews never had 'the pleasure of journeying through life with a father', he has journeyed through life with his father's spirit. Apart from his pride in his father's heroism and the enormous vacuum caused by his loss, he has measured himself continually against his father's achievements. David's children, too, cite their grandfather's bravery as a potent influence in their own lives. Lionel's 'larger than life' personality, his achievements both before and during the war, and his heroism have provided not only his family but also his colleagues and friends with a powerful role model for strength in adversity.

David and his mother, who had been living in Adelaide since Lionel left for Malaya, were not forgotten after the war. Once they were back home in Adelaide, Stan Woods and other ex-POW friends banded together to ensure that Lionel's young son was able to continue his education at King's College in Adelaide, the school his mother had chosen for him. This small group of ex-POWs continued to pay David's school fees until he left school in 1955, without ever, David said, commenting on his academic results.[2]

In 1999, David Matthews and Elizabeth Moore (Dr and Mrs Taylor's daughter) were invited to join the Commonwealth Department of Veterans' Affairs Sandakan mission to Borneo. David wrote two articles for the *Advertiser* which are presented below. In the first, a tribute to his father, he is preparing himself for his first visit to Borneo.[3]

It was the small letter from the International Red Cross, which created the wound in my mother's heart. A small letter, but with a huge impact on my life. And I remember it with such clarity it could have been delivered yesterday.

Mum and I had returned home to Marryatville from a visit to my father's parents at Stepney one Friday night in April, 1945, when she received the letter which had come in the afternoon post. Her mother handed it to her and we all entered the living room as Mum opened it. The shock was instant. My father Captain Lionel Matthews had been executed by the Japanese at Kuching on 2 March 1944. I recall my mother, grandmother and an aunt all crying, so I cried, too.

A six-year-old may not understand the grief of a grown-up but he knows something traumatic has entered his mother's life. From that moment, life changed for me. Instantly I had joined the legions of Legacy Club boys who had lost their fathers.

I would never have the pleasure of journeying through life with a father but as the years have passed, I have formed a strong image of what he was like. Physically, he was a big man for his era. He stood 186 centimetres and weighed 102.6 kilograms. Trained as a lifesaver (beltman for the Holdfast Bay Lifesaving Club), he was a strong swimmer who also made money during the Great Australian Depression boxing the professionals in the travelling boxing shows. As a youth he twice was stroke of the Norwood Sea Scout unit's whaler crew, the crew that won the head of the river for Sea Scouts on the Port River in Adelaide.

He was strong physically and, obviously, mentally. He also had a gentler side. He played cornet and was a competent ballroom dancer. A fine artist, he was employed in Melbourne during the 1930s as a wallpaper salesman for the firm Brooks Robinsons. During this period he designed a wallpaper in black and gold that won an international wallpaper design competition in London. Languages were a hobby of his and he learnt Esperanto, could speak some French and Spanish and tackled Malay and Japanese successfully during his time in the Far East.

It was a fine effort for a man who had not even sat for his Intermediate Certificate. The Depression had arrived and he left Norwood High School early to help swell the family finances.

Scouting had been a major interest for him. After leaving the Norwood Sea Scouts in the late 1920s, he formed the 1st Leabrook Scout Troop as its scoutmaster and later became scoutmaster of a Rover Troop at Pentridge Gaol in Melbourne. It was during his time with the prisoners at Pentridge that he apparently learnt various survival tactics employed by them in captivity. One of these, I'm told, was to split a match into eight useable parts. These experiences apparently helped him during his captivity.

He had an infectious sense of humour. One of my senior colleagues on *The Advertiser*, legendary police roundsman the late Bob Whitington, had served in my father's unit, 8th Division Signals. Bob told me once that he always knew when Lionel Matthews was in the officers' mess by the uproar and laughter. It was this sense of humour and larking about that often drew stern disapproval from his commanding officer, Lieutenant Colonel (later Brigadier) James Thyer. Brigadier Thyer once told Mum that he had more trouble with my father than any officer under his command but he realised Dad was the best soldier he had commanded.

One of my favourite photos of Dad is on the front cover of *Weekend* (the magazine section of the weekend *Advertiser*). It was our last portrait as a family as Dad departed half an hour later for Spencer Street train station in Melbourne.

Dad's George Cross (GC) was earned as senior intelligence officer in charge of the underground at Sandakan camp, where he organised the admission of medical supplies, building of a wireless set and the escape of

LIONEL WITH LORNA AND DAVID
ON HIS FINAL LEAVE IN MELBOURNE, 1941

men from the camp. He was also appointed commanding officer of the British North Borneo Constabulary, which he ran as a guerilla unit outside the camp. When his organisation was uncovered, he was taken to Kuching and submitted to appalling torture without revealing information and was subsequently executed.

His Military Cross (MC) had been earned at Gemas in Malaya, where the Australian forces first encountered the Japanese in the war. He was also recommended for a Military Cross on Singapore Island, but the two recommendations were combined to give him one award.

Armed with this knowledge of the man, as well as many tales related to me over the years by men who served with him in Malaya and Borneo, it is not difficult to see how a young boy could build a picture of his heroic father. He has been a guiding light to me throughout life. It seems he has almost dictated to me from the grave, for never a day passes in which I don't think of him and his dreadful treatment at the hands of the Japanese in Borneo.

Borneo. As a child the very word 'Borneo' filled me with impressions of wild hills men who hunted and lived in the jungle beside fearsome orang-utans. Perhaps I read too many *Boys Own Annuals*. The island has always remained one of mystery and romance to me. Now, for the first time, I have the chance to visit Borneo, where my father became a legend, and form my own impressions. It won't be an easy trip for me, just as life has not been easy living in the shadow of a war-hero father. I have a feeling of trepidation and abject humility at confronting his grave in the war cemetery on Labuan Island off the Borneo coast.

Will I break down and blubber like a two-year-old for a man whom I have really only known through folklore? If I am going to have an emotional tour, and it is inevitable, then how difficult must it be for those few among the twenty-four in the party who actually endured those dreadful conditions at Sandakan? They include Owen Campbell, the sole remaining survivor of the Sandakan to Ranau marches. We will be travelling along the Death Track to Ranau where Owen was one of the six men who escaped to live to tell the tale. If it is going to be hard for me the memories will surely be torture for him.

Dad was executed when he was thirty-one years old, having had an amazingly adventurous life. What would he have been like had he survived the war after the treatment handed out to him by his brutal captors? Would he have been the kind man who left Australia to defend the Empire in a far country, or would he have been a hard man, tempered by constant torture? It is questions such as this that have tormented me over the years and still do, despite my having reached the age of sixty. I feel it is unfair that I have been granted such a long life compared to his fortunes.

Sadly he was not the only relative of mine to die in World War II. Dad's brother, Fred Matthews, was a regular Army bombardier with the heavy artillery battery captured at Rabaul and lost his life with the other POWs who were all drowned when the Japanese tramp steamer *Montevideo Maru* was sunk off the Phillipines on its way to Japan.

My mother's brother, Flying Officer Gethen Lane, died in 1944 when his plane crashed near Adelaide River in the Northern Territory. He survived the crash but died a few days later from burns suffered while re-entering the burning plane to rescue the pilot and co-pilot. The pilot survived. The price of war was harsh in our household.

Now it is my turn to travel to Borneo to be given the opportunity to pay my respects to my father and to all those men who endured the privations and hardship as POWs at Sandakan under such a savage taskmaster.

I am thrilled to have been selected in the official party and to be part of such an historic occasion, but I feel it is a pity the authorities have taken so many years to recognise the bravery of these Australian soldiers. It is so long after the war, and many of the survivors of Sandakan camp are now dead, leaving just a few to enjoy the heritage they created.

In the second article, written after he returned to Adelaide, David describes his visit to Sandakan and to his father's grave in the Commonwealth War Graves Cemetery at Labuan, an island off the west coast of Borneo. After fifty-eight years, he was able to say goodbye to a father he had never known.[4]

A simple comment in the foyer of the Hyatt Regency Hotel in Sabah's city of Kota Kinabalu caused my first emotional attack on a pilgrimage to Borneo. 'One of the Duke's men had to be here.'

Speaking to me was C.W. 'Snowy' Marsh, eighty-three, of Cairns, who had travelled to Sabah at his own expense for the opening of the Commemorative Pavilion and the dedication of the memorial on the site of the infamous World War II Japanese prison camp. Snowy had come because of his tremendous respect for my dad, known as 'the Duke' because of his uncanny resemblance to the Duke of Gloucester. He had been a motorcycle dispatch rider in the Malayan campaign and was one of twenty-seven men in E Section, 8th Division Signals, trained by my father, Captain Lionel Matthews, GC, MC.

Dad was executed by the Japanese at Kuching on 2 March 1944 — defying them to the bitter end. I was choked with emotion meeting Snowy, whom I had not seen since the early 1980s. As we hugged each other in the foyer, the tears flowed.

Here was a man who had travelled thousands of kilometres to be with me when I attended the official ceremonies and visited Dad's grave. It was Snowy's first visit to Borneo, because his time as a prisoner of war had been in Japan.

I was in a party of twenty-four veterans and relatives of deceased veterans who had been farewelled by the prime minister, Mr Howard, at Sydney's Victoria Barracks. We went to Singapore for a ceremony at Kranji War Memorial and were delighted by the Australian International School Choir. At the end of the singing, the children lightened the atmosphere somewhat by scampering around to gather autographs from veterans on the tour. A service at Changi Gaol followed and included our first taste of tropical rain.

The next day we headed for Kota Kinabalu, known during World

War II days as Jesselton. Here we took part in a most unusual church service; it rained so heavily the chaplain decided to hold the service at Petagas War Memorial on the bus outside the cemetery. The memorial commemorates the 150 local people massacred by the Japanese in reprisal for an uprising led by Lieutenant Alex Kwok in 1943.

By contrast, the services at Sandakan were held in warm, humid weather. It is difficult to imagine what it would have been like in Sandakan POW camp during the war. In those days, the area surrounding the camp was flattened of foliage. Today, much of the original camp site is covered in thick jungle-tall trees, creeper and thick grass. As we sat during the cere-monies, butterflies flitted among the onlookers and squirrels could be seen playing high in the trees. No shouting now of Japanese guards as work par-ties moved out for another day's toil under the merciless sun.

The Sandakan memorial ceremony was very moving as the twelve-member Army band from Kapooka, New South Wales, played hymns and the paratroopers of the catafalque party from the 3rd Battalion, Royal Austra-lian Regiment, stood motionless around the stone memorial. It was difficult not to be affected by the ceremony and many of the veterans were teary-eyed.

Among the guests at the ceremony were local men who had been part of the underground organisation controlled by my father. It was an honour to meet them.

Other ceremonies were held at Ranau and finally at the Allied war cemetery on Labuan Island. At each ceremony, the tour leader, Repatria-tion Commissioner Major General Paul Stevens, chose members of the party to take part in either speaking roles or in the laying of wreaths. My turn came at Labuan, where I recited the prayer for world peace a mere 30 metres from Dad's grave.

After the ceremony I met Snowy Marsh again. He was the only person I saw wearing a coat in the hot, humid afternoon. I asked him why. 'Your father would have commanded it,' was his reply. 'He was a very natty dresser, you know, and every man in his section had to be well turned out.' So Snowy accompanied me to Dad's grave. I laid a beautiful sheaf of flowers kindly given to me by Mrs Joan Scott, wife of the Veterans' Affairs Minister Mr Bruce Scott. Snowy's tribute was simple — a single poppy from a man to his former leader. Snowy had delivered his final dispatch.

I feel at peace now about my father's demise. I know that he rests forever with his mates in tranquil surrounds at Labuan.

It's a comforting thought.

Reflections

ANGELA GUNN

Captain Colin Percival Juttner (SX14044)
2/9th Field Ambulance, AIF
POW: Changi, Kranji; Burma-Thailand Railway

Colin Juttner was married, with a young son, when he enlisted as a medical officer with the 2/13th Australian General Hospital (AGH) on 16 April 1941. He was sent to Malaya later that year where he was transferred to the 2/9th Field Ambulance. After the Allied surrender, he spent the next fourteen months in both Changi and Kranji camps in Singapore. In April 1943 Colin went to Thailand as one of ten Australian medical officers on F Force. He was based at Kami Sonkurai, the most northern camp occupied by the Australians, about 10 kilometres from the Burmese border.

Only thirty-four Australian medical officers accompanied the more than 13,000 Australian POWs working along the entire length of the Burma-Thailand Railway.[1] Like the other Allied medical officers they had to make do with supplies they had brought from Singapore and any bits and pieces they had managed to collect along the way. To most Allied POWs, these railway medicos were heroes or even 'saints' as they struggled to look after the men, performing complicated amputations and other operations with minimal equipment and drugs. They managed to improvise and design extraordinary pieces of surgical equipment to assist them and their patients but despite their efforts, nearly 3000 Australian POWs labouring on the railway died through sickness, starvation, injuries and violence. In May and June 1943, cholera broke out in the camps and F Force was particularly badly hit by the disease.

The railway was completed in October 1943 and by December the Japanese had shipped most of the railway survivors back to Singapore. By then, 29 per cent of the 3664 Australians in F Force had died.[2]

Colin Juttner remained in Singapore until his liberation. Back home in South Australia he returned to his general medical practice at Woodside and he and Pat had their second child, their daughter Angela.

In November 2004, sixteen months after her father's death, Angela and her husband travelled to Thailand for the Remembrance Day services at the Burma-Thailand Railway. They were able to visit the site of the camp at Kami Sonkurai where her father had spent seven months in 1943.

I was born in June 1947, two years after the end of World War II and two years after my father returned from three and a half years as a POW in Changi and later on the Burma-Thailand Railway.

From the moment I became cognisant, his war experiences became part of my life. I could not compare the personality of the man who went to war with the one that returned. I just accepted the way he was. As a small child I didn't give a great deal of thought to what he had been through, other than to listen to his stories. However, I did realise that his health was affected.

After marrying my mother in 1938, they had travelled to England to enable him to study for a scholarship in surgery. War broke out, the course was cancelled and they returned to Australia. My brother was born in 1940, Dad enlisted and was sent to Malaya.

During the war years my mother lived in the Adelaide Hills with her mother and my brother. Dad had established a medical practice before departing and Mum oversaw the running of the practice with a series of locums. She wrote constantly to Dad throughout the war and, until the fall of Singapore and his subsequent imprisonment, he wrote wonderful letters to her. Dad was reported missing and for much of the duration of the war she did not know whether he was dead or alive.

Mum's only brother, Peter Seppelt, was also reported missing after the sinking of the *Perth* in the Sunda Strait in February 1942. His body was never found.

In 1944, after my father's return to Changi from the Burma railway, he received twenty-seven backdated letters from my mother in one day. All the letters between my parents, as well as telegrams and government reports have been preserved. They are an amazing resource that I have only recently read, following the death of my mother in 2004. They capture the period and their separation with such clarity.

After the war life seemed like a precious gift. The men were told they probably wouldn't live beyond fifty. Dad was frail and unwell and decided not to take up the government's offer to return to study, but rather to remain in general practice in the Adelaide Hills and enjoy life with his young family.

Dad had a number of health problems. His gall bladder had to be removed as a result of the palm oil consumed while a POW, he suffered from long strain malaria and was subject to debilitating effects of the disease for twenty-five years. He also suffered from severe migraine headaches until well into his seventies.

He was a great believer in the powers of physical fitness. He took up riding with a vengeance, exercised every day of his life when he got up,

PAT, COLIN, ANGELA AND HER BABY DAUGHTER ALICE, JANUARY 1977

practised yoga, waterskied and worked hard on the property. His health gradually improved and he died as a result of a fall, just before his ninety-third birthday. He remained active and at home until the end — rather an amazing outcome given his projected life expectancy!

Today soldiers return from war and receive counselling — this did not happen then. Dad found it hard to adjust to civilian life. He was traumatised by his memories, couldn't sleep, and felt totally displaced among people who hadn't experienced the brutality of war. I heard only recently about a woman who had been the matron at the Woodside hospital after the war. She said that Dad would often visit and sit with his patients in the middle of the night, because sleep eluded him at home.

Dad was a very complex person. How much his personality was affected by the war I don't know. My mother was always very protective of him and wouldn't discuss the matter. He could be moody, blunt or fly into a temper easily. He always wanted to be in control and he upset a lot of people, but my mother never censured him. He could equally be urbane and charming. He was widely read and had the most inquiring, searching mind of anyone I have ever met. My birth was a great joy to him and we were always very close. I always tried to please him and we shared many interests. I was always instinctively well behaved — life with Dad was like treading on eggshells.

I used to wonder what Dad would be like as a grandparent — whether he would be tolerant or very strict. As it turned out, he was wonderful in the role. He adored our three children, followed their development with great interest and treated them all as individuals. When they reached maturity he treated them as adults and valued their opinions. He also had a lot of fun with them.

In his last years, Dad suffered from quite severe depression. War memories flooded back and plagued him and he became more moody. In the few weeks between his fall and his death, he seemed obsessed with his POW years and talked about them with me a great deal.

In November 2004, sixteen months after Dad's death, my husband and I went on a Burma-Thailand Railway trip organised by Lieutenant Colonel Peter Winstanley from the Defence Reserves Association. My father never went back to the railway. My mother wasn't interested in going with him. He once planned to take me but Mum became ill so we didn't go. This trip proved to be a cathartic experience for me. We travelled along parts of the railway, saw the feats of construction, visited museums and the place names that had been imprinted on my mind since childhood.

There were three wonderful old POWs on the trip. They gave us horrific accounts of treatment meted out to individuals by the guards and vivid impressions of the squalor, disease and hopelessness of the situation. Dad always played that side down — I realised there was much he wanted left unsaid.

Dad's camp was at Kami Sonkurai. This was the most northerly camp, near the Thai-Burma border. The area is still largely undeveloped. During the monsoon, the POWs were marched by night over 300 kilometres through virgin jungle to the more remote camps. One can scarcely imagine what it must have been like, but I found myself constantly looking into the jungle with its giant bamboos. Turning back time, imagining the journey, I just wish that my father had known that I had trodden in his footsteps. I don't think he would have been surprised and I know he would have been thrilled.

A Fighter Right to the End

SUE BYRNE

Signalman Henry John Fletcher Sweet (NX69992)
8th Division Signals, AIF
POW: Changi; Naoetsu

Henry Sweet was born in Paddington, New South Wales, on 14 May 1920. He had served with the 1st Battalion in the Australian Militia Force (AMF) for two years before he enlisted in the AIF on 13 March 1941. Signalman Henry Sweet sailed from Australia with 8th Division Signals second and third reinforcements and joined the unit in Malaya on 15 August 1941. Six months later he became a POW.

On 29 November 1942, he was transported with C Force from Singapore to Naoetsu in northern Japan, where he worked in factories and on the wharves unloading coal ships (sometimes in blinding snowstorms) until the end of the war. In September 1945, Henry returned from Japan on the *Tjitjalengha*, a hospital ship. He met his wife Maureen in 1946 at the first 8th Division Younger Set ball, held at the Trocadero in Sydney when Maureen made her debut to General Gordon Bennett. They were married on 24 December 1948 and Henry and Maureen's only daughter Sue was born in 1953.

Sue wrote the story below shortly after her father died in June, 2001.

Today is Father's Day and just three months since my dad, Henry, died. He had gradually become increasingly frail, and was confined to a wheelchair for the last eighteen months of his life. My daughter and I were sitting with him, holding his hands, when he took his last breath. Dad was a fighter right to the end.

He had cancer of the prostate with secondaries throughout his abdomen. We only realised he was suffering immense pain in the last week of his life, when it became evident that the weight of a blanket on his stomach caused him terrible discomfort. Even then, he found it hard to admit to his agony, still saying he was 'all right'. A few days before he died he finally confessed to the doctor that the pain was unbearable and getting worse every day. He had the mindset of a soldier, a POW, who had seen and endured terrible atrocities with courage, dignity and a very stoic attitude.

His death was an immensely spiritual experience. Dad's breathing was very laboured all day before he died, but he still struggled valiantly on. Eventually, his grip on our hands slackened and he just concentrated on the terrible effort to breathe as life slipped away. Shortly before he died, I was filled with an intense certainty that his spirit was calling out to me, saying, 'I have to go now. Will you be all right?' Even in the act of death, he was still being my dad, my protector, whose last thoughts were for his only child and her family.

When I was born in 1953, Mum and Dad were living in Epping in Sydney. I was very loved and doted on by both parents, and they appeared very happy together.

Tragically, my brother John, who was born four years later, was severely affected by RH incompatibility and only survived a few weeks after birth. I can still remember the phone call in the middle of the night to say he had died, and the inconsolable grief of my parents. As a mother now, I have some understanding of how great their agony must have been. Because of the RH factor they were counselled that the risk to other subsequent children would be even greater, so they were dealt a double blow. Dad was already drinking heavily, and Mum and Dad separated when I was seven.

Dad, absolutely devastated, went through a very bad time that I don't think he would have survived without the love and support of his sister, other family members and some wonderful friends.

SUE AND HENRY, 1966

From my earliest memories, I knew that Dad had been a POW and I was smugly proud of the fact. Dad was in L Section, 8th Division Signals, and, after the fall of Singapore, he was taken as a POW to Naoetsu in northern Japan. Whenever he was asked why he thought he survived Naoetsu, he would shrug his shoulders and say, 'Well, I think it was because I was extremely fit to start off with.' My dad had been very involved with amateur athletics and before enlisting he was New South Wales Junior Champion Walker.

When I was a child, Dad recounted to me tales of the terrible cold and snow in Japan, of not having enough blankets or warm clothes, and of eating watery rice stew with seaweed. I knew he had worked in coalmines and loaded and unloaded ships.

His story about some American soldiers landing at the end of World War II, who gave a group of Japanese children their first taste of chewing gum, has always remained a vivid memory. Apparently, the Japanese kids thought they had developed lockjaw when their teeth started to stick together with the chewing gum. I can also remember Dad saying how foolish he felt when, after the war, he was walking along a city street and a car backfired close by. Dad thought he was being shot at and ducked for cover.

He was strangely reticent about discussing atrocities committed in camp, saying it gave him nightmares to do so. After he died, I found nine pages that he had handwritten in pencil, hidden among old family photos. They were details of some of the atrocities committed on him and other POW's at the Naoetsu prison camp. Although Dad testified at the war crimes trial of the Naoetsu camp guards, he held no animosity towards the younger Japanese generation.

My dad Henry was an intelligent, dynamic person who loved sport, a drink, parties and pretty women. He had a booming voice and he could be very blunt. He was determined and pig-headed and I realise that these traits helped him to survive the POW camp. He also had a very strong code of ethics. He was always there for me and I greatly miss his amazing and unconditional love.

My Hero

PETER O'DONNELL

Sergeant Jack Herbert O'Donnell (NX59210)
2/10th Australian General Hospital, AIF
POW: Changi

Sergeant Jack O'Donnell was born in Singleton, New South Wales, on 27 May 1909. He trained as a schoolteacher and taught until his enlistment in the AIF on 15 July 1940. Jack sailed on the *Queen Mary* with the 2/10th Australian General Hospital (AGH) and remained with the AGH in Changi during his imprisonment.

Jack managed to continue irregular entries in his diary while he was imprisoned and just weeks after their capture he noted that most of the 'boys' had 'already lost a stone or more in weight' (6 kilograms) and that more than 400 of the men already had dysentery.[1]

On 12 May 1943, Jack wrote that the high rate of sickness among the AIF men remaining on Singapore (approximately 2000 on the island, with 1000 of them in the hospital area) meant that he and other able-bodied hospital staff would volunteer to go out on work parties.

Have been in a wood trailer party every second day for past month — on my day off. A nine mile trip on rice, pulling like horses is not the best, and many men are incapable of doing it — hence a few of us in the AGHs have been doing it voluntarily… Ninety per cent of the troops have suffered with deficiency diseases — Happy feet,[2] Eczema Scrotum, Blurred vision, sore throats, tongues and swollen lips — this shortage of food and medical supplies is sure becoming serious. I personally have always been reasonably fit and I am sure it has stood me in good stead while here. I've had feet, tongue and throat trouble but fortunately not serious, while my eyesight is still unimpaired. Green grass soup seems to be doing more good for the eyes than anything else. Sweet potato tops, hibiscus leaves and couch grass are part of our daily diet; in fact we not only work like horses, we eat like them too.[3]

Three days after the Japanese surrender in 1945, Jack noted that despite the Japanese surrender it was 'work for the Imperial Japanese Army as usual'. He was now 8 stone 10 lbs [55 kilograms] and 'one of the heavyweights in camp'.[4] Twelve days later on 30 August he commented that although there was now plenty of food from Red Cross parcels, he still hadn't left the camp and was taking things very easy. 'My ulcers and tropical pemphigus [sic][5] still not so good. Bandages on four limbs — all the lads tell me I must have fallen at the last hurdle.'[6]

Jack was finally repatriated on the *Duntroon*, sailing from Singapore on 20 September 1945. According to Stella, his wife, he was a 'real wreck' when he returned. 'He had malaria, dysentery, beri-beri, you name it there was a big long list of things wrong. He used to say he was the fittest man in Australia until the Japanese got him.'

Jack and Stella had only just met when he left for Malaya.

They met up again when he returned and were married at St Peter's Church, Richmond, on 14 December 1946. Stella who was eleven years younger than Jack and who 'comes from a family of soldiers', had also enlisted. She joined the Australian Women's Army Service (AWAS) when she was twenty-one.[7]

Peter, Stella and Jack's third child, was born six years after his older siblings, twins Margaret and Ross. Like their father, Peter and Margaret are both schoolteachers. Peter lives with and cares for his mother in their family home at North Richmond in New South Wales.

Dad was one of ten children, five boys and five girls. Before the war he became a teacher and he was stationed at several National Fitness Camps, including Broken Bay. He loved all sports and was a champion tennis player, winning many tournaments and championships. Dad was seeded in the top ten in New South Wales in the glory days of our many Davis Cup victories. As well as tennis, he played cricket, bowls, golf and many indoor sports proficiently.

In 1937 Dad was appointed to Tennyson Public School, a one-teacher school, near North Richmond. He used to ride his bike down from where he boarded in Kurmond, until the day he joined the Army in 1939.

After he was captured in 1942, Dad spent three and a half years as a POW of the Japanese in Changi prison camp. During this period he wrote a diary of events, which he hid inside a hollowed broom:[8]

This small book of reminiscences has been written, not with the idea of having my fast fading memories penned to paper, but just as a means of wiling [sic] away a few monotonous hours as a POW.

We still have his original diary, and excerpts from it can be found on the Internet on the website 'Australia's War 1939–1945'.[9]

Dad returned to Australia in 1945 and married my mum, Stella, in 1946. He was reappointed to Tennyson School in 1948 and purchased a house across the road from the school. Power was installed only one week

JACK WITH THE TWINS, MARGARET AND ROSS

before my parents moved in. My brother and sister, Ross and Margaret (twins), were born in 1947. Mum and I still live in the house today.

Tennyson School closed in 1952 and Dad moved to nearby Richmond Primary School, where he taught until his death in 1968. He transported many local kids to school in his car. My brother, sister and I attended Dad's school; it was pleasant having him there.

After the war Dad suffered from constant ill health. He battled malaria, beri-beri, tropical and stomach ulcers, anaemia and high blood pressure. Before the war he was 'the fittest man in Australia', but he returned weighing only half his original body weight as a result of sickness and starvation.

He couldn't eat big meals as his stomach had shrunk. He suffered nightmares and probably depression, although no counselling services were available in those days. Despite his illnesses, Dad was a wonderful father. He liked getting out and about and took us kids on many outings. One of my fondest memories was of our family gatherings for Christmas at Swansea on Lake Macquarie. We went swimming, fishing and exploring with all my cousins, uncles, aunts and grandparents.

With 3 acres and 200 fruit trees, our little property at Tennyson was a perfect place to grow up, with many adventures, pets to care for and a lovely little creek as our bottom boundary. We kids spent countless hours building things and keeping ourselves amused, as there was no TV. We always had poultry — chooks, geese and ducks, many dogs, cats, guinea pigs, goats, rabbits, mice and horses. Some of our wild visitors included echidnas, possums, flying foxes, and birds of all descriptions, foxes, snakes, goannas, lizards and hares. Growing up in Tennyson was paradise for kids, with neighbours and friends dropping in regularly. Some of the local parties were great, with lots of singing, dancing, poetry and fun.

Dad's willpower kept him going, despite his problems. He didn't like talking about the war, but I can remember that he would never buy any Japanese products.

Whether consciously or subconsciously, I have lived my life similarly to Dad's. I enjoy a beer, a smoke, fishing and sports and I share his love of animals and the outdoors. I am also a teacher, as is my sister. Dad enjoyed growing plants, fruit and vegetables, as I do.

During the early days in Tennyson, Dad and Mum resurrected Tennyson Bush Fire Brigade and when there were federal and state elections polling booths were placed on our verandah. Dad was highly respected, both as a member of our small community and as a local schoolteacher. I wouldn't swap my special upbringing by both my parents, for anyone's! Sometimes I feel cheated that, due to his imprisonment, I was robbed of my father before his time.

I was only fourteen when my dad died but I still feel him around, quite often. I can remember feeling devastated at the time, but as the years have gone by, I feel his moral and social influences on me have stood me in good stead. Like most boys, my dad was my hero!

PETER WITH HIS FATHER'S AUSTIN A-40

Hugh Waring: My Father

DIANA VALLANCE

Lieutenant Hugh Waring (NX65585)
8th Division Headquarters, AIF
POW: Changi; Sandakan/Kuching

Hugh Waring, who was born in 1917, believes he was 'just the right age' to be a POW, not too young and not too old. He also believes there were many positive moments during his incarceration — particularly in Lintang Barracks in Kuching — and that it was 'not necessarily a life of constant fear and unpredictable violence...many people who survived never went back to a complacent life ... they knew they could do anything they put their mind to'.[1] Hugh certainly did — his life changed dramatically after he was liberated in 1945. As a young and newly promoted lieutenant he had lived with other POWs from a variety of backgrounds, many of whom had academic qualifications. He was also fortunate to be in a camp in which these men organised an academic program for the benefit of their fellow prisoners. Having left school early, Hugh was determined never to return to the office life and clerical work he had done before the war.

In July 1942, Hugh was sent with B Force from Changi to Sandakan. Once there, he and the other officers were put into work parties. In 1943, when the Japanese discovered the underground network, they separated most of the officers from the men and Hugh was part of the group sent to Kuching in October 1943. His promotion 'in the field' to lieutenant probably saved his life: of the POWs who remained at Sandakan in 1943, only six survived.

After their liberation from Kuching, Hugh returned to Sydney on the *Wanganella* in October 1945. He enrolled at the University of Sydney where he studied to become a forest soil scientist under the Commonwealth Reconstruction Training Scheme. He also met Adele Perrin, whom he married in 1947. They produced seven children: four daughters and three sons. Hugh and Del live at Robertson in the Southern Highlands of New South Wales and together they have more energy than most people half their ages.

Diana, Hugh and Del's eldest daughter, remembers a conversation with her father when they were shopping together in Moss Vale one day. They were talking about security codes for the personal identification of credit cards and Hugh told her that during his conversation with the bank he had asked them: 'Did it have to be a number?' 'No,' they said. 'So I used a word I knew I would never forget — "Sandakan"!'

Sandakan — Kuching it took years to sort out the stories.
For years it was relics in the dining room cupboard
in suburban Canberra —
wooden clogs, a bible with hand writing
around the margin of each page,
some marmite and fish paste,
two faded sketches of a prison camp,
a book of posters for musical performances
and a photo of a young soldier on the lowboy
in our parent's bedroom.
Oh, and the rats that nibbled their toe nails
as they lay on their three boards haunted my childhood.
There was the coming home photo in the box
of family photos in the foyer cupboard
— all the Warings and Dunlops at the repat hospital in Sydney —
Hugh's face bloated and everyone smiling.
He never went to Anzac Day marches,
never wore the medals in his sock drawer
but usually attended reunions.
But all through the 60s and 70s the war stories we heard
were of a massive life changing adventure.
His mates' personalities larger than ordinary life:
the ones with a sense of humour, musical skills, organising activities,
the crazy brave ones the Japs hated,
the clever ones with multiple degrees, the career soldiers,
the ones with pre-war families.
How lucky he was in his hut-mates — what terrific people
they were — how they supported each other.

Hugh lives his life according to a personal philosophy that was forged largely from his experiences as a prisoner of war for three and a half years in Sandakan/Kuching during World War II. His life post-war has had goals and integrity and has been directed by his personal choices. He chose to study for a science degree and a professional career as a soil scientist. An abiding interest in the environment and in botany — in particular, trees — has been his lifelong personal passion. He chose personal fulfilment: marriage and seven children. After the war, he left behind organised

HUGH AND DEL WARING WITH THEIR FAMILY, FEBRUARY 1992

religion and a narrow focus on life. He has lived, he says, each day as a bonus.

As I write these words about my father, Hugh Waring, I am aware that I share him with my six siblings. However, he is of course my father as well as our father. My view of Hugh, as a father, is just that — one view out of seven. One seventh of the possible views of Hugh as a father. My view started in 1950, five years after the end of the war that changed his life and loomed large in my/our lives. In 1950 Hugh was studying for his science degree at the University of Sydney, taking full advantage of the educational opportunities offered to returned servicemen. His younger brother Stan was at university too and our half of our shared house in Hornsby in north-west Sydney was given over to study and babies, as I joined my two-year-old brother Tom, my mother Del, and the other students. We frequently visited our maternal grandparents in Tea Gardens, on the Myall River north of Newcastle, where Hugh and Del met within months of his return from prison camp at the end of 1945. Hugh still has the letters he wrote to his mother from the hospital ship as he planned his fateful post-war holiday in Tea Gardens, a holiday based on fishing stories told in the prison camp about local fisherman Tom Perrin, Adele's father.

Our family life depended on Hugh's choice of partner. He chose a tall, challenging, forthright, smart, good-looking young woman of twenty-two: Adele Perrin. She chose a youngish, serious, philosophical, curious, committed, loyal man of twenty-nine. Both were mad keen to get on with their lives after the war. During the war Del worked in a munitions factory making machined parts for the rear sights for Bren guns. They married in 1947. She became a ferocious and committed pacifist.

Both my parents had left school at fourteen to seek work in the aftermath of the Great Depression. Del worked with her father in his boat hire business on the Myall River at Tea Gardens. Hugh went to work in Sydney in various junior positions in a range of businesses, mainly as a messenger boy in the Sydney CBD. He spent his leisure time involved in church activities associated with the Methodist church at Thornleigh. He imagined he would marry a good Methodist girl who played the piano. His mother imagined that Hugh would become a Methodist minister. The war changed all those plans. Del's father's boats were confiscated and hidden for the duration of the war and Hugh volunteered for the AIF. He was considered well qualified as he and his older brother George had been keen rabbit shooters all through the 1930s. A beautiful rabbit skin rug adorned my parent's bed all through my early childhood as a legacy of those hunting skills.

After completing his science degree at Sydney University and an honours thesis on the soils of the Pillaga Scrub, Hugh won a prestigious Harkness scholarship to travel and study in the United States for a year. Joan, who was born in February 1952, had to be weaned and then she and I stayed with Dad's brother George and his wife Dot, while Tom stayed with Del's parents for all of 1953. What an amazing adventure it was for them; what a long wait it was for us. They travelled by air and boat, camped out and stayed with fascinating and influential people in the USA and came home via Britain and Europe, which were both still recovering from the war. Hugh could have stayed and worked in America, a very wealthy country compared to Australia in those days. Instead, they came home determined to start Hugh's career and to continue with their family life in Canberra, where Hugh was to work for the Forestry and Timber Bureau.

The coniferous forests of America and Europe, as well as his work in Australia growing radiata pine softwood forests, had inspired Hugh. Once he and Del were back at home, he started looking for land to grow trees. He persuaded his brother George and his wife Dot to become partners and by 1955 he had narrowed his search to the rich, red volcanic soil of Robertson in the Southern Highlands of New South Wales. They bought 30 acres of bracken- and blackberry-covered steep hillsides that included 5 acres of scrub—remnant temperate rainforest. Our families set to work on weekends to clear land, build a shack, pile up stones, plant potatoes, import and germinate tree seeds, set out nurseries, trap rabbits and build fences — all by hand. Tools were bracken hooks, spades, picks, machetes and axes. We used kerosene tins as buckets, had a drop toilet, a kerosene fridge, pressure lanterns and washed up in a dish with water from a small galvanised tank. We, the children, ran wild. Dressed in jodhpurs and windcheaters, we built cubbyhouses, swung on ropes like Tarzan in the rainforest, made bows and arrows, trapped, skinned and ate rabbits, walked to the next door farm for fresh whole milk in a billy and to another farm to catch yabbies and fish from a dam. We cooked on a wood stove and for years used the smart camping equipment (aluminium plates and red sleeping bags) that Hugh and Del had brought back from America.

Our 4 x 8 metre hut was also full of ex-army surplus gear as our Uncle George still worked for the Army ordnance depot at Liverpool. We had army greatcoats, boots, trousers and rain capes, while our cupboards and stools were made out of ammunition boxes. We were wild hill tree farmers for nearly every second weekend and most school holidays throughout the 1950s and 1960s.

When we went home, it was to an orderly life in a red-brick bungalow in suburban Canberra with all the mod cons, manicured gardens, paved footpaths, excellent schools and an ever-increasing family. In 1954 Megan was born, followed by Brett in 1957. Great Aunt Mary came to live with us in about 1958 and Roger was born in 1960. By now, our suburban villa was overflowing and Hugh and Del took out a war service loan to extend the house and we luxuriated in the extra space. Paula was born in 1966.

The tree farm at Robertson is my father's personal indulgence and yet, as an enterprise, it was never entirely personal. It functioned as an extended family meeting place until Dot and George sold their share to Hugh and Del in the mid-seventies. During the big development years of the fifties to mid-sixties, the combined manual labour of the two families was crucial and meant that the brothers met frequently, accompanied by at least a couple of their children. Sitting around fires listening to Hugh and George discuss politics, philosophy, religion and the war and reminisce about their boyhoods and their extended family was central to the Robertson experience. There were spirited discussions about how, when and where to do things and at any moment the discussions on any of these topics could become loud arguments from firmly entrenched positions. I learned that it is possible to argue, disagree and yet remain friends.

For Hugh and George, it perhaps operated as a place outside their regular work and family lives where they could do dangerous and challenging physical work, make all the decisions themselves and see the results of their labours, in effect, to say and do whatever they liked. Del's contribution to this boys' own adventure should not be underestimated. She had to deal with Hugh's frequent absences, organise and wash all the filthy work gear, have the food for the weekends organised, plan the Robertson family holidays and agree to spend scarce family financial resources on the enterprise. 'Robertson clothes' referred to particular items of clothing that were separate from school clothes and good clothes.

Folklore has it that some time in the mid-sixties Del suggested they cut trees at Christmas and sell them in Wollongong to help defray the costs of the farm. We started by thinning existing plantings of Douglas fir and the first trees were, by our recent standards, sparse misshapen things. Hugh, Del, Dot and George decided to cooperate in the selling enterprise. Dot and George took their caravan to a site in an abandoned quarry at the back of the North Wollongong Caltex service station and basically ran the selling site for nearly thirty years. Hugh and Del stayed at the farm and ran the teams of family members and friends who worked as cutters, loaders and drivers and who prepared the trees for sale. So for a crazy ten to twelve days each December, our families have run a Christmas tree sale every year for the last forty years. Dot and George stopped selling about ten years ago and we have wound back the selling in Wollongong and now mainly sell from the farm.

For Hugh though, his heart is in the trees he has grown, not the sales. He has small forests of radiata pines and Douglas firs and smaller stands of firs, spruce and pines from Europe and the USA. He has some fine eucalypts and plantings of rainforest trees, such as Morteon Bay, chestnut and red cedar. There is a memorial grove of ginkgo trees, dedicated to his late daughter Joan, and some Japanese trees, such as sugi and hinoke. Since his retirement Hugh has greatly enjoyed planting a range of specimen trees around the farm. The result is a personal arboretum of over 200 species, which after his family, is his pride and joy.

Robertson, in effect, embodies my father. He chose it because of its rich volcanic soil. He has dedicated all his spare time and money to it for the last fifty years. All his passion and knowledge about trees and the world of nature is exemplified in the plantings at Robertson. In Hugh and Del's retirement, Robertson has become a joint venture for both of them and a beautiful place for family and friends to visit. The other by-product of the tree farm has been the logs that were thinned from the Douglas fir forest in the early 1980s by Ray, Hugh's son-in-law, other family members and some German backpackers. They were stored and dried for about five years in a shed built on traditional local lines. We then built a log cabin onto the original Robertson hut that has been Hugh and Del's retirement home since 1988. At Easter 2005, Hugh and Del hosted a gathering of over two hundred family and friends to celebrate fifty years of tree planting at Robertson and the sixtieth year of Hugh's post-war survival.

Hugh has no personal animosity towards the Japanese people as a result of his war experiences. He does say ironically that things were so dire by August 1945 that their lives were literally saved by the dropping of the atomic bomb on Japan. To this day, he enjoys eating rice, he still sings camp songs and he is grateful to the Japanese government for the seven years of tertiary education they provided to his daughter Joan. On his best days he wonders why the Japanese bothered keeping the prisoners alive at all, once their work as coolies was over. Through Joan's language and research skills, Hugh has in his latter years come to personally know a former guard from his camp. He and our family have thus been able to witness and participate in war reconciliation and reparation on a very personal level.

Hugh has attended the funerals of most of his wartime friends and prepared moving eulogies for many of them. 'Who will talk for me?' he mused one day, knowing that he will never know and also knowing that the passing of his generation of war survivors and their values is a great historical event.

Questions from my childhood

How come you survived the prison camp, Dad?
1 My mother fed me porridge as a baby.
2 I learned to live like a coolie and like it.
3 They dropped the bombs on Japan.

How come you survived after the war, Dad?
1 I met and married Del and had my seven children.
2 I did my degree at Sydney uni and had an interesting career.
3 I grew trees at Robertson.

What changed you the most, Dad?
1 I lost my religious belief.
2 I found a zest for life through science.
3 I learned to live each day as a bonus.

What scars do you have, Dad?
1 Tropical ulcers like sunbursts on my legs.
2 Mid-life fear of dying — survival guilt?
3 Recurring dreams — fear and loss?

Who helped you survive, Dad?
1 Colonel Stahle who promoted me in the field.
2 My friends Eddie, Bunny, Johnny, Slugo.
3 My parents, George and Polly.

How did you survive your survival, Dad?
1 I developed a personal philosophy.
2 I committed myself to my family.
3 I grounded myself in nature.

What do I need to survive, Dad?
1 Learn to be a good camper.
2 Have a gold bar as a doorstop.
3 Hoard a drum of rice.

What skills do I need to survive, Dad?
1 Tolerate discomfort.
2 Turn adversity into fun.
3 View life as an adventure, but be careful.

What philosophy do I need to survive, Dad?
1 All living things are interrelated.
2 Develop carefully considered values.
3 Death is the one great mystery.

How come you really survived Dad?
1 Luck.
2 Fate.
3 Chance.

Honto ni honto ni setsunai ne
(Truly, Truly a Pitiful Sight)

JOAN KWEK

Lieutenant Hugh Waring (NX65585)
8th Division Headquarters, AIF
POW: Changi; Sandakan/Kuching

In many respects, Joan's story is a sequel to Diana's account of growing up in the Waring family. Joan, Hugh and Del Waring's second daughter, wrote 'Honto ni honto ni setsunai ne' (Truly, Truly a Pitiful Sight) in 1995, three years before her death in Canberra. Joan spent the last years of her too brief life trying to make sense of the POW experience. Her father Hugh encouraged me to include her essay, believing it should be read by anyone interested in the POW experience. I needed no encouragement; in fact, Joan's essay has been the impetus for this collection.

Joan Kwek died in March 1998, just months after she was diagnosed with liver cancer. Her parents believe that Joan's intense preoccupation with her father's POW experiences may have been a factor that caused her to neglect her health.

I first met Joan at the Australian War Memorial in 1995. She was in the Sandakan area of the new 'Victory in the Pacific' exhibition, explaining her father's POW experiences to her family. Thus we began our all too brief friendship. Joan's enthusiasm and knowledge of the POWs and their captors was impressive and rather daunting and, although we met originally through our mutual interest in Sandakan, Joan was determined to assist me with my own research. Whenever she found someone or something she thought would be useful to me, she would send me little notes, often scribbled on request slips from the War Memorial, the National Archives or the National Library.

Joan had spent seven years studying in Japan and had met and married her Chinese Malaysian husband Hong while she was living there. In 1995 she located and translated a small booklet she found in the National Library. It had been written by a Formosan guard from the Kuching POW camp in western Borneo, the camp in which her father had spent the last two years of the war. The guard, Hayashi Miki, felt he had been most unjustly vilified and imprisoned for his prison camp role during World War II and he responded enthusiastically when Joan wrote to him.

Some months after I met Joan, I had the opportunity to travel to North Borneo to visit the site of the Sandakan POW camp. Soon after I returned Joan sent me her account of her correspondence with Hayashi. She told me later that she had sent it to a handful of people whom she thought might be interested to read of her activities but that I was the only one who had responded. It confirmed her belief that many Australians were not yet ready for an open discussion about the POW experience, one that incorporates the experiences of both the protagonists.

During this time, Joan continued to correspond with Hayashi who was clearly overjoyed with his new-found Australian friend. He was so keen to meet Joan that he organised to visit her in Canberra almost immediately. His timing could not have been worse. Joan's illness had just been diagnosed and she wrote, asking him not to come. Undeterred, he travelled to Canberra anyway. Although Joan was able to meet him, she was not well enough to spend much time with him and it was her parents and a local Japanese friend who were given the task of showing their visitor around Canberra.

Being merely an observer, I had not expected to meet Hayashi. However, Joan's Japanese friend introduced him to me when she was showing him around the War Memorial. Would anyone working around me in the Research Centre have even believed that this small and very polite Formosan tourist was a convicted war criminal?

Despite her illness, Joan kept on with her research, continuing to contact people who had been involved with Sandakan and Kuching. She would sit propped up in bed with her laptop, seemingly pragmatic about the medical paraphernalia that had necessarily overtaken her body and her bedroom. She was determined to keep working as long as she could.

Joan's years in Japan were reflected in the style of both her home and her cooking. She particularly loved ginkgo trees,[1] often placing one of the distinctive leaves in among her correspondence. She propagated the seedlings in small pots around her front door, distributing them later to her family and friends.

It wasn't until I heard the eulogies at Joan's funeral that I realised she had worked just as enthusiastically within the Waring family and the Canberra community as within the POWsphere, organising most of their family functions as well as participating in her children's school committees and other local groups. Joan Kwek was an exceptional woman with a unique ability to pursue and interpret the POW experience.

Sandakan is a name I have lived with all my life, from back when nobody had ever heard of the place. Sandakan was the reason my father Hugh cooked *nasi goreng*, when other people ate rice with milk and sugar, and Sandakan was the place where Dad made his wooden clogs. They sat then, as they do now, on top of the bookshelf near the front door, along with the tiny bible with the scribbles in the margins and the two stained pencil sketches of huts with thatched roofs.

Dad said it was at Sandakan that he learned to eat comfortably lying down, like at a picnic with no chairs. At Sandakan they used to debate for hours whether it was better to eat fast and enjoy it, or chew carefully for a long time. They couldn't decide. At Sandakan Dad got the scar on his leg from the tropical ulcer that wouldn't heal, and on long trips in the car he taught us a song from the Celebes, 'Pagi pagi belayar di laut' (Every day I sail the seas) in mangled Malay.

Sandakan was also somehow the reason why my father went to

Diana (Vallance) and Joan (Kwek), c. 1966

university to study science, even though he hadn't finished high school, and the reason why I went to university in Japan, after my father saw a notice about Japanese government scholarships, pinned up over the water cooler at work. It may have been the reason he ended up having seven kids after the war when he wasn't even Catholic, and it was certainly the reason why he stopped going to church, never wore his medals, and never marched in Anzac Day parades.

He did, however, disappear off to Sydney once a year for the reunion of Old Sandakians. Here he met up with friends to whom you didn't have to explain anything because they already knew everything. We never did get to hear much about life at Sandakan from him. We got more from other ex-POWs when they visited, bearing colourful stories about split-toed Japanese Army boots, and about tricking guards into forcing the prisoners to eat raw eggs because they were supposed to be so disgusting.

But the best images we got were from the strange book *Borneo Burlesque*, also up on the bookcase, which was put together on the boat back to Australia. This book amused us endlessly with its 'programs' for the countless musicals and plays that were put on in camp, and the hilarious pencil sketches of the wild-eyed, skinny men wearing lap-laps. My dad was in the choir called 'The Sextet'.

I later learned that Sandakan was only half the story, as my father and his reunion mates were moved to the Japanese Army Borneo headquarters at Kuching about halfway through the war because they were officers. All but six of the couple of thousand that stayed behind died, through sickness, violence or on the death marches. But it was at Sandakan that my father learned to become a coolie, building the airstrip, while it was at Kuching that he had the chance to read, devouring the personal library confiscated from a British civilian who marked his books 'Ex Libris Johnsoni'. In all, he was interned for three and a half years.

The Old Sandakians' Association has an interesting logo, nicknamed the 'potato man' by certain disrespectful wives. It is a little roundish man, the shape of Borneo, marching along with a hoe over his shoulder. I was sharply reminded of the potato man recently when in the course of my research job I came across a mocking song in a Japanese language book held in the National Library of Australia. The book was written by, of all people, a former guard at Kuching prison camp and the song was a *kae-itta*, a parody of a popular Japanese tune, set with catchy new words by the Kuching guards. The bulk of the book is heavy with outdated military terms and is a bit hard to read, but the song itself is quite simple. It goes:

Kuching meisho wa san mairu
Naka ni haireba shuyo-jo
Shiro ya kuro no furyo-tachi ga
Kuwa o katsuide kashira migi
Honto ni honto ni setsunai ne.

The most famous sight at Kuching is three miles hence
If you go inside you'll find that it's a prison camp
Enemy prisoners both black and white
Hoes over their shoulders, eyes right
Truly, truly a pitiable sight.

(my translation)

The 'black' prisoners, I have since been told, were probably Indians.

The title of the book translates as *City of the Colonial Soldiers Imprisoned as War Criminals*,[2] and it was written by a colonial guard from Formosa, with not a hoe but a very large chip on his shoulder. While the song might mock, the book itself was a cry of resentment against the Japanese who taught him to be a guard; the Australians who convicted him as a war criminal with a sentence of fifteen years; the Australians who mistreated him during his ten years on remote island prisons near Borneo and New Guinea; the Japanese who said he was no longer Japanese after he finally finished his sentence, and the Japanese who continue to deny him any form of compensation or pension for his sacrifices in the name of the emperor.

With the song being so like the sort of song the prisoners themselves used to make up, I decided to prepare a souvenir copy of it for the upcoming fiftieth anniversary reunion of the Old Sandakians Association. But at the reunion, the little song, printed first in characters, then in transliterated Japanese pronunciation and then in English translation, caused only a small ripple, as did the various photocopies of the guard's book, and extracts from two other Japanese language books on the subject of Japanese prostitutes working in Sandakan town during wartime.

(Interesting, certainly, but did one need to know these things about guards and prostitutes? After all, one had got on so well without them for a very long time.)

So I was unprepared when one of the ladies present whispered urgently in my ear, 'Why have you brought Japanese language to this place?' I answered carefully that I thought it was just part of the picture, that there was nothing good about it, that the picture was necessarily a pretty grim one. I offered a copy of the song, but she let it flutter to the floor, saying, 'No! No! I can't even touch it.'

Having paid a lot of money to get Japanese on my computer and being very proud of my crisp true-type fonts, I was stunned and chastened.

'— But I'd like a copy of that.'

The still-shaking woman was pointing to a list of convicted Kuching Formosan prison guards, with their date and length of sentence, which I had copied from a file at the War Memorial. This list was the document that had told me that the guard who wrote the book had changed his name since the war. I could tell because while he had changed the reading of his name when it was written in ABC alphabet, he had not altered his original Chinese characters, which had also been handwritten onto the list.

The next day I had a further surprise when I discovered that the Japanese language materials that had caused one woman so much distress, had been very carefully perused by the one man who learned to speak Japanese properly while in camp.

'I don't have much opportunity to speak Japanese these days,' he said, 'but I do occasionally work my way through Japanese obstetrics articles.'

I, with my years in Japan, would certainly not tackle the terminological tortures of a topic like obstetrics voluntarily. Yet Ted Esler, camp interpreter turned obstetrician, learned Japanese with no textbooks, and was beaten up regularly for his efforts at mediating in disputes.[3] Almost every day the guards would send chills down spines when they ran through the compound calling, 'Ezura! Ezura!' when they required an interpreter.

Ted wanted to get hold of a copy of the book, to read it, cover to cover. I suggested inter-library loan, but Ted alone had noticed that the book was privately published and included the address of the author for the place of publication.

I caught on quickly and beamed. I felt a lightening of the weight on my shoulders. Ted Esler, never officially rewarded for translation in the face of extreme peril, was telling me in his quiet way, the sort of way that mollified excitable guards, that he was going to write to the Formosan guard himself, in Japanese.

I felt hugely relieved, because now I could reveal what I had told nobody, not even my husband or my father — that I had written to the guard myself on the exact date of the fiftieth anniversary of the surrender of Borneo, and had sent him a copy of the War Memorial's fiftieth anniversary 'War and Peace' booklet, with its eight pages on the atrocities of Sandakan. I did not want to do it, or know how to do it, but as the date approached I felt I should attempt it because I thought (mistakenly, as it turned out) that no member of the Kuching camp generation could countenance it, and because the likelihood that another person would come along with both some interest in the events as well as enough Japanese to write would be very small. Thank you, Ezura, for proving me wrong. But, of course, facing up to acute situations with Japanese guards has long been your speciality.

What can you say to a resentful former war criminal? I was mindful of the obsessive tone of the book, of the minute hand-inserted corrections of typos that only an author would bother to correct, and of the handwritten insert slipped into the back cover, summarising yet again his main grievances, in case you had missed them. The book had obviously been donated to the National Library by the author himself.

Haikei.

On the occasion of the fiftieth anniversary of the end of the war in Borneo, I extend my greetings from Canberra, the capital of Australia.

Somehow, the cry of one colonial soldier has reached me here.

I am the daughter of a former enemy prisoner of Kuching and Sandakan prison camps. Wanting to understand what little I can about my father's experiences in the war, I have begun reading your book at the National Library of Australia.

In it is written that while the warm hand of assistance has been offered to convicted war prisoners by the government, this applies only to Japanese war criminals and not to colonial war criminals. The human qualification of being 'Japanese' is distinguished by a frame not unlike the perimeter fence of a prison camp. It is a qualification obviously not possessed by foreign enemy prisoners, but what of the colonial soldiers who stand at the edge, or rather, who guard it as part of their patrol duties, more assiduously than any Japanese? Do colonial soldiers possess it, do they not possess it, can they ever possess it? It is the sort of question that one could not hope to comprehend at the young age of eighteen or nineteen, and it is the sort of grey problem that never seems to get resolved, no matter how much time passes. I feel sorry for you.

In the present world that tries to stress human rights rather than these kinds of frames, perhaps we can sense a little wind of progress. At the same age as you and my father in wartime, I went to study in Japan with the encouragement of my father. There I got married at Meiji Shrine to a fellow foreign student who was a Chinese Malaysian. (His dialect is Teochiu, which is close to your own dialect of Hokkien.) Our children with their slightly Chinesey faces do not appear to worry very much about whether they belong inside a certain frame or outside it.

At the end of this week a reunion of former Sandakan prisoners will be held in Sydney. Because it is the fiftieth anniversary, I will be attending, for the first time, along with my husband and children. Many of the POWs are getting very old, and I fear this will be the last gathering for a number of them.

Thanks to your efforts, Mr Hayashi/Okabayashi, the misery of war is brought home to me across the distance of fifty years. As you yourself said, 'Truly, truly a pitiable sight.'

Keigu

By putting both of his names, I wanted it known that I had a key to the story of his war, apart from his own book. In a number of ways it was not entirely a gentle letter, and neither was the War Memorial booklet.

I returned to my research occupation, this time at the War Memorial, because I needed to know why it was that a young guard who was rewarded for good service ended up with a quite severe sentence of fifteen years. In spite of my qualms about privacy, I needed to know, and a general administrative file from the war crimes trial at Labuan in 1946 revealed the following petition of appeal against the sentence:

> *35. Okabayashi Takemitsu was sentenced to imprisonment for 15 years as the penalty for beating 6 prisoners. He seems to have been sentenced so severely because one of the six prisoners was a lady. On a certain day of 'Strict Salute Week' the accused passed in front of the kitchen in the women's compound whilst he was supervising as an assistant orderly and one of the five or six ladies there did not take off her head dress and he gave notice in Japanese but as the lady could not understand he gestured for her to take it off. Suddenly, misunderstanding his gesture probably, she bashed him on the face and being, [sic] insulted the dignity of a soldier on supervising duty before others he gave her a few slaps in the face on the spur of the moment. It is a matter-of-course also in the Oriental ethics that man treat the gentle sex kindly but on the side of women, gentleness and obedience are also demanded as her highest virtue and we cannot even imagine, from our Oriental point of view, that any woman dares to beat a man, even her slave, before others.*
>
> *We humbly beg, you to take the fact into consideration that he was brought up under Oriental ethics and that in this case faults were on both sides and judge his responsibility generously on re-examination.*[4]

I have to say that as one who was warming to the guard's theme that the penalties meted out to colonial soldiers were discriminatory on both sides, and that the human rights of war criminals have perhaps been violated, I found the proffering of this kind of defence startling. I was not the least bit surprised that a woman who slapped a guard got worked over.

However, as one who has ended up marrying an 'Oriental', I was thinking I should go back and check the fine print on my contract.

In the future, perhaps the best I can do is to offer this man a trade-off. I will acknowledge that war criminals, too, have basic rights and may have suffered injustices, if he will acknowledge the injustice of implying that any woman is necessarily a step lower in the striking hierarchy than the basest male. 'Ethics' is a strange word to describe the attempt of the unjustly lowly to force others even lower. There is no Geneva Convention on the treatment of women.

Nettled, I went looking for more details, but I found them in a strange quarter. If the Formosan guard was involved in an incident in the women's camp, I am told by my father, it is sure to be described in the book *Three Came Home* that the American author Agnes Newton Keith wrote after the war about her experiences at Kuching Lintang Barracks. Where to find a war narrative published in 1948? In your local public library, fortunately, and I discovered that in my large print edition the incident in question occupied six pages, while the full chronicle of the situation leading up to it stretched for fifty.

The twist, and I am finding that there usually is a twist, was that the tense situation that resulted in the bashing of the woman in the kitchen was due in no small measure to the writer, Agnes Keith herself, after she formally complained that a guard had tried to rape her. When she refused to retract her complaint, even after having several ribs broken in the interrogation, the officials then turned on the guards and disciplined them severely. In retaliation, the guards in turn commenced a strict 'work-to-rules' that resulted in prisoners in all parts of the camp being beaten for small infractions such as bowing with a cigarette in the hand.

The six women who bore the injured prisoner on a stretcher to the main camp office for charging, all swore that she had not actually hit back at the guard, only tried to fend off his blows. 'The guard declares that the prisoners are lying, as of course they are,' says Keith. The young guard was 'known to us as Wife Beater because he was the kind of man who would'.

My father's only comment was that the women in camp were protected remarkably well, considering that they were surrounded by thousands of rough men and impetuous armed guards.

In commemoration of the fiftieth anniversary, there was one more item that I had prepared for the reunion, apart from the Kuching guards' song. This was a set of prints made from the Sandakan pictures, the sketches of the huts with thatched roofs, the artist of which was unknown.

A family friend offered to scan them onto computer disk and retouch them to near-original condition. On the computer screen, as the patchy stains were lifted, the crease marks erased and the insect gnawings repaired, there emerged two subtly shaded scenes of meticulous detail. Such was their detail that an acquaintance asked whether the photographer was still alive. I explained that they were only pencil drawings, and that the artist had died at Sandakan along with everyone else.

Later, at the War Memorial, I sat down in the little corner of the end-of-war exhibition that is devoted to the tragedy of Sandakan. Under the gaze of countless small portraits of dead men, I combed the roll book of names for one that might fit the initials in the bottom corner of the pictures.

(Joan identified the artist, located his family and wrote to them.)

My apologies for surprising you with my call yesterday. I'm sure the loss of your father has caused you much grief over the years, and sad as it is to bring it to mind again fifty years on, I feel certain you will be glad to have this small 'contact' with the meticulous artistry of your father. Or just enjoy the privilege of seeing as he saw things around him in camp in Borneo, by way of his pictures.

With this letter I also enclose a copy of the booklet that the War Memorial has prepared as part of the fiftieth anniversary celebrations. You will note that some eight pages are devoted to telling the Sandakan story. Now I, like yourself, have lived with this story for most of my life, and I have to say that this is the first time that I have seen it discussed in detail in a 'public'-oriented publication of this kind, as opposed to an 'in-house' publication prepared by and for veterans or historians. It seems to have taken fifty years for this event to be properly acknowledged, perhaps because of the guilt many have felt for letting it happen.

My father says he did not know your father personally, which is why he has had so much difficulty remembering the particulars. However, he did commission your father to draw his own bunkroom and the parade area outside, and paid for the sketches in Japanese yen. Such pictures were not permitted by the guards, and my father says the reason why they are now so stained is that he often had to hide them up in the atap (palm leaf) thatching of the roof.

Regarding the parade ground picture, a number of people at the Sandakian reunion said that there seemed to be too many features telescoped into one drawing: that there did not seem to be enough space between buildings, as they remembered them. However, my father is adamant that this is not so. He insists that your father moved around until he found a particular oblique vantage point that incorporated all the main features of interest. Apart from 'the big tree' in the centre of the camp and the first of the prisoners' huts, it shows one of the 'cages' that were used for punishment, the wire perimeter fence, the original main gate, and the guard house. A road ran beside the guard house and in through the gate. The trees in the background with the flat branches are kapok trees, whose pod fluff is used for stuffing mattresses, while the palm branches visible are those of the oil palm tree...

... The hut seen immediately behind the big tree was the one my father slept in, and its interior is shown in the second picture. (I believe my father's bed was the third from the back on the right.) I was also told at the reunion that later on most huts were converted by the prisoners into bunk-style, so that more space was created in the centre of the room. When I remarked that the room looked very tidy, they said that because they didn't have many belongings there never was much clutter.

That is probably all I can say about the pictures at this stage.

I recently suggested to my father that some sort of trees could be planted on the site of the Sandakan camp, to remind visitors of the original setting. My suggestion was to replace the 'big tree', or perhaps plant some kapok trees, but my father said that what he would like to see would be some cinnamon trees, as these grew close enough by that the prisoners could pull off a bit of bark, and later grate a little over their rice ration, using a home-made grater, to make it a bit more palatable.

Continuing the culinary theme, as a side dish they would eat boiled kang kong, a tropical swamp vegetable that likes growing in open drains and thrives on sewerage and gunk. I recently found a number of packets of kang kong seeds in a Vietnamese grocery shop in Canberra, and passed them on to my father, thinking he might distribute them to some of his friends when he writes to them. But I notice that he hasn't. Apparently he thinks they would not take it too well, that there is no humour in reminding these people of starvation on a kang kong diet. I myself ate a lot of kang kong while living in Malaysia, where it is a typical low-class but nutritious side dish, along with bean sprouts, for anyone who doesn't have much money. Perhaps you would like to grow some this summer? Anyway, I am going to.

At the recent War Memorial War History Conference, we met a Dr John Pritchard, whose speciality is British war crimes trials, and who sometimes comes into contact with the families of British soldiers who died at Sandakan (there were no British survivors). He was keen to distribute photocopies of the prints to them, and felt that some family members of British Sandakians might wish to write to Australian survivors. He said that what they seemed to want is an image of what their son/sibling/father might have become had they survived.

My father said that should they write, he would tell them that it was not such a bad thing to die in camp, because you died surrounded by good friends, many more friends than you would have in ordinary life which can be pretty lonely sometimes. He says that once you got used to the life of a coolie, and understood what to expect, it was not necessarily a life of constant fear and unpredictable violence. That there were some positive moments too, such as the songs and performances they used to put on regularly, the sharing of books, and the opportunity to talk endlessly with people from all walks of life: farmers, academics, surveyors, shipwrights... He says many people who survived

*never went back to a complacent life, and they knew they could
do anything they put their mind to.*

*The Padre at the commemorative service in the naval chapel on South
Head said that at the distance of fifty years, one finds oneself, surprisingly, closer to the truth about events in the war. Maybe wanting to
find the face behind the Sandakan pictures, which lived for my entire
childhood on the top shelf of the bookcase near the front door, is
another part of that need to know how it really was. As far as I can tell,
these are the only surviving pictures of Sandakan POW camp, which
was of course burnt to the ground in an attempt to obliterate it. But
burning didn't work because, thanks to your father's skill, we still know.*

Meanwhile I had received a reply from the Formosan guard, now living on
the southern Japanese island of Kyushu. There were many pages, copies of
petitions that he had unsuccessfully sent to a succession of eight prime min-
isters, a newspaper clipping with a photo of him working away at his word
processor, and a short letter setting out yet again his main grievances in case
I may not have grasped them. The pages were warm to the touch with red
underlining, bold capitals, star points, and handwritten additions, saying,
for instance, that he was now preparing to take his case to the Human
Rights Office of the United Nations.

He also put a message on the end for me to convey to Sticpewich, the
survivor of the death march, who had saved his friend Takada Kunio with
his testimony. Takada, I was informed, had died in June last year (1994) at
the age of seventy-two. Unfortunately, Sticpewich himself died in a car
crash in 1977, but I thought that Ted Esler, to whom I was more than willing to pass responsibility, might best convey this news to him. I had made
my contribution by breaking the ice, and felt that others were more qualified to take on from there.

But then another letter came. This time the storm had broken. In
fact, the letter had much to do with the state of the weather and the season.
He described the passing that day, 24 September, of typhoon no. 14, and
recollected the many evening squalls he had experienced on Borneo Island,
Morotai Island, Rabaul Island and Manus Island where he had passed
around from prison to prison. Apparently he had distributed copies of my
letter to a number of his friends and supporters, and letters of congratu-
lations were now starting to arrive.

In autumn, just as coloured leaves are beginning to fall, it suddenly seems as if the petals of spring flowers are fluttering down instead. But when you take time to think about it, she is writing from the southern hemisphere…

How lucky that you went to the trouble to write your personal story, and what a good outcome for your sending a copy to the National Library of Australia.

He is fortunate to have good friends who can write these words for him. With the letter came a copy of a newly published book by a Japanese woman author, telling the story of 'four Taiwanese friends who ended up as Japanese war criminals'. The book includes a photo of the ever fresh-faced Hayashi Miki, he who had so much difficulty enforcing discipline in his youth because of his angelic features, this time spruce in the uniform of a parking attendant.

It is barely a month since I first surreptitiously sent off a letter to Hayashi, a few days before the Old Sandakian reunion, and the earth has certainly turned a few degrees since then. My one remaining task is to answer the request for a copy of the list of Formosan war criminal convictions, for the lady who could not touch the paper on which Japanese words were written. This I will do now, but I will supply a lot of other information about the guard as well. That he had a home in Taiwan, that he had a mother tongue before he learned Japanese, that one of the incidents which earned him his conviction was there for all to read about in Agnes Keith's book, that he hasn't gone to hell but is here among us still, fuming away.

Through revealing to her the identity of Hayashi as the 'Wife Beater', I realise that I am betraying him, making him the sacrificial victim of my imprudent push towards some kind of progress on the fiftieth anniversary of the end of the war. By so parading his humiliation, I am hoping that acceptance, reflection, and even one step beyond that may all be possible once the initial shock has passed. I am also hoping that even more closely held secrets — not those of the war crime trials, but rather the sad truths that were deemed necessary to withhold from the families of our own soldiers — may also creep forth from the recesses and be examined lucidly for their lesson.

According to my father, under the strict socialist ethic of the Australian prison camp, and more so than in other prison camps, most prisoners were sustained by the firm conviction that a strong community spirit and a commitment to friends and the common good, rather than personal advantage, was the guiding tenet that would deliver them all home safely. Some never adhered to this rule from the outset, and chose quite rationally to be outlaws who looked out for number one in all situations. Others started to waver only when the going got tough and the outlook increasingly bleak. One man was caught taking double rations and literally died of shame when his transgression was announced to the full assembly of Australian prisoners. What survivor would ever be able to relate these in-house 'war crimes' to the families back home?

Even more pathetic was the recognition that the guiding tenet did not necessarily keep generous individuals alive. Witness the pillar of camp community life who was, it was obvious to all except himself, killing himself with his voluntary duties. Would there never come a point when he would decline and conserve his precious energy? Witness also the remarkably low survival rate of the death marches, on which selfless devotion to hopeless mates kept many marching on to oblivion. It is an aching irony in the Sandakan version of the war that the immediate reward for not succumbing was noble death of the self without achieving life for any, let alone many.

It has been my rule through all of this to counterbalance grief, shame and anger with cool, bald facts; the dropping of simplistic edifices and disguises, and the acknowledgement of human weaknesses. However, I realise with resignation that it is far easier to write to a former convicted Japanese war criminal than it is to confront the personal devastation that evidence of the warping or weakening of sacred tenets may bring. I, like everyone else, will probably have to cover for it, and some cool, cruel facts will have to stay buried for more years than fifty.

Postscript

Hayashi had always been keen to visit Joan's memorial 'rock' on her parents' property and early in October 2004 he returned to visit Hugh and Adele. There, in the Southern Highlands of New South Wales, Hayashi the former prison guard placed incense sticks around the rock and conducted his own memorial service for Joan, the daughter of one of the POWs from Kuching.

Letter to My Father

FRAN DE GROEN

Sergeant Geoff de Groen (NX67344)
2/19th Battalion, AIF
POW: Changi; Keijo; Omine

Geoff de Groen, an assistant manager with Mayfair Cinemas in Sydney during the 1930s, embarked with Heron Force in January 1941, just days after joining the AIF. He returned from the Pacific in September 1941 to join the 2/19th Battalion in Malaya, disembarking in Singapore on 5 October 1941. In January 1942 his battalion was involved in fierce fighting against the Japanese at Parit Sulong in Malaya before making their way back to Singapore where Geoff was wounded on 11 February. He spent the first five months after the Allied surrender in Selarang Barracks at Changi, but in August 1942 left Singapore on the *Fukai Maru* with Japan Party B. He was sent first to Keijo in Korea and then in October 1944 he was moved via Jinsen to Omine, near Fukuoka, in Japan.

In Keijo he was one of the 'sew sew' group of prisoners, men who spent their working hours sewing buttons on the uniforms of their captors. It was a much easier life there than it was at Omine where he joined other POWs working long hours in the coalmines. Geoff remained in Japan until they were liberated by the Americans in September 1945. He returned to Sydney, met and married Prudence Palmer and they had two daughters.

Geoff's eldest daughter, Fran, has spent the last six years researching the experiences of the POWs in Japan Party B. She has made research trips to Korea, Japan and the United States and in 2002 she presented a paper 'Prisoners on Parade: Japan Party "B"'[1] at the 2002 History Conference held by the War Memorial in Canberra. Fran cheerfully admits that her research into the POW experience has changed her life.

Not long ago I found a letter that I had written to you during the early 1970s but never posted. It gave me a shock, the kind of shock you get when you come unexpectedly upon a mirror or old photograph and cannot at first recognise yourself in it.

The letter is dated significantly '26 April' — the day after Anzac Day — and it reveals me reaching out to offer you comfort and hope. I can't recall precisely what prompted me to put biro to paper. At the time I was with an older man, a man old enough, in fact, to have been my father. You lived only a few blocks from us and sometimes used to take your little white poodle, André, for walks in our direction. You must have dropped in to see us. You must also have seemed very unhappy. I remember D. describing you as 'sad' and 'silent'.

The letter begins clumsily and rather childishly: 'Dear Daddy, It made me very miserable to see you so sad last night. I felt I should write something to you.' It continues in an embarrassingly gauche manner, pontificating about the melancholy nature of 'the human condition' and the 'value' of suffering, and passing judgement on the resolute but sometimes dismissive cheerfulness of my mother (your wife). It offers a backhanded apology for our failure to communicate, in effect exonerating myself and blaming you: 'You are not an easy person to talk to'. I even presume to advise you how to cope patiently with life's worries: 'You would probably say that you learned more about life from your war experiences than from any other source'. It ends by identifying with you: 'So, from one melancholy old pessimist to another, Cheers'.

I am relieved that I did not post it. What did I know of your 'war experiences' and how on earth, at twenty-two years of age and with very little experience of the world, could I possibly have understood what they might mean? To me you were distant, silent and pathetic. You smoked heavily — eighty cigarettes a day — until your first heart attack at sixty forced you abruptly to quit. Never violent or noisy, you drank yourself into a boozy stupor in front of the TV set almost every night. For years I had been unable to give you a hug or take your part in family arguments. Indeed, I was your main antagonist — the 'hare-brained intellectual' with her 'head in the clouds'. I envied girls who could talk freely and affectionately with their fathers. In 1975, when you proudly showed me the account you had written of your experiences as a POW for your battalion history, I patronised you by praising something that I had not even made the effort to read. Sure, I held the volume in my hands, felt its considerable weight, glanced at the four or five pages you had contributed — but that was all. I did not bother to register the significance of the historical information that you had condensed into a fluent and sardonic short essay, nor appreciate your sense of having been a part of something larger and more intense than the post-war life you led as husband, father and wage-slave in a dreary outer Sydney 'fibro' suburb. A few years later, while I was teaching in a College of Advanced Education, a senior colleague who had served briefly as a combat soldier in the dying stages of the Pacific War told me that he had been 'honoured' to meet you. I found his enthusiasm effusive, sentimental and ultimately phoney. It amazed me that he could hold you in such esteem. Not long afterwards, I told an eminent American poet that I despised you.

I am only now coming to terms with the shame. Rejecting you, I was also rejecting myself — or rather those parts of myself that I associated with you. Having recently learned a little more about you, I realise that I have inherited many of your traits, worthy as well as unworthy. I am a worrier, as you were, biting your nails as I still can in times of stress. If you never verbalised your fear of the future, I am 'the voice of doom'. You once told me that when you were required to recite Hebrew scriptures at the ceremony marking your bar mitzvah, you froze and were speechless, provoking disapproving head-shaking and 'tch tch tch' tongue-clicks from rows of bearded patriarchs. I, too, find speaking in public an ordeal — even when I have important things to say and long to say them with passionate conviction. Before the war you had been involved with a theatre group in Kings Cross. You told us about it — you, on the stage, in company with Gwen 'Pussy' Plumb? I can't imagine it. Your one successful theatrical appearance, however, lacked dialogue — you played the 'author', seated at a desk, stage left, silently writing the action that unfolded for the audience through the words and deeds of other actors.

In 1951 when you were exhibiting physical symptoms of anxiety, including nervous vomiting, a Repatriation Department psychiatrist assessing your state of mind, diagnosed a 'slight tendency to anticipate trouble'. (If only he had known. You had good cause to be terrified, but I will not remind you about it here as it will only cause embarrassment.) On a more positive note, you were a humanist and a card-carrying atheist. You affirmed the golden rule — 'Do unto others as you would have them do unto you'. If you honoured that rule more in the breach than the observance, no matter — it stays with me. You gave voice to what I now regard as the sole basis for decent social relations — empathy — and although I have no firm evidence, I suspect that you were a closet socialist.

In your will, you demanded 'an atheist's funeral' — and what a desperately sad, poorly subscribed affair it turned out to be. The only mourners were your immediate family — on your wife's side. None of your Jewish relatives showed up. Did they know you had gone? Had all your friends died? Where were they? Did you in fact have any friends? How lonely you must have been.

Before you died in early 1982, we made a guarded peace. I bought a townhouse a few suburbs away from you and Mum. (I was concerned that if she died first I wanted to be geographically close enough to do your washing but not so close that I would have to see you on a daily basis.) I asked you to help me create a garden for my tiny backyard and we pottered around quite happily together on weekends. You would bring me plants from your own garden and give advice about where to put them — and I'd 'argue the toss' until we came to a compromise. Meanwhile, I'd try unsuccessfully to make contact with you on the 'big' questions — and I suppose in a desultory way we did discuss them. But I never felt that I really knew *you* or that we were really *talking*. Perhaps I had missed my cue by failing to read carefully what you had written about your time as a POW. Perhaps you *wanted* me to ask questions about those experiences, but by then it was too late. You had never shared much information about yourself with us. You rarely told stories about yourself. You always seemed 'otherwise engaged' (to quote the title of a Simon Grey play): gazing into the distance (where? at what?), lighting up a fresh cigarette with the old one only half-smoked, jiggling your foot, or drumming insistent fingers on the dinner table or the steering wheel or the arm of your chair.

What was it that you were so nervously 'anticipating', that preoccupied you so intensely? By my mid-twenties you were drinking more than your failing system could handle, vomiting and passing out, and leaving Mum to clean up the mess. By choosing to live just out of 'harm's way', as it were, I consoled myself that were you to be left a widower I could be helpful at a distance without taking on 'the whole catastrophe'. You were so unhappy, so depressed, so unreachable — I couldn't see how anyone could cope with you. As it turned out, you saved me the bother.

About two years before your death, you travelled alone by train to Brisbane to try to locate an old wartime buddy. To this day, although I have since recovered your army kitbag from a gentle old man in Brisbane who had been in Omine camp with you, I still don't know for certain who it was you were looking for — you never told us. 'Dad's big trip,' we said ('we' meaning my mother, my sister and myself). We were very pleased. It seemed as though you were taking an interest in life again. But you stayed one night only, telephoning us in tears the next morning with flight details and asking for someone to come and pick you up from the airport. Unable to find your old mate, you had checked into a dismal room in the 'People's Palace', spent one miserable night there and could not bear to stay another moment. You wanted to come home immediately, no matter the cost. We collected you from the airport and teased you unmercifully. 'Dad's big trip: one night away from home!' I realise now that you must have been lonely and frightened, perhaps worrying that you would die alone in a strange room. (You really were quite ill with serious cardiovascular disease, not that I was aware of it or particularly interested. I was too immersed in my own life and believed you to be a hypochondriac whose worst health problems were self-inflicted, the result of excessive smoking and drinking.) Anyway, you were glad to be driven home and, if my memory is correct, you even shed a few tears. When you died not long afterwards, I confess I felt relieved. I no longer had to worry about your unhappiness.

Now that it is too late to ask, I want to find out more about you. I want to know what, if anything, your silences held and how, if at all, they were related to the sufferings you underwent between 1942 and 1945. How were these years significant in shaping the rest of your life? To what extent did they make you the 'sad, silent man' that you became? You must have valued these wartime and captivity experiences because, apart from writing them up for your battalion history, you left behind a carefully preserved cache of documents and photographs testifying to their historicity and tantalising me with their enigmatic significance.

The documents record your 'official' dealings with the military and give an intriguing insight into your subjection as a prisoner. The photographs you kept from this period are the only ones you bothered to put into albums — carved-leather albums that you kept hidden away. They reveal you in a variety of guises: proud in militia uniform at a Tamworth army camp and casually elegant in khaki drill on the back platform of a Singapore bus; skylarking with anonymous buddies in waist-high, open air, woven-bamboo shower stalls; writing a letter on the verandah steps of your tropical quarters. Not too long afterwards, they show you standing at attention behind sandbagged fortifications looking decidedly scared, in a tin hat and clutching the rifle you told Mum that you never fired. You had rested it against a tree, you said, when an anti-personnel bomb arrived and put you out of action. (Mum said you had probably put the rifle down to light up a last cigarette.) How you ever would have accurately fired it is a mystery to me. Your enlistment papers categorise you as class IIA because of a 'slight disability right hand'. The description, 'multiple scars right hand; scar right inguinal area', understates the mutilation you suffered as a child when you slipped and fell under a Bronte tram. Even more puzzling is the fact that at Keijo camp you were assigned to the 'sew sews', the group of POWs who mended Japanese uniforms, attaching buttons and knitting. (Somebody was clearly being kind to you as this was the easiest — and warmest — job to be had.)

In many ways you were lucky to be held in Keijo — a 'show camp' generating Japanese propaganda via the 'satisfactory' reports communicated by the International Red Cross after the annual visits permitted by your captors. The letter you wrote to your widowed mother from Keijo offers glimpses of a man I cannot quite get into focus — articulate, succinct, wry:

Once again I'm able to write and let you know that I'm in the best of health and spirits.

For those of us who have not yet heard from home, the Super- intendent of this camp has granted special permission to write this letter which will leave on the ship which is to effect the transfer of nationals this month. The British troops received mail some days ago and I hope that letters for the A.I.F. are not far behind.

Under the circumstances, life in the prison camp is not unpleasant and, as I have mentioned in previous cards, the Superintendent does all he can to improve our lot. At present I am employed in the tailor's shop and (don't laugh too much) have learned to knit. My job is repairing pullovers, gloves and sox.

In reading the papers I see that the Labour [sic] Government was returned with an overwhelming majority and also that the cities near Darwin have been bombed. I hope that they did not fare too badly.

In this country, the climate reaches the extremes — very hot in summer and very cold in winter. At present the summer is on its last legs and, consequently, the weather now is most pleasant.

Once again, don't worry about me, as I'm quite okay and have no complaints. Sooner or later this war will be over. In the meantime keep your chin up. (3/9/1943)

To what extent are your bland, yet intriguing, statements designed to allay your mother's fears and please the Japanese censors? A subsequent card repeats your praise for the 'Superintendent', Colonel Yuzuru Noguchi, who was later tried as a war criminal and sentenced to twenty-two years hard labour — but that's another story.

Your collection of photographs reveals a curiously pragmatic interest in 'show biz'. Before the war you had been assistant manager at the Mayfair cinema in Sydney. (Family rumour has it that you were sacked after a scandal involving a showgirl.) In Kuala Lumpur and Singapore you seem to have visited the local movie theatres and introduced yourself to the management before taking 'snaps' of the buildings and staff with your brownie box camera. The images live on in your albums. In the diary of one of your fellow Pay Corps NCOs, I discovered that you and he had become acquainted with Guan Yu, the Chinese proprietor of the Pavilion Theatre in Kuala Lumpur, who invited you both to a Chinese banquet. Your Australian friend, Alex, recorded that for him the meal was 'not a success'. For you, however, it was and it became one of the rare stories about 'the war' that you sometimes shared with us. More than the exotic food, you appreciated the ministrations of dainty waitresses who arrived between courses with steaming hot towels to mop your brow and wipe your hands. You retained your enjoyment of Asian cuisine, treating us to cheap Chinese meals in local suburban cafés and more expensive Korean and Japanese food in the first restaurants to bring such foreign fare to Sydney. Some of my happiest 'family' memories feature 'bamboo inns' and 'sukiyaki houses', where you introduced us to good food and wine and were a generous host, even if you could not afford to be.

Other photographs are even more intriguing, showing smiling men in shabby greatcoats, crouching eagerly over Red Cross parcels, with Japanese guards in the background. I have since learned that the Kempei Tei who took these propaganda photographs also sold copies to the prisoners. Among your collections are wistful scenes showing British officers and a padre attending a funeral being conducted under pine trees. There are postcards of a Japanese mining company office and a Japanese bathhouse and more formal shots of recently liberated POWs, yourself among them, dressed in American Army uniforms, staring dazed into the camera, like sleepers awakening. The most puzzling of all are those taken by somebody Japanese during the war — shots of a woman, Yoshiko, and child at a railway station; a street scene with children; photographs of beautiful young Japanese women. Some of these have names, dates and places in Japanese script. One photograph shows a very young Japanese man in what looks to be an American uniform. It bears the inscription, in your handwriting: Hoshino Teiki. Who was Hoshino Teiki and why do you have his photograph? In your later years, the only social life you enjoyed beyond the immediate family was as a member of your battalion association. You must have had some 'inner' life that focused on your contact with Asia because

FRAN AND HER FATHER, 1949

you accumulated and assiduously read (but never discussed) a magazine that as a child I found unutterably boring — *Korea Survey* I think it was called. You remained interested in what was happening to the country where you spent two and a half years of captivity. (You also subscribed to the *Saturday Evening Post*.) Perhaps, before you surrendered completely to alcohol, you had the makings of a closet intellectual.

When my sister and I were children, you were our hero. You had black hair and a black moustache and brown eyes and we thought you were very handsome. People used to say you looked like Robert Taylor. (Who was Robert Taylor?) We knew you had been a soldier 'in the war'. You wore medals on Anzac Day and went to the dawn service. We sometimes went to the march in town with Mum and waved to you when you swung past. You also occasionally took us to the Cenotaph in Hyde Park, but it was boring for us to be quiet and well behaved inside the big marble room, and we'd skip disrespectfully up and down the steps or race outside to play chasings around the Pool of Remembrance. Once my sister slipped in and wet her shoes and socks and you were cross. I was surprised at how shallow the pool was.

At night when you came home after work we'd greet you eagerly:

'Show us your scar Daddy'. You'd roll up your trouser leg to the knee to reveal a long white lesion about an inch wide running right down your shin. We'd pester you with questions that you dodged or deflected: 'How did you get your scar Daddy?' 'Shrapnel.' 'What's shrapnel?' 'You wouldn't understand.' 'Did it hurt?' 'Mmmm…' 'Did it? Did it? Well, did it?' '…' At bedtime we'd beg you to tell us stories. 'Tell us a story, Dad.' (Wasn't there a song with a title something like that?) Every night we'd beg and every night you'd peep around the door and solemnly chant: 'There was a fly upon a wall. Buzz, buzz. That's all.'

'Tell us a story Daddy, tell us a story.' We longed for stories about the 'olden days' and especially about 'the war' but you always refused. 'Buzz buzz. That's all.'

You must have had hundreds of stories about your time in the military. The few that you did tell were either humorous or in the nature of a warning. I can remember only two. The first concerned a diminutive, bespectacled Japanese guard who needed to stand on a box to belt prisoners across the face. He once so aggravated a large POW that the prisoner hoisted him high off the ground and shook him for several minutes, like a terrier shaking a rat. 'Mind my glasses, mind my glasses,' he squeaked, until he was let go. The second story focused on prophylactics. As a pay clerk you were required to dock the wages of all AIF troops reporting with VD. The stupidity of the repeat offenders amazed and amused you.

I wish you had been able to tell us something. You spent eight months with Special Force Heron in Ocean Island and Nauru — but I can't seem to find out anything about this tour of duty, although I do seem to recall your nostalgic enthusiasm for the pawpaws and other tropical fruits that hung ripe for the picking, just outside your army hut windows. Why didn't you tell us about Malaya, where your unit faced the brunt of the well-trained Japanese Imperial Guard and briefly held them? (Mum told me recently that your 2/19th commanding officer, Col. Anderson, VC, was your hero.) And what about the bombardment of Singapore Island, the terror of being under fire, of being wounded and patched up and of being held captive for three and a half years — first in Changi, where you went down with dengue fever and missed going to Borneo by a whisker; then in Keijo camp, Korea; and finally Omine, Kyushu, where you spent a year, slaving in a coalmine.

I am only now discovering some of these stories and the unexpected depths they conceal. I register and appreciate, for example, the objectivity you demonstrate in the war crimes depositions you made, your dry sense of humour, your willingness to celebrate the bravery of others, the more so when, by your own admission, you preferred to avoid trouble by 'falling down' when blows were being dealt. (Better to be a live dog than a dead lion.) At the same time, you were fair-minded, recognising and stating that the 'discipline' you and your fellow POWs were forced to observe was no different from that meted out to lower ranks in the Japanese Army. My mother tells me that you felt great pity for the suffering of the Japanese people at the end of the war and had no desire for vengeance. I was therefore surprised when one of your ex-Omine pals told me how, after the capitulation, a guard who had persecuted a sick prisoner on the same squad now came bowing and scraping obsequiously into POW quarters wanting to be 'friends' and you kicked him in the rear, propelling him ignominiously downstairs, to the mirth of all present. This Chaplinesque act of revenge seems as out of character as his description of you as a cheerful chap who liked a joke.

As children we felt that you were not interested in us. We sensed I suppose, even then, that you were 'otherwise engaged'. We had no comprehension of what the empty Corio whisky bottles meant, or why, whenever we went for a drive with you in the Ford Prefect (your first car), we had to wait patiently while you called into several hotels along the way 'to see a man about a dog'. When we asked you to play French cricket or piggy-in-the middle you'd refuse because you had 'a bone in your leg'. On one memorable occasion, you passed out at the dinner table with your in-laws present, your face falling into your dessert. You did, however, sometimes take us fishing for tiddlers on the wharves around Sydney Harbour. (Perhaps you would have been happier with sons.) You also dutifully chauffeured us to sporting fixtures and social engagements during our busy adolescent years. You loved gardening and you had a 'green thumb' and, although I did not appreciate these qualities when you were alive, I can now see that despite your inability to relate to us, you were gentle, compassionate and generous. If you were not what the world would call 'successful', you were 'a good provider'. You always gave us titbits from your own plate and spoiled us with packets of exquisite tiny boiled sweets ('Bo Peeps', I think they were called). You carpentered and painted a perfect half-size 'early kooka' stove for us to play 'house' with. You bought us a duckling each to rear, bred budgerigars, canaries and finches in an aviary you built yourself, and once tried to save a half-fledged baby sparrow that had fallen from its nest by keeping it in a shoebox and feeding it with an eye-dropper. You gave in to our pleas for a puppy and bought us a silly black cocker-spaniel-cross. After he committed harakiri on the main road, you again relented and brought home a smarter (if more neurotic) fox terrier that emulated its predecessor's traffic-defying bravado but escaped with merely a broken hip. Tuppence — I don't know why we named her this, perhaps because she wasn't worth much — chewed off her plaster cast, twice. On recovery she resumed her busy life, barking at cats, eating frogs and plucking naked any delinquent chook that had the misfortune to make its way from the yard next door through our decaying paling fence into her domain. When she eventually died, you replaced her with the miniature poodle that you doted on and that outlived you.

A TV addict in later life, you would weep in sentimental movies (I do, too) and although you could curse furiously (as can I) with frustration when unable to assemble a kit wheelbarrow or start the lawnmower, you were not a physically violent man. I know this for a fact from your reaction when you administered my one and only 'belting'. I can't remember what I had done but it must have been extraordinarily naughty because the razor-strop (often threatened, never before wielded) was the instrument of punishment. I tried to negotiate a lighter penalty but you were adamant and delivered one or two stinging lashes to my legs. Did I cry? You left the room abruptly but returned almost immediately, weeping and apologising. With my child's logic I despised you for being weak.

Now, fifty years later, I want to exhume your buried stories, to fill in the blanks, to listen for the cues I ignored when you were living. So far, I have discovered very little. You kept a remarkably low profile. Perhaps I won't discover layers of complexity — perhaps, after all, there aren't any. Perhaps you were simply an ordinary man faced for a time with extraordinary trials and then afterwards, an office equipment salesman defeated by life. (D. called you a Willy Loman, but you were a better gardener than Willy — your roses bloomed abundantly.) Whatever I discover about you will be a bonus. Everyone has a story — many stories — and, as Arthur Miller reminds us at the end of *Death of a Salesman*, 'attention must be paid'.

'A Bonza Bloke ... for an Officer'

KERIN MOSIERE

Captain Kenneth George Mosher (NX34857)
2/18th Battalion, AIF
POW: Changi; Sandakan/Kuching

Ken Mosher was born on 30 October 1913 in Sydney. He was educated at Sydney Boys' High School and Sydney University, where he studied geology. He enlisted in the AIF on 28 June 1940, just a few months after his marriage to Imelda, and in February 1941 he sailed for Singapore with the 22nd Brigade.

Ken was widely respected by his fellow officers and his men. He was recognised as 'a real soldier' and he was a popular leader. In July 1942 Ken went to Sandakan in Borneo with B Force. Like most of the officers at Sandakan he was removed to Kuching after the work of the underground network was revealed to the Japanese.

After the war Ken returned to geology and he and Imelda built a house at Killara in Sydney. They had two children, Kerin and Max. Ken's profession as a geologist meant that he spent long periods away from his home and family, leaving Imelda to bring up the children and run the home front. According to Kerin, her father was a highly respected geologist, known as the 'doyen' or 'grandfather' of the coal industry in New South Wales. But, despite his evident popularity among his colleagues and friends, Kerin found living with her father difficult.

Some years ago Kerin accompanied her mother to a POW reunion where she met another Sandakan/Kuching veteran, Hugh Waring. Hugh talked briefly to Kerin about her father and their POW years together. He told her that her father was one of a handful of men who had been responsible for changing many of the men's lives. Lacking education himself, Hugh claims he would never have had the interaction with such a diverse range of military and academic men were it not for the POW experience. With these men as role models, Hugh and other young officers from Kuching were encouraged to take advantage of the educational opportunities available through the post-war Reconstruction Training Scheme — opportunities they would never otherwise have been offered. Hugh was the first person to have spoken to Kerin about some of the positive outcomes of the POW experience. Kerin recently met another of the men who had served with and admired her father. 'He was a bonza bloke … for an officer,' he told her.

Kerin has not only written her own story, but has also encouraged others in her POW-family network to contribute their stories to this collection.

My earliest impressions of my father's character have been formed by comments from family and close friends who knew him during the decade of his life from the age of sixteen to twenty-six. A young man of high principles and ethics, my father prided himself on being impeccably honest. Always the nucleus of pranks, he had a love of fun and a good sense of humour. He was a man in a hurry and was regularly referred to as 'the mighty atom'! My father had a passion for learning and was highly intelligent. He was a great organiser and he relished the odd argument. He also lacked commonsense and practicality. His brother, who was unfortunately killed in New Guinea, would comment that my father never had his feet on the ground. All these traits were unchanged post-war and through my adolescent years.

My father was the eldest of three children. His father was a gentle businessman married to a more dominant woman. He was a high achiever at Sydney Boys' High School and he went on to study at Sydney University. Institutionalised activities played an important role in his life. He thrived on order and thus the scouting movement and the Army were his primary activities before the war. My parents met through the scout movement and were married in 1940. Consequently, at the onset of war, my father was educated, had an established career and was happily married. The war whipped the carpet from under his established feet and had a profound effect on his later life.

Although it was the beginning of uncertain times, my parents shared the power of positive thinking. The day my father sailed for Malaya, Mum purchased a magnificent tablecloth ready for their first meal together when he returned. Nearly five years later they did use it for their first meal together in their new home — draped over the packing box they were using as a table![1] My father too had made a small carpet, which he had deliberately left unfinished. His plan was to complete it on his return, which he duly did!

During the war years my mother studied nursing, but once she learned that my father had become a POW, she chose to enlist as an ambulance driver. This gave her close contact with the injured and their stories. At the end of the war, one of the medicos who had only recently seen my mother reported to my father that she was fit and well and had short, wavy brown hair. My father replied, 'That's funny, she was blonde when I last saw her'. Not only had his wife's hair changed colour naturally during the period of his absence, but she herself had also experienced five years in a vastly different workforce from the one that existed prior to their marriage.

The thrill of my father's return soon gave way to the difficulties of readjustment. These were many and varied. In the early days after the war my parents would be walking down the street one minute and the next instant my father would have disappeared, sometimes for days on end. There were the nightmares, the mood swings and the feelings of claustrophobia. Strategies were put into place. The cloisonné vase on the mantelpiece in the lounge room would be turned upside down. It was an indicator that my father himself recognised that he was in an impossible mood where arguments would be useless.

At one point, soon after his return, my mother was feeling unwell. She visited the local doctor who duly patted her on the back and told her not to worry as she was obviously suffering from a nervous reaction to my father's homecoming. With time this 'nervous reaction' became more obvious and I was the result! After their release the ex-POWs had been told that there was a likelihood of impotence or sterility. That theory was shortlived. I was the frontrunner in the unit's £150 stake for the first-born post-war baby but two others pipped me at the post. Since both my father and I needed constant attention during the first 12 months of my life, Mum not only had one baby but sometimes two to contend with at that time.

My early childhood photos show my father playing and having fun with me but this was shortlived. His pre-war activities soon resumed. Was it his personality that thrived on these activities or did the busyness of his life keep the demons at bay? There were neither guidelines nor therapy sessions to help returned servicemen assimilate back into civvy street; not that my father would have availed himself of such services! I believe that as POWs the men would spend hours each day dreaming up recipes, planning the family home and imagining family life post-war. Until recently I questioned why these dreams were so effective in captivity and yet, post-war, our family was just taken for granted. I received my answer only weeks ago from a daughter of one of the POWs, who simply said that realism alters many a dream.

We were raised on a 'Do as I say, not as I do' policy and Father used this quote unashamedly on more than one occasion. The rearing of my own children has been the reverse. Father was an early riser and had the idea that we all should follow suit. For years we would be woken at daybreak by him chanting 'The sun is shining, the birds are singing ... time to get up!'

He would present Mum with a cup of tea, which was his pièce de résistance and the brew that fixed all ailments.

Mum was the peacemaker and would have us bathed and fed prior to Father coming home from work. My parents would retreat into the lounge room with sherries in hand, while Father unwound and recounted the day's events. On weekends he would ensconce himself in his lounge chair and read for hours on end, while listening to Beethoven's *Emperor Concerto*. Strangely and quite by chance, we heard this piece on three different occasions the day he died.

My father's CMF (Citizen Military Forces) career escalated and peaked in my mid-teens, thus giving me an entrée into the glamour of balls and rounds of cocktail parties from the age of fourteen. My father was patron of one of the University societies, a position that eventually led to the introduction to my future husband. Socially I had a ball because of my father's connections. At home the story was very different.

Mum was both parents in one. She held the family together and staunchly supported my father personally as well as his many activities. She too enjoyed a rich social life, including interaction with high dignitaries, and was always a true lady. My father was awarded honours for both military and civil careers but the old adage 'Behind every successful man is a woman' held true.

Family life? I can't say we really had one. I cannot recall ever going out as a family save for work-related functions, the odd visit to the paternal family and our summer holidays. Father had his life and we had ours. Mum's support for all of Father's associations often put demands upon her. Once, daunted by the task of delivering an important speech to nearly two thousand people, she questioned her ability to do so. Father's reaction was 'Get on with it woman — just do it'. He expected and she produced! Annual events such as Guy Fawkes and Easter were celebrated with family friends in the absence of Father due to his other commitments. School functions would come and go without him and even my school reports would pass him without comment. It may have been disinterest or simply that he knew my mother coped with every aspect of our lives, including our education. Father was well read and had a vast general knowledge. Unfortunately, any discussion soon turned into a lecture and I consequently decided that educated people were boring. My school results subsequently reflected this attitude.

Our annual summer holidays took the form of a military exercise.

The car would be serviced in readiness for the two-hour drive. Lists were made for every conceivable facet, while Mum undertook the annual spring clean of the family home! The evening prior to departure would see Father announce 'I can move an army more easily than this family. Look — I'll show you how I can pack everything in ten minutes!' Mum's reply was: 'Yes, I could too if I had the flunkies to do all the work!'…and so it went on.

On arrival the 'list of food requirements' would be taken down to the local store and Father would return with sufficient supplies to feed an army for a month! Forbidden foods, such as jam and sweet biscuits, were consumed with haste and Father would take on the role of resident chef. He would stuff pumpkins with mince steak, make delicious pots of goulash and serve us blue potatoes![2] He would then leave the unholy mess for the rest of us to clean up. Chinese cooking was his speciality, as was his chilli sauce that would lift the head off many an unsuspecting taster. These were, no doubt, the legacy of the numerous recipes dreamt up while imprisoned. Mum would often comment that the cleaning up would take longer than the preparation, but no one could deny that his finished products could compete favourably with any reputable Chinese restaurant. I have inherited the old seasoned quali,[3] which lives a very sedate life these days, only turning out the odd stir-fry.

Another year, Father purchased a live chicken, which he intended to cook. Unfortunately, we kids fell in love with it between purchase time and the pot, but somehow Father was able to whip it away undetected for the deadly chop. His act was soon discovered when, to our horror and dismay, a headless chook was seen running around the backyard! Needless to say, my brother Max and I became vegetarians for that meal!

Those holidays were the only time we really spent as a family. My brother and I still remember fishing with Father off the rocks, proudly returning home with the catch of the day. Unfortunately the numerous yellowtails never did provide us with a substantial meal! In my early teens my own agenda took over from the family activities. Once my suntan was in place, the social life would begin, and I hardly saw the folks save for mealtime and the compulsory rest period each afternoon. Father would meet his mates at the beach in the morning but by afternoon it was drink in hand, personality change and sleep. I question which fuelled what.

Preparation for departure was another logistical exercise as the holiday house had to be given its annual spring clean too. This meant we had to change all the drawer linings again. The pages of the *Sydney Morning Herald* imprinted with the previous year's departure date were replaced with the current issue. For Father it was a matter of pride that the Austin A40 would make the pilgrimage to the holiday house and back to Sydney without boiling. It never did join the multitude of cars on the side of the road with bonnets up and steam gushing from the radiator!

As we grew older, we would enjoy Father's absence; it was far more peaceful without him. My childhood recollection is that he did not suffer fools. In my eyes, he was a street angel and a house devil. He was dictatorial, unbending, impatient, intolerant, unrealistic, argumentative, unreasonable, self-centred, uncommunicative in so far as he would talk at you, not with you and lastly, a know-all! There was little room for discussion and real communication was non-existent. If we needed to talk to him we would have to 'toe the line', which was either the edge of the carpet or a floorboard, and state our case in between the movements of his favourite concerto. At times Father would become totally out of hand and Mum would warn us that fireworks were about to erupt. She would give him a serve, pull him back into line and he would eat out of her hand for a short time until the cycle started all over again.

Mealtime was a big issue. Grace consisted of Father saying 'We have food to eat. Thank God!' If we laboured over finishing our meal, we would have to sit through the discourse of 'Eat it! You don't know what it's like to be hungry!! Think of all the starving people in the world!' 'Then give it to them!' I would reply. We were often forced to eat everything on our plate and no food was ever thrown out in our household. It was saved for Father's bubble and squeak. Even in his later life, during each hospital stay Father would stow his stash of biscuits or old toast in the top drawer of his bedside table. Mum once commented to the nurse that he was a health hazard, but the nurse just asked her whether he had been a POW.

The subject of 'the war' had a huge impact on our childhood although, in retrospect, specifics were never discussed. The starvation and the 'Japs' were ever-present. We were allowed neither guns nor Japanese-made toys. Father's hatred of the Japanese men was foremost, but not so for the Japanese women. At one point, my father was regularly dealing with the Japanese in business. At the conclusion of a lengthy discussion held in Japanese, most likely intended to exclude him, he would delight in throwing away the odd Japanese word. The businessmen never really knew how much Japanese he had understood and that delighted him. Much later, a

Japanese family moved next door, but there was no friendly welcome from us, their neighbours. Father could never bring himself to face the husband and Mum subsequently felt obliged to explain the situation. As for their poor dog — if it so much as set a foot on our property, Father would bristle with rage and hound it away. The poor dog would have been Australian born and bred, but Father never saw it that way!

What was the effect of this on me? I am not prejudiced against the Japanese people but neither do I have any interest in visiting Japan. I worked alongside a beautiful Japanese lady for a time and caught myself thinking how years before our fathers would have instantly killed each other: the irony of history and the futility of war.

War books were plentiful at home and many conversations revolved around military history. As a result, I do not engage in anything pertaining to war, nor have I read any books written about the atrocities my father endured. 'Suga', the Borneo trunk that stored the treasures at the conclusion of the war, was like a family member.[4] The hand-made clogs, carved from wood with tyre rubber tops, were everyday wear around the house. Military shorts and shirts were father's weekend knockabout clothing and the old Japanese key box from the camp now holds my son's bow ties. Father's best shirt for fronting the Japanese officers is more a patchwork quilt than a shirt and the size is markedly small. This shirt and the clogs now do the rounds of groups and clubs wishing to hear of the plight of the POWs.[5]

Names of mates from 'the clink' were commonplace and it is interesting to now be meeting their offspring. In my mid-teens Father announced that a daughter of one of his friends was at a nearby boarding school. Being a country girl, wrenched from her family for educational purposes and therefore supposedly lonely, father took pity on her and invited her home. We were given the rounds of the kitchen and told to make her feel welcome as it would be a daunting experience for her to walk into an unknown family. I was expecting a quiet, retiring, rather fragile convent girl and had the odd conversation ready at hand. Father drove in with the said girl in tow. We heard her long before we laid eyes on her. The country convent girl, presumably of few words, was none other than Ethnee McLoughlin, daughter of George. Anyone who knows Ethnee will understand why our sides were aching from laughter by the end of the night. She has been a proxy member of our family and medicine for our souls ever since!

Father's fiftieth birthday was a night to remember! All went well until 'the speech'! Joviality was replaced by a sombre discourse, which disclosed that this would be his last birthday. He finished his speech and went off to bed. Apparently, not only were the POWs told that they could not father a child, but also that they would be dead by fifty! Proved wrong in the first instance, Father lived to a ripe old age of seventy-six — well past his designated cut-off point and a credit to his constitution, considering the abuse he gave it. A heavy smoker of more than seventy cigarettes per day, with a cough that would announce his presence anywhere, he was told by an Army medico that he would be dead in six months if he continued the smoking habit. In true form, Father went cold turkey and gave up his lifetime vice overnight. This vice, however, was replaced with food and an odd 2 stone (12.5 kilograms) soon made its way around his girth. Unfortunately the formidable cough remained with him and caused me many an embarrassing moment.

Personalities and relationships within the family were wide and varied. Mum and my brother were the carers and the peacemakers who inevitably tried to please my father. Both took his negative serves to heart and the more they were hurt, the more they tried. I, on the other hand, was much more of my father's personality and will, even today, proudly claim his good traits. As time went on and Father's behaviour became more erratic, unreasonable and dictatorial, I chose to remove myself from the 'eye of the storm', namely him. I saw my father as the negative force within an otherwise positive family unit. Where my brother and mother would visibly crumble at the tirades, I would give father tit for tat and he loved it. Bullies love to be bullied! The more outrageous his behaviour, the more outrageous were my serves. I saw my role as being the confronter for the tribe with the ability to 'change the course of the war'. It was effective and it worked.

As time went on, names changed. There were the usual teenage referrals to the folks such as 'the olds, the cheese, his masters voice, TOM (The Old Man) and he who is to be obeyed'. My brother nicknamed my mother 'Snooks', while I chose to be more familiar and called her by a derivation of her Christian name. Father became 'Father' or was referred to by his initials and all names are still in place today. The metaphors are as indelible as the names. At primary school, my brother was asked to draw a picture of his father — he drew an armoured tank.

Father was a force of nature and his entrance in the evening, always signalled by the family cat, was like a hurricane. In the silence of the night,

KERIN'S BROTHER MAX DREW THIS PICTURE OF HIS FATHER FOR HIS BIRTHDAY

the cat would suddenly go into panic mode and race around the house until it found an exit point. On a few occasions its exit coincided with Father's entry and the electricity between them was something to be seen. Father had no affiliation with animals and they had no love for him either. He refused to have the cat desexed and would pride himself on regularly supplying the university with its offspring for scientific purposes. This never sat well with us.

My courting years were another story. I lost more than one suitor because of my father: the fear and trepidation of him outweighed the thrill of the chase of me! Many a time I would return home and invite my date in for a coffee. There, sitting in the lounge chair with nothing on, save for a skimpy pair of pyjama pants, would be my father. Book in hand at 2 a.m., he would look the picture of innocence. Later he graduated to the even more embarrassing tactic of circling the parked car with torch in hand.

The command performance came when I was about twenty years of age. The proud owner of my own car and holding down one-and-a-half responsible jobs, I was almost independent and I had a date with a very desirable dental student. Unfortunately, the dean of his faculty happened to be in the lounge room as my date entered the arena for the grand introduction. The poor boy took one look at the dean and Father obviously sensed his discomfort. Dictatorship rose to the fore and we were duly told to be home by midnight. I pleaded for extended time, without success, and was eventually delivered home by the stated hour of midnight. It was New Year's Eve!

Surprisingly, I did eventually marry and I moved to Penang not long afterwards. This gave Father the opportunity to visit us and to take a trip down memory lane. It opened a Pandora's box. He was once more on familiar territory and we endured the war yet again. He knew it all and became the navigator and director. He had me entering expressways in Singapore from the exit points and his 'white man's supremacy' overruled the locals. He spoke down to shopkeepers, argued with all and sundry and took on the 'colonial rule' mentality. My parents then continued on to Borneo where his behaviour worsened. It culminated in a local black ban where no taxi would transport them to the airport and my parents subsequently missed their flight.

My father was a man of great contrasts. His ability to command men within the military system was outstanding and his influence has had an immense impact on some very prominent men. As a father, however, I found him ineffective — almost non-existent in presence and input. He could be the life of the party, a mischief-maker and very much one of the boys. He could also fall into bouts of depression, which caused great concern to us on more than one occasion. Although his catch cry was 'There's a place for everything and everything in its place', the rule was for everyone bar him. He would arrive home after work and there would be a trail of disaster from the front door to the back room. His hat would be in the kitchen, his shoes in the lounge room, while other personal objects would be strewn hither, thither and yon. He never wiped his feet at the door, or picked up after himself. The office at home was a disaster area and resembled a war zone. I once used it as a shock tactic for my young daughter who was going through a messy stage of her life and it worked wonders. On another occasion a work colleague rang to ask the whereabouts of a certain item. When told it was on my father's desk, he replied 'Oh, it's all right, I'm not in that much of a hurry!' The batman had his job in the Army and in civvy street the wife automatically replaced him.

Father was a great one for plans and lists but that was often where the project would both start and finish. Everything had to be filed and order was the desire but not always the outcome. After his death, Mum and I had the daunting task of wading through his documented life, which uncovered many items now housed in a museum. Father had a soft side but that was rarely exposed. He would do anything for anyone but only to a point. There was a demarcation line over which one could not step — prohibiting entry to his world of vulnerability, intimacy or reliance. His inherent ability to be able to read men and act accordingly, to be in command of situations, was sometimes quite the opposite outside the 'system'.

The military system suited my father to the ground. Every action had a reaction and every command had a counter-command. There were those above and those below and he thrived in such order. He was supported by the system and the system supported him. This was not so in his personal life. After retirement, without personal interests or hobbies, my father's life spiralled downwards, totally out of control. His workaholic tendencies gave way to isolation and the spare time that he had never before experienced now perhaps allowed him to think and possibly to meet his demons. In retrospect, my father must have been very bored, but he lacked the strategies to overcome his predicament. One task he could have undertaken, the documentation of his life's work, was never attempted. Unfortunately, much of his precious knowledge of the coal industry was subsequently lost because on his own, without any supporting infrastructure (or lackies), he lacked the resources to organise and record it.

The dreaded amber liquid engulfed him and he was eventually institutionalised. Once again he rallied. He knew many of the doctors and he would successfully dictate to them. He had an innate ability to be able to pull the wool over people's eyes but this eventually hurt him. Mum, recognising the contrast in his behaviour, asked why he happily did whatever the nurses requested of him. He replied, 'Oh, they have authority'. He thus imprisoned himself and never saw the outside world again.

Often unpredictable, Father's behaviour was most predictable each February and September, coinciding with the fall of Singapore and his release from Kuching camp in Borneo. He would experience strong mood changes, become depressed and retreat into himself. It was in the month of February in 1990 that my father eventually died.

Who Is This Man?

JOHN 'PADDY' O'BRIEN

Major Charles O'Brien (NX34793)
2/18th Battalion, AIF
POW: Changi; Burma-Thailand Railway

Charles O'Brien was born on 29 December 1906. He trained as a schoolteacher and became a captain in the Sydney University Regiment. In July 1940 he was seconded from the University Regiment and appointed commanding officer of B Company, 2/18th Battalion. When Charles sailed from Sydney to Singapore with the 22nd Brigade in 1941, he left behind his wife Vera and their two small sons, John 'Paddy' born in 1938 and Paul born in 1939.

In July 1941 Charles was promoted to the rank of major. On 26–27 January 1942, his battalion suffered heavy losses during fighting against the Japanese in the Mersing and Jemualang (Nithsdale Estate) areas in Malaya. On 12 February 1942, he was appointed to replace Colonel Varley as commanding officer of the 2/18th Battalion. Major O'Brien was sent from Changi to Burma with A Force in May 1942. Much of his time was spent in hospital camps where he was the senior or joint senior Australian officer.

Charles O'Brien returned from Singapore in November 1945 on the *Circassia*. He left the Army in December 1945 and returned to teaching. He and his wife had two more sons, born in 1946 and 1951. Paddy's mother was 'not interested in anything to do with Charlie's war service and did not want to partake in Anzac Day activities. After Charlie retired, December 1971, on his sixty-fifth birthday, as part of planned travel, he wanted to revisit Singapore, Malaysia etc — this elicited a very firm "not on your life" from his wife'.[1] Charles O'Brien never went back.

In 1986 he was diagnosed with stomach cancer and he died on 10 August 1991. Ethnee Brooks, Captain George McLoughlin's daughter, remembers nursing Charles O'Brien when she was a community nurse. Her patient was embarrassed that the daughter of one of his 2/18th colleagues was showering him. Ethnee remembers telling him that 'if he could face the Japanese for three and a half years he could face her for a few moments in the shower'.[2]

In 1967, when Paddy was a warrant officer in the RAN, he visited the Kanchanaburi War Cemetery during a ship's visit to Bangkok. He made a second visit on Anzac Day 2000, when he laid a wreath on behalf of the 2/18th Battalion after attending the dawn service at Hellfire Pass.

I was too young to remember Father before he left Australia. I was only three years old when he embarked from Sydney on the *Queen Mary* in February 1941. However, I do have a very clear memory of Father's return to Australia in November 1945, meeting his ship at Pyrmont in Sydney, and arriving at our rented home in Earlwood.

My earliest memories are of Young in western New South Wales, where my mother and younger brother Paul and I lived with my maternal grandmother. We had been living in Sydney, and the move to Young would have taken place while my father was at the training camp at Glanmire, just outside Bathurst — probably in November or December 1940. I have a photograph of my father and mother, with myself and younger brother Paul, on the front steps of our home in Young. I suspect it was taken during the 'pre-embarkation leave' in December 1940.

I recall that in Young there were few men around. My mother used to go with other women to pick fruit at the weekends, climbing up onto trucks outside the post office. However, in the 'circle' of people I knew, a number of families had fathers, and I can recall wondering why we didn't. In 1942, my mother went back to teaching at the Young High School.

I hold copies of correspondence from my father's sister to her twin brother, John Hill O'Brien, who was also a POW, but who spent his time on

Vera, Paul, Paddy and Charlie, Young, c. 1940

Blakang Mati Island[3] off Singapore. My aunt's letters show that my mother did not really know whether my father was still alive until September 1945. On 20 September 1945, my aunt wrote that she had received a telegram from my mother: my father had been reported alive in Siam (Thailand), and he had sent a cable to her saying that he was well.

Apparently, next of kin were informed that their 'man' was a POW in early 1943, and then there was no further word, at least in respect of my father until September 1945. At some stage in 1945 my mother moved us back to Sydney, and this could have been after this advice had been received, or even later, after my father had contacted her. I've never seen any copies of correspondence between my mother and father, so I can only presume that all such correspondence was destroyed many years ago, most likely once my father returned home, if not before.

I don't remember my mother speaking about my father before she received the news that he was alive. After that, she started to show us photographs that he had sent to her from Malaya before the Japanese landings and invasion. I remember being taken into her bedroom in Earlwood, being shown some photographs, and being told this is your father, he has been to war, and he would be home soon.

My father arrived back in Sydney in November 1945. We had decorated the house in Earlwood with small Australian and British flags, and a banner across the front of the house, proclaiming 'Welcome home'. My mother, Paul and I were taken from Earlwood to Pyrmont in a Red Cross car with a uniformed driver. Our mother pointed out our father as he walked along the wharf towards us. I still have a fairly clear memory of seeing my father on the wharf for the first time. Here was a man with straight white hair, quite unlike the brown wavy hair that we had seen in the photographs we had been shown.

I can only assume that the car, which took the four of us back to Earlwood, was provided on the basis that my father had been required to remain in Thailand. Because of his rank and his position there, the Army Military History Section interviewed him at Nakhon Pathom on 23 September 1945. My father was also given a couple of days at home before he was required to attend the Ingleburn army camp, unlike his brother who had to go direct to Ingleburn before being allowed to go home to Melbourne. In a letter to his brother, who had already been repatriated to Australia, my father said that he was on the last transport (apart from hospital ships) carrying POWs out of Singapore to Australia.[4]

I can remember that I had no idea how I should feel about this man, a man that I didn't even know. What was he like? Was he the reason we had left Young? Young had been, and still is, a very special place. Our grandmother really brought us up when my mother went back to teaching during the war years and we visited Young frequently after the war. I still go there occasionally to visit my grandmother's grave: she is buried there alongside my mother's sister.

On arrival back at Earlwood we were given some army gear to play with. We had to stay outside with my mother's sister who was living with us. This, at that time (I was two months from turning eight), hurt. I didn't know why we were to stay outside — I felt that this stranger had arrived and taken my mother away from me. I could not, at that time, and for some years after, understand why I felt hurt.

The years 1946–47 in Earlwood were good fun, at least for my younger brother and myself, as we rode scooters around the nearby suburbs. I cannot recall much to do with my father who had returned to his teaching career. My mother remained at home, and a third boy was born in September 1946. My father seemed to be a severe man, and hard to get to know. I vaguely recall that I had trouble relating to him, and did not really know who he was.

In 1948 we moved to Stroud, a small country town around 80 kilometres north of Newcastle, on the old Pacific Highway. Here I probably got to know my father a little more — he was the principal of the school we attended. But my memory leads me to think that the relationship was a little difficult. I still seemed unsure of who he was, and why. In 1950 I was sent to boarding school in Sydney. I was told that this was because there was insufficient local secondary schooling available, and if I had to go away to school, and board, then it may as well be in Sydney.

I hated this decision. At the time, I felt that my parents no longer loved me. It seemed to me that this father coming into our life was the cause of this upheaval. Of course, later as I grew older, I could understand the rationale of being sent to boarding school, but at that time, I was too young to know what 'rationale' meant. However, by the time I left boarding school, I had made a solemn promise to myself that, should I have children, they would never ever be sent to boarding school.

I finished boarding school in 1953. I could no longer cope with it, and my education, if going anywhere, was going backwards. My younger brother, who had joined me there in 1952, left with me. I completed my schooling living at home in Coonabarabran in 1954.

Those earlier years I cannot remember feeling any great love for my father. I am not sure why, but it is a strong recollection. I must admit that there were times when I thought he was 'all right' — usually during holiday times and particularly during our visits to Melbourne over the Christmas school holidays. We did that every three years and I joined them on those holidays until January 1954.

As children do, I grew up and left home. I became independent, was working, and spent some time living away from home, which was then at Woolgoolga in New South Wales. In 1960, I joined the RAN. In 1963, my father and the family returned, at his request, to teaching in Sydney. That year my father asked me to accompany him to both the Anzac Day march and the 2/18th Battalion reunion following the march.

From this point, our relationship improved. From listening to what was being said, not only that 1963 Anzac Day, but on many others, as I often went along (I enjoy the privilege of associate membership of the 2/18th Battalion Association), I began to realise what my father and many others had gone through. While none of them talked at length of their POW experiences, I was able to realise the enormity of their plight and suffering on the Burma railway.

If my parents ever discussed my father's POW days, it was without my knowledge. My father did not discuss it with me either, apart from a few fleeting moments, after which he would always change the subject. Nothing was ever said at home about the war years. My mother did not discuss the war either, her experiences, or anything to do with that period of her (and my) life.

I believe that the war and subsequently the POW days took something away from me. To have a father suddenly thrust upon you took some getting used too. Particularly when, for as long as I could remember, until I was almost eight years old, I had known only one parent (not forgetting my grandmother who did a lot of parenting in Young). Maybe my father also had some difficulties coming to grips with being a father again, having two sons who were nearly five years older than when he had last seen them.

My mother once said that my father had returned from overseas a very changed man. I do not know exactly what this meant. Although I asked her at the time, she did not want to discuss the subject.

My mother, who died in July 1989, was considered by my late youngest brother and me to be rather 'unloving'. Could this have happened because of the war? Because little or nothing was heard of the men after Singapore fell? Maybe this and her belief that my father was a changed man when he came back, are the reasons why I always felt that she was 'unloving'.

As I watched my widowed father 'fading away' in his last couple of years, in a nursing home, I felt that he had aged very quickly. At the time of his death, he was eighty-four, 'going on ninety-four'. He had a number of health issues and most of them were probably attributable to his days as a POW. It was sad to see him suffer.

Had there been no war, or had my father not gone to war, I would have grown up with him and maybe had a better relationship in those very early, formative years. Conversely, maybe my father would have had exactly the same temperament and characteristics if had he not gone to war and become a POW. Who knows? It is also possible that the strained relationship between my parents may not have been as evident, had my father not been away for nearly five years, leaving my mother to cope with two young sons, not knowing what was happening to her husband, after the fall of Singapore.

Hunter Valley Hero

ETHNEE BROOKS

Captain George James McLoughlin, MID (NX12496)
2/18th Battalion, AIF
POW: Changi

Many recognise George's contribution to the betterment of mankind as outstanding. He was a mentor to many and his influence will have a profound and lasting effect on all he loved and helped.[1]

George McLoughlin was born at Scone in New South Wales on 18 August 1912. After finishing school at De La Salle College in Armidale, he worked for his father and uncles on their various properties in and around the Hunter Valley. He enlisted in the

AIF in May 1940 and left for Malaya in February 1941, just weeks before his wife Catherine delivered their first son.

Captain George McLoughlin became the second-in-command of C Company, 2/18th Battalion. He was a popular officer and after the war received a number of letters from the men in his battalion thanking him for his leadership. His Mentioned in Dispatches (MID) cited his 'distinguished service while in the Australian Military Forces' when it was gazetted in March 1947.[2]

Ethnee, the second of George and Catherine McLoughlin's four children and their only daughter, was born in 1946. She grew up knowing all her father's ex-POW friends and says they were close to them all. She spent a lot of her school years with the Mosher family. Ken Mosher was master of ceremonies at Ethnee's wedding and in later years introduced Ethnee's son Matthew to the scouts.

Ethnee went to Anzac Day marches with her father and was always very conscious of his popularity among his troops. At home in the Hunter Valley he was generous, even extravagant, with a great deal of style and Ethnee's friends loved him: 'There he was a war hero but they didn't see what went on behind the scenes'. And, she says, they didn't see that he drank heavily; nor did they see the demands that he placed on his children, particularly his eldest son. He was very hard on them all and had very high expectations for them: 'Second place was never good enough; we had to be first'.

Ethnee is a nursing sister and counsellor and feels that now, many years later, her attitude has changed.

I fully understand what my fun-loving, warm and brave dad had to face: starvation, fear, loneliness, torture, tropical disease, loss of brave friends on a daily basis. I wish I had possessed the wisdom to be kinder to my dad and to help him with his emotions — instead, as a liberated young nurse, I flew the banner of equality for women and argued with him. We adored each other but a soldier is trained to be brave, silent and self-sufficient in order to survive and to protect his men.

*Now as the mother of a young soldier (now a sergeant) in
1RAR who has received a military commendation for his
'outstanding performance of duty while serving on
Operation CITADEL in East Timor', I have not made the
same mistakes again. I listen carefully and watch for signs
of inner conflict and pain and Matt and I do talk about his
experiences in Timor and how atrocities there affected
him. So, yes, I have used the lessons learned from my POW
father to be a nurturer of others.[3]*

My father returned from Changi on the troopship *Arawa* in October
1945. He was 8 stone (50 kilograms), 6 feet 2 inches (1.88 metres),
suffered from a severely compromised immune system, pernicious anaemia
and emotional scars. My father also had a charismatic personality with a
hearty laugh, a good sense of humour and he could laugh at himself. He
was very popular with family and friends and commanded respect — a
born leader. He had progressive ideas and introduced electric light to the
valley; he was president of the local sports/rodeo committee and loved
community involvement.

My father was delighted to meet the son who had been born a few
weeks after he had sailed to Singapore and he was delighted to settle the
three of them into Yanolee, their beautiful grazing property in the upper
Hunter Valley. After all they had been through during the war, he and
Catherine planned that they would make Yanolee a home away from home
for all their friends. Yanolee became renowned for its hospitality, both on
the national and international level.

My father deeply loved my beautiful, gentle and nurturing mother
Catherine, but like most returning servicemen, he found it hard to readjust
to life with his 'newly found' son, George Junior. It was unconscious but he
was hard on my brother. This made my mother anxious and upset. She had
depended on my brother. He was all she had during the eighteen months
when she had not known if Dad was dead or alive. This dependence on her
son exacerbated the problem and this was a common occurrence for many
returned soldiers.

I arrived in September 1946 and Dad felt able to put all his pent-up emotions into loving me — he carried me about and sang Irish lullabies like 'Toora loora loora' to me. I was 'his little mate' and from the age of two years I rode with him on a pony called Bantum, in a pad with bucket stir-rups. My parents had two more sons, Timothy and Patrick, but as the only daughter, I felt special.

Even though the years to follow would be mixed with struggles, my innate confidence from that early love has endured. As I grew, I stood up to my strong father. I defended my brother George Junior and my mother Catherine if I thought he was out of line. He found my behaviour hard to deal with and consequently we were often at loggerheads.

Dad drank at times for two reasons: firstly, he was very sociable and loved company; and secondly, he had many bad memories. My mother said that in the early days after the war he would wake screaming. The combi-nation of his weakened immune system and strong drink could make him verbally abusive. My mother was a devoted wife and mother and, being shy and kind, she did suffer very much.

I grew up with a father who was recognised as a war hero in the Upper Hunter Valley. He was always asked to chair meetings and to be the master of ceremonies at functions. I was proud to be a McLoughlin with my wonderful family of three special brothers. Dad educated us at the best pri-vate boarding schools in Sydney and he loved the company of educated people. His good friends included Weary Dunlop, Adrian Curlewis and many more. Dad loved Shakespeare and frequently quoted him, a favour-ite quote being: 'To thine own self be true and it follows as the night the day you cannot then be false to any man'. He taught us to be 'the best you can be and be generous'.

Like many children, I worried about my dad having such high expectations for my brothers and me. I tried many times to calm him down and 'make it right' and, when I couldn't, I felt sad and frustrated — too big a job for a little girl growing up. I always tried to live up to what Dad wanted. My mother understood this and she knew how hard we kids tried to please him. Mum's deep understanding of Dad kept him going; she put up with a lot because she knew how truly wonderful he was. They were different times. The man was the head of the household and, on the whole, women coped with domestic matters. However, Mum was the inner strength and he coped with readjustment after his war experiences until, after sixty years of marriage, he passed away at the age of eighty-two.

GEORGE AND CATHERINE MCLOUGHLIN WITH PATRICK, ETHNEE AND TIMOTHY AT THE
WEDDING OF THEIR OLDER BROTHER, GEORGE JUNIOR, NEWCASTLE, 1969

I met many of Dad's officer friends and their families when I became a boarder at Loreto Convent at Normanhurst in Sydney. Colonel Ken Mosher, his wife Imelda and their children — Kerin, who had beaten me by a few months in the baby stakes,[4] and Max — became my family as well. This friendship began when I was twelve years old. I was somewhat nervous of Colonel Mosher, but I loved him, and many years later he became one of my patients when I was working as a community nurse in Sydney.

Kerin and I are still great friends. After my brothers and I have marched with the 2/18th men on Anzac Day, Kerin, her mother Imelda and I attend the 2/18th Battalion Anzac Day luncheon together. On the Sunday after Anzac Day the Battalion families attend a service at the Garrison Church at Gordon and share a light lunch afterwards. Great friendships have been developed and maintained. The Changi network still functions very well.

Life Is for Getting on With

JACQUI HICKSON

Lieutenant Russell Winthrop Ewin (NX76171)
8th Division Signals, AIF
POW: Changi; Sandakan/Kuching

On 10 September 1945, Russ Ewin wrote to his wife Joyce from Kuching camp:

Conditions have been far from easy, yet I have been fortunate; I am probably one of the fittest in our camp, at least the experience has broadened me in many ways & I think improved my whole character and outlook. I yearn

for you, to be together again will be paradise complete —
how eagerly I look forward to holiday & home building
together.[1]

They had known each other since they were teenagers but
Russ and Joyce had only been married for a week when he left
with the 27th Brigade for Malaya in July 1941. Now, four and a
half years later, they were soon to be reunited. Russ Ewin's
daughter Jacqui does not remember her father's POW experiences ever playing a prominent role within their family; in fact,
she is almost self-conscious about their minimal effect on her
own life. Clearly though, when Russ wrote to Joyce again from
the hospital ship *Wanganella* on its way back to Australia in late
September, he was aware that despite their love for each other,
there would need to be some accommodation of the changes
that had occurred in both their lives:

I'm certain that there must be a fair amount of
readjustment between us, for we both will have changed
to a certain extent. Yet I feel that those things are not
going to be too difficult for us, loving each other as we do.
Just a little tolerance for me please, lady; you'll probably
have to be a bit firm with me too.[2]

Russ was born on 5 November 1916 at Summer Hill in
Sydney, the eldest of five boys. He and his younger brother Les
both joined the AIF.[3]

In July 1942, five months after the Allied surrender, Russ
was transported from Changi to Sandakan with B Force. He
became involved in the underground network established and
operated by Lionel Matthews and Dr James Taylor, helping to
smuggle radio parts, messages, medical supplies and money into
the camp when he went on working parties. Although not
implicated when the underground group was betrayed, he was
moved to Lintang Barracks at Kuching with most of the officers
from Sandakan. After their liberation in 1945, Russ returned
from Kuching with Maurie Arvier, Ken Mosher, Vic Sinfield,
Hugh Waring and Stan Woods on the *Wanganella*.

Russ resumed his job at the Tax Office in Sydney, working there until he retired as Assistant Deputy Tax Commissioner in New South Wales. He has always remained in close contact with his Sigs colleagues and for some years now has been editor of *Vic Eddy*,[4] the official journal of the 8th Division Signals Association. He has also been a valuable point of contact for Sigs relatives, most particularly for sons and daughters searching for information about their fathers' war service. In June 1996 he initiated a new section in *Vic Eddy*, called 'Did You Know Him?'.

I hope this will also encourage our members to respond readily to any plea for news of a loved one. Please don't think that someone else will do it, or that your little smattering of information will not be of great value. I assure you it is not so. It is remarkable how one source of information can frequently start a chain reaction, leading to other sources. There is a real craving for any little snippet — sometimes children have no knowledge of their soldier father's character or his lifetime experiences. The reaction when a picture begins to unfold makes it so evident that pent-up tensions over the years are at last being removed.[5]

Russ and Joyce live in Belrose in New South Wales. They will celebrate their sixty-fourth wedding anniversary in 2005.

Born in 1949 and growing up in Sydney, I was not aware throughout my childhood of the horrors my father, Russell Ewin, had been exposed to as a POW. He had spent a few months in Malaya in the 8th Division Signals, enjoying the work of setting up communication lines and learning about the country and its people. When the Japanese invaded from the north, his group retreated south, and finally was captured at the surrender of Singapore. Originally incarcerated in Changi, after a few months he was transferred to Sandakan, and then to Kuching. The atrocities committed by the Japanese captors in these camps have been well documented.

Dad never mentioned his war experiences at home. Most of what I have learned of his experiences came from reading books recommended by my father, when I was well into my teens and later. My mother sometimes remarked about the nightmares Dad had, waking up shouting, but nothing more was said in front of me and possibly not even spoken about further between the two of them. I certainly never felt there were secrets being kept from me. Nor did I have any inkling of what my father had been through in the not so distant past.

Even later, after I had read the recommended books, we didn't discuss them much. Perhaps I was reticent to bring up the topic directly. I don't know. I do know that he still becomes very emotional when speaking publicly about his experiences and maybe I shied away from such emotional confrontation.

We often (my recollection — probably once a year, maybe less) went to POW reunions. My memory of those is meeting a lot of Dad's friends

RUSS AND JACQUI IN THE SNOW AT ORANGE, C. 1959

who came from all over the country and were always very friendly to me. To me they were large-scale picnics that Dad looked forward to, where he and his friends stood around and talked a lot. I did know at the time that these 'picnics' and these friends were very important to him, without being particularly aware of the context of their friendships. We also visited several of these friends over the years, but again, I knew them as Dad's friends, not fellow soldiers or POWs.

Looking back many times over the years, I have been amazed at how racially tolerant my parents are. This certainly didn't occur to me during my childhood — I was not aware of some people's intolerance to other human beings until well into my teens. Only after I read about Dad's experiences did I begin to wonder about how he coped with the influx of Japanese people and products into our lives in suburban Sydney. He never showed any sign of prejudice or even bitterness towards the race as a whole or towards any individuals who had not been involved.

Before writing this, I asked him if I had simply not been perceptive or perhaps sensitive to behaviour of his which might have been caused by his POW experiences. His reply was that what had happened was in the past: when the POWs returned little was made of their suffering (another story in itself), so that relatives and non-POW friends were not aware of what they had been through. Life was for getting on with.

No Complaints

CAROLYN NEWMAN

Captain Wilfred D'Arcy Fawcett (NX70392)
8th Division Signals, AIF
POW: Changi; Keijo

Wilf Fawcett was born in Kapunda in South Australia in 1907, the youngest of eight surviving children. He studied engineering at Adelaide University and worked as a design engineer with the Adelaide Electric Supply Company (later the Electricity Trust of SA (ETSA) before transferring from the Militia to the AIF In 1940.

Wilf joined 8th Division Signals and sailed from Sydney to Singapore with the 22nd Brigade and attached troops in February 1941. During the next months, his M Section 'flying squad' travelled around Malaya repairing and maintaining communications equipment, spending the final days before the Allied surrender in the Singapore Botanical Gardens. In August 1942 Wilf was transported from Singapore to Korea, where he took over the role of senior Australian officer in the Keijo POW camp. Three years later, on 9 September 1945, American troops liberated the camp. He went by sea to Manila in the Philippines where he recuperated in No. 3 Australian PW Reception camp before flying home. Wilf returned to his job with ETSA and married Joan, a Royal Australian Air Force nursing sister. They were settling down to family life with their two young children, when Wilf was killed in a traffic accident.

It was a wet Friday night in October 1954. A young male driver collided with my father as he walked across North Terrace in Adelaide. Although the accident was just metres from the Royal Adelaide Hospital, they couldn't save him. My father was shockingly injured and he died two days later without regaining consciousness.

That may have been when I first realised he had been a POW. The adults' muffled voices and mutterings about fate and what awful luck after surviving the prison camp. Small snippets of conversation that we probably remembered later.

Our first invitations to the Legacy Christmas party arrived soon after our father's death. They continued until we were almost teenagers, a reminder that my brother and I were different from our friends. I'm not sure if we really understood why we received the invitations or why a man who seemed much older than our parents suddenly appeared to 'look after us' and take us out for Sunday afternoon drives. We did understand that our father had left forever and we missed him. We didn't talk about him very much: our mother cried whenever we mentioned him, so we stopped mentioning him. He faded from our lives. We lost contact with my father's family and, some years later, our mother remarried.

It was not until I was in my twenties and backpacking through Thailand that I remember thinking much about my father's POW experiences.

WILF WITH CAROLYN AND BILL, FLINDERS RANGES, 1954

Two Japanese businessmen gave my friend and me a lift and I wondered what my father would have thought about it. When I told my mother later she replied that our hitchhiking would have worried him more than their nationality. It was the first time that she and I had really spoken about my father's POW experiences and it must have reminded her to show me an article he had written more than twenty-five years earlier. It was a brief account of his POW days. I was interested to read something my father had written and surprised by his lack of bitterness, but he still remained quite remote from my life.

Twenty years later, in 1996, I met a group of 8th Division Signals veterans at the War Memorial in Canberra. A couple of the men could remember my father and, for the first time in forty years, I was being introduced as Wilf Fawcett's daughter. The men took my details and within days I had received the 8th Division Signals unit magazine, *Vic Eddy*, and a copy of the unit history, *Through*. I wrote to thank Russ Ewin, the editor of *Vic Eddy*, telling him how much my meeting with the men had meant to me. I asked if anyone else who knew my father could contact me.

Russ published my letter in the next issue. I received phone calls, a couple of letters and one of the veterans even sent me his autobiography. He and my father had gone on leave together to the hill station at Frazer's Hill in Selangor in Malaya in December 1941 and I could read about it on page

46.[1] Excitedly I read about their journey from Johore Bahru to the government bungalow at the hill station where they planned to spend a week. They didn't. When the steward brought their first round of drinks, he also brought them each a telegram. Their leave was cancelled and they were to return to their unit headquarters. They left the next morning. I read and re-read page 46. I was glad to read that 'Wilf Fawcett was a pleasant easygoing companion',[2] but I kept wondering about the 'round of drinks'. I realised I had no idea what he liked to drink.

Feeling somewhat euphoric after that generous gift, I received even more surprises the next day. I had been sent some photos and bits and pieces of memorabilia from Keijo camp in Korea where my father had spent most of his POW years.

I was amazed and very touched that these men could find the time and energy to contact me so many years afterwards. But it was not only the veterans who contacted me, so did some of their sons, daughters and even nephews. One man whose uncle was in my father's section sent me a photocopy of the menu from their final meal at the Bathurst camp. It was the first time that I had seen my father's signature. I wondered what my mother would have thought of all this. Had she known any of these men? She must have heard some of my father's stories. Too late to ask, of course. My mother had also died in the month of October, in 1986.

During my own search I was also discovering that many other ex-POW offspring were just as busy as I was, chasing their fathers' stories. Some of them had only recently lost their fathers and I was surprised at how little they knew about them. A couple of the women I met had only recently discovered that their fathers had been POWs. Having felt somewhat disadvantaged by the paucity of my own information, I was beginning to realise that having a father around didn't necessarily mean being told about his experiences, nor did it guarantee a happy family life. Now I was starting to hear some very personal details from people who contacted me through *Vic Eddy* and who wanted to share their experiences with me. There were some harrowing stories.

One of my callers was very keen for me to help him and he rang hoping that I may have found some information relating to his father as well as mine. His father had died on the railway in Thailand, leaving his grieving mother with two small boys. After their mother's (far-too-early) death, he and his brother had cleared out all her personal memorabilia, including their father's letters and possessions. They made a bonfire and burnt everything — even the few photos of their father. Everything to do with him and the war, everything that had brought them and their mother so much unhappiness. Now, years later, he said that apart from themselves, he and his brother had no tangible evidence of their father's existence, but they had at least found their father's name in the nominal roll in *Through*. I have remained in contact with him but, so far, have found nothing for him to add to his meagre collection.

Despite possessing far more evidence of my own father's existence, I remembered I had checked for his name immediately I received my own copy of the unit history. Now years later, I still have bright pink 'Post It' notes attached to those pages that mention him.

Then, quite unexpectedly, one of my aunts sent me some letters my father had written from Malaya. I hadn't known they existed but I was not surprised they had been kept in his family. My father was a son and brother, rather than a husband and father during the war. My aunt had included one of the portrait postcards that many of the men sent home. My father looked so young and so like my son. Best of all, however, was a long letter he had written about his wartime experiences. It was addressed to his brother in Western Australia and it is clear it was prepared especially for him. The letter is dated 26 December 1945 — Boxing Day — so I'm sure he wrote it then. I've learnt that he was a very methodical man. I sat looking at his photo. I tried to picture him sitting outside on the verandah of his old family home at Kapunda, meticulously writing page after page. He had left Korea just a few months earlier. Was he reliving it all again as he wrote?

There are some wonderful descriptions of his early months in Singapore and Malaya — he loved the tropical plants, birds and animals. Apparently though, his section's technical equipment was problematic and they 'did not function according to the text books'. He wrote that he had 'small detachments scattered all over the State of Johore' and he had to travel about 200 miles to visit them all. *Through* also mentions these 'flying squads'.[3] The final position his section occupied before the surrender was in the Singapore Botanical Gardens. On the first morning they woke to discover that they were in the front line: the troops that they thought were covering them had been relocated. They all 'relaxed a little' once some British infantry moved in front of them. Admitting that his memories of the final days before the surrender were 'a bit hazy', his letter concentrated more on describing his first few months of imprisonment.

My father seemed to take a keen interest in everything. For example, he noted how quickly the men's pulse rates had dropped once they were deprived of their normal diets. His own dropped to forty-two within the first few weeks at Changi. He also talked about the onset of beri-beri which had appeared in the men much more swiftly than the doctors seemed to expect. He added that he was fortunate and had 'only rarely showed mild signs of it', but he pondered on their individual susceptibility. I had read in his unit history that during their early days in Changi he supervised a yeast factory for the unit, presumably because of his engineering background.[4] He also mentioned it in his letter to his brother: 'one of my jobs for a time was the making of yeast from a proportion of our rice ration, as it was hoped to be of some use in preventing beri-beri'.

I was interested too that my father had thought of escape. He wrote that they had considered the possibilities, that it 'was never far from our thoughts', but that they 'had abandoned the idea'. I wondered who 'they' were. Fortunately for him it seems that his men abandoned the idea as well:

Incidentally an order was issued by the Japs that if anyone tried to escape, the officer next senior to him would be held responsible. When we passed this order on to our troops we asked them to give us a run for our money and not get caught just over the skyline. Fortunately none of my men tried it so I do not know whether the Japs' threat was serious.

Food too was a constant theme.

Of course everyone thought and talked of food, until we made it a forbidden topic. Greens, to supplement the rice diet were very scarce, and hybiscus [sic] leaves, raw or boiled became popular, as there were hedges of this plant around the barracks. When we got the garden going sweet potato leaves and a type of spinach became available. Some of the chaps preferred grass to the hybiscus, but I stuck to hybiscus.

Reading his culinary recommendation I feel embarrassed that I've lived with a hibiscus in my garden for many years and I still haven't tasted the leaves, either raw or boiled.

In August 1942 my father left the tropical climate of Singapore to travel to Korea on the *Fukai Maru* with Japan Party B:

On 16 Aug 42 a party of 1000 PWs embarked from S'pore docks in the Fukai Maru *(pronounce it as you wish!) a Japanese tramp of about 4000 tons; built in Belfast very many years before. The Australians in the party numbered 93, including 6 officers (one of them a doctor) and a Red Cross Representative.*

With 1000 all ranks living in the 4 upper holds of a ship that size you can imagine that we were fairly crowded. The lower holds were filled with bauxite, which had the advantage of making the little ship very steady in rough weather.

Our living space below decks averaged 6 ft x 2 ft (1.83 m x .6 m) per man, with about 5 ft (1.52 m) headroom. The centre of the hold was stacked with rice, and we lived on two wooden platforms, one a few inches off the 'floor' and the other some 5 feet above. These platforms surrounded the hatch area.

Since my father was about 1.88 metres tall, he must have struggled to fold himself into that space. It was a shocking trip and he wrote that by the time they reached Formosa at the end of August, 40 per cent of the men were sick, one with diphtheria. However, he pointed out that it could have been even worse if the other 300 or so POWs in the Senior Officers Party had stayed on board as the Japanese originally intended.

Given the awful conditions on the *Fukai Maru* and the uncertainty of the men's futures, both in terms of survival and reproduction, it would no doubt have been unimaginable to Geoff de Groen, Alex Johnstone and Wilf that their (as yet, unborn) daughters would meet each other fifty-eight years after their fathers' voyage to Korea.

It took another month to reach Pusan in South Korea. They had been transported from Singapore for propaganda purposes and the debilitated men were disembarked and paraded through the streets of Pusan to the railway station. There are a number of images on the War Memorial database which show them marching through the crowded streets but they don't seem to look quite as weak and defeated as they were supposed to be.

The POWs were split into different groups and my father, in a group of about 400 British and 60 Australian POWs, went by train to Keijo (Seoul). On 25 September 1942, they were marched into the Keijo camp — an empty factory plus a few huts and a small compound. He spent the next three years there, the senior Australian officer in a small group of Australians.

Another of my discoveries was my father's war crimes affidavit[5] in which he mentioned the conditions in Keijo camp. He wrote that they were 'cold and hungry' and that the outside temperature during the winter months 'was frequently 30°–40°F below freezing point' but he also noted that, despite their deprivations, there were no Australian deaths during his detention at Keijo.

Within months the extraordinary links within the POW network led me to another valuable discovery. I heard that a man in Victoria owned a collection of sketches done by an artist in Keijo and that his collection apparently included a sketch of my father. I had never heard his name and he was not on the Sigs nominal roll. I thought immediately of Carol Cooper (whom I met in Canberra in 2000) and her father's diary. I wrote to Doug Phillips, the owner of the sketches, explaining who I was. Immediately he received my letter, he telephoned me and invited me down to stay with them in south-eastern Victoria.

I went just as soon as I could. Doug's father Richard had been the Red Cross representative who travelled with Wilf on the voyage to Korea. Too old to enlist, Richard Phillips had instead become a Red Cross representative with the 8th Division. Incarcerated in Changi with everyone else, he joined Japan Party B on the *Fukai Maru*. In Keijo he had commissioned one of the British prisoners to sketch five of the POWs, including my father. Doug had the sketches sitting there ready to show me, together with the meticulous diaries that his father had kept while he was in Keijo.

This generous couple, Doug and Yvonne Phillips, set me up in their study with my laptop and the diaries. I was amazed at their hospitality and commented on Doug's trust. When I suggested that I could have been 'just anyone' he surprised me by telling me that he knew exactly who I was. Apparently he had visited my parents in Adelaide just after I was born. Was there no limit to this POW network?

I spent two days scouring the pages of tiny handwriting for references to my father. There were many. They revealed that he had suffered three brutal beatings by the guards. The third incident had been on 14 September 1944 when he had written that 'Wilf Fawcett, one of the quietest

men in camp, was again for the third time a victim of savage brutality'.[6]
My father's affidavit to the war crimes tribunal states simply:

That although face-slappings and beatings were common, punishments rarely had lasting ill-effects. The Camp Commandant was difficult in minor ways but generally endeavoured to give fair treatment to prisoners. All things considered, his administration was good though frequently his subordinates did not follow his example.[7]

Doug's father had reported innumerable meetings with the camp commandant as he and my father endeavoured to improve conditions for the men. Some Red Cross parcels were distributed but, despite their efforts, food was limited and the men became very thin. Their low body weight is obvious in many of the official propaganda photographs. I learned later from Fran de Groen that the POWs could buy those photos from the Kempei Tei photographers. I have seen a number of almost identical collections of the tiny square photos so it must have been lucrative.

I could have spent many more hours reading Richard Phillips' diaries. Not only had his notes answered many of my own questions about the POWs' existence in Keijo, but I had been made to feel so welcome by the Phillips. As I was packing to leave, Doug handed me the sketch of my father.

Meanwhile my search continued to link me with other offspring. We shared our memories and our research and I was interested to see the close bonds that developed among those of us with similar stories. Not so different probably from any group with shared experiences, but comforting nevertheless. There also seemed to be a particularly strong link between some of the women, an 'inexplicable affinity' was how one of them described it. I was surprised too by the general honesty and openness about quite personal incidents — as though it was 'all in the family'. Indeed, the 'POW family' is a common theme in this collection.

One of my most significant meetings during my decade of discovery was with Joan Kwek. I had met her in 1995 when I was busy on another project. I hadn't yet met the veterans then and hadn't really started to think about my father. Joan's father Hugh was an ex-POW and Joan's enthusiasm was infectious. She was determined to find information about my father and she would contact me with snippets of information or names of veterans who might have known him.

As mentioned in the introduction to Joan's story, her fascinating account of her research, 'Honto ni honto ni setsunai ne', became the starting point for this collection. I felt that story should be shared more widely, but so should many of the other stories I'd heard. Could they be written down so others could share them? I didn't know if anyone would be prepared to write about their lives but I kept asking if they would. It is one thing to share experiences during a telephone call or within a social setting and quite another to commit them to paper. To their credit, a number of people have done so.

Meanwhile in Canberra, Sigs veteran Harry Fletcher provided me with more details of my father's personality. Harry is over ninety now. He was sent from Changi to the shipyards in Japan but he knew my father in the early days of the Sigs unit at Bathurst in New South Wales. Strangely I was in Bathurst when I heard another story about my father. I met a contemporary of Harry's, also a Sigs veteran, who was interested to know whether I had heard about my father's nickname. He revealed that because of my father's height he was called 'Pull' by some of the men in the unit. Apparently it was from the expression 'pull through'. I was relieved to be told that it is the long thin piece of string that is pulled through the barrel of a rifle to clean it. It probably suited him — he was always tall and thin. I remember my mother saying he weighed about 6 stone (40 kilograms) when he was liberated in 1945. But I do wonder whether he knew they called him that.

My father didn't die of war-related causes; nor, as far as I know, did he suffer from any post-traumatic stress. I don't know whether — like these other men — he was warned he would die at fifty (he didn't even live that long) or if he was told he would probably be infertile. (Thank goodness he wasn't.) But I do wonder now whether he achieved any of his prison camp dreams during those too few post-war years. Maybe he didn't dream, I will never know. In *Australians under Nippon*, one former prisoner is quoted as saying 'that if all the men who had talked about poultry farms had actually started them, Australia would have sunk under the weight of chooks'.[8] We had a lovely big old bluestone home in the Adelaide foothills, with plenty of room for chooks but we didn't have them. Claire Woods did. I've just discovered that her father Stan Woods was a good friend of my father. They grew up in nearby country towns and presumably stayed in touch with each other after the war. The strange thing is that I didn't know this when Claire, Angie Gunn and I were at school together. I never knew that Angie Gunn's father was a medico on the Burma railroad and Angie says she never realised I didn't have a father. What did we all talk about at school? As Di Elliott asks repeatedly in her story: Why didn't we discuss these things? Why didn't we know?

Now, so many years afterwards, it is difficult to explain why I left it so late to look for my father. But quite simply, he was not part of our lives. As small children we were so sensitive to our mother's distress that we packed him away, and we deserted him.

I can never know what our lives would have been like if my father had survived but I've often wondered about it. I like to think that he would have continued on like so many of the other ex-POWs, making the best he could of his life. I feel there's a clue at the beginning of his Boxing Day letter to his brother:

> *Fortunately for me I missed most of the experiences that have made headline news in the papers. Most of the chaps concerned in those were not lucky enough to get home. Maybe my luck was out when I joined the Army instead of staying where I might have been able to be of some use to the war effort, but after that one slip my luck held extremely well and I have no complaints!*[9]

I have no complaints either. Of course I wish I'd really known my father — I'd love to have grown up with him by my side. But now he's no longer a stranger.

I've been told that when my father died 'it was as though a light had gone out in the Fawcett family'. I can't turn the light on again but from where I am now, I don't think it's quite as dark as it was. Everyone has a different story of the impact of their father's POW experiences on their lives. This is mine.

Part of the Larger POW Family

RON GILCHRIST

Lance Corporal Stanley Robert (Bob) Gilchrist (VX47839)
2/10th Ordnance Field Park, AIF
POW: Changi; Burma-Thailand Railway; various camps in Indochina

Bob Gilchrist was born on 28 July 1903 at Donald in Victoria. He worked as a farmer, drover and road contractor before he enlisted in the AIF in June 1940. He married Sheila Gellert from Willaura in Victoria in June 1941. In January 1942 Bob left Australia for Singapore and one month later he was a POW in Changi. Sheila and Bob's first child was born in June 1942, just after he went with A Force to Burma.

The POWs worked first in southern Burma, levelling the ground for airfields, and then by September were moved up to Thanbyuzayat and organised into work parties to construct the Burma-Thailand Railway. The line was completed in October 1943 and Bob was among those returned to Singapore. In February 1945 he was shipped to Saigon in Indochina where he worked on the docks and at a nearby aerodrome before being taken up the Saigon River to a camp in a rubber plantation near Bien Hoa. For the next two months, between bouts of illness, he worked on an airfield in Bien Hoa. On 25 April Bob was taken north to the mountains at Dran (near Da Lat) and marched into a new camp at Lien Khang where he spent time working on the construction of an aerodrome before being selected to herd cattle. At the beginning of August he was part of a small group of Australians ordered to accompany a group of British POWs up the Mekong River to Phnom Penh in Cambodia. The Japanese surrendered while he was in Cambodia and the men were returned to Saigon. Bob was liberated in Saigon and on 21 September 1945 he flew to Bangkok on a Dakota aircraft. He returned to his wife and daughter in Australia in October 1945.

In 1946, the Gilchrist family moved to Gippsland in Victoria and Bob retrained as a carpenter with the State Electricity Commission power complex at Yallourn. He built his own home at Newborough and he and Sheila had three more children. In 1968 they retired to Seaford near Melbourne, where Sheila still lives. Bob died on 3 May 1980.

Our father's state of health determined how our family operated. My earliest recollections of the early to mid-1950s are of an awareness of his health. He suffered heavy bouts of malaria, perhaps triggered by the cold, wet working conditions of central Gippsland. Other associated 'POW illnesses' involved regular train trips to the 'Repat' at Heidelberg for hospital care and check-ups. Despite an improvement in his health, we were always conscious of the fact that something might happen to him at any time. As country children we enjoyed a great deal of freedom: the only real restriction on our activities was that our parents wanted to know where we going, 'just in case something happened to Dad'.

My father was one of the older members of his unit: he was thirty-seven when he enlisted. Before the war he had actively played sport. Sadly this interest could not be undertaken after the war as his health did not allow it. Despite the presence of four active young children, he seemed to have lost the energy to play with them or to closely follow them in their various sporting activities.

In 1965 Dad developed an unusual growth on the inside of his leg. A casual word with a local doctor brought to light the fact that the diary he maintained through much of his time on the railway recorded a knock to this leg following a fall through the roof of an *atap* (bamboo and palm leaf) hut in Thailand. The Repatriation Department accepted the view that the knock most likely started the growth along its twenty-two-year journey. However, during further contact with the new Department of Veterans' Affairs (DVA) in the early 1970s they were not so forthcoming. As he approached his seventieth birthday, my father increasingly began to suffer health problems most commonly associated with the long-term effects of malnutrition, malaria, beri-beri, and so on. Under family pressure, he sought an increase in his meagre service pension. My father was devastated when DVA rejected his application. His concern, as I vividly recall, was not for himself, but rather that he would not be able to adequately provide for our mother should something happen to him. Years later, upon checking aspects of his death certificate and relating these to DVA papers concerning their acceptance of our mother as a 'war widow', I was struck by the similarity of reasons given for his death and the initial submission to DVA in the early 1970s. The sense of callousness on the part of government and bureaucracy has stayed with me to this day.

Our family life

Dad met and married our mother — who was fifteen years younger — after a brief romance. They were married in June 1941 and my father was posted overseas in January 1942. My eldest sister Lilian was born in June 1942 at a time when Dad was 'Posted Missing, Believed Dead'. He didn't become aware of his daughter's existence until late 1944 when he received the

BOB WITH HIS FOUR CHILDREN (LEFT TO RIGHT)
JOHN, HEATHER, RON AND LILIAN, C. 1954

photograph of my mother and sister. He carried that original photo for the remainder of his captivity and for many years after. However, adjusting to a 'new wife' and a three and a half-year-old daughter on his return took some time. Always the favourite with Dad, our eldest sister Lilian did have to endure a stricter upbringing than the three of us who followed her. We all received gentle guidance in the values that our parents held, namely honesty, hard work and participation within your own community.

My father purchased several blocks of land with the backpay he received from the Army. In later years these were sold off to assist with our education. Dad valued education and understood the possibilities that it offered to us. I sense some of this came about as a result of the people he had met and listened to in the various POW camps. Struggling through the Depression and the subsequent years of captivity had given him survival skills. He wanted his children to move beyond that point.

The POW experience

Dad was a strong supporter of the POW Association and the work they attempted on behalf of all ex-POWs. He always wore his membership badge proudly. *Barbed Wire and Bamboo*, the journal of the Ex-POWs Association of Australia, was a constant in our home throughout my childhood. Through its pages I came to know many of the characters of the 8th Division, their units and the events that shaped their experiences. I attended the annual POW Association Christmas party at Keast Park, Seaford, until I was a teenager. It was probably one of the few times that my father had an opportunity to enjoy the company of some former members of his unit. He rarely attended Anzac Day services and, although a member of the RSL (Returned and Services League), he did not participate in or like the political nature of the organisation. The war had blunted him to the whims and pursuits of those seeking public office.

A highlight for our family was the annual 'Test' cricket match between the Chillingsworth and Gilchrist families fought out in the backyard of the Chillingsworth home at Mordialloc in Victoria. Mr Chillingsworth was an even older member of the unit. He had survived German captivity in France in World War I and later migrated to Australia from the UK. He and my father teamed up early during the war, possibly for sanity, as many members of that unit were quite young. Dad lost his closest mates, Frank Watson and Ron Hankinson, when they were sent on separate work parties from Singapore. Both later perished, one at Sandakan, the other on the Sandakan-Ranau death march in 1945. I was named after these two fine friends.

In Thailand Dad met and teamed up with an English soldier from Pontefract, Yorkshire. Our family had migrated from Pontefract in the 1850s and thus mutual acquaintances existed. After the war my parents sponsored various families from Pontefract to our district. Unfortunately, my father's mate was not among this group: his wife was reluctant to leave Yorkshire. We did, however, receive the delights of tins of Pontefract liquorice for some years after the war.

During the 1950s large numbers of migrants, many of them displaced persons from central Europe, were directed to the power complex at Yallourn. My parents were active and generous in supporting these 'New Australians' as this large group came to terms with a new language, customs and laws. I believe that my father saw the need to help these people based on his POW experience. He understood that helping and mateship were the keys to survival, whether in Burma or Victoria. Similarly, my parents were involved in a large range of community groups as their new community established itself from bushland in the late 1940s and early 1950s.

Because of the Depression and his POW captivity, my father and his subsequent family were frugal. Little was wasted and wanton wastage was not tolerated. Recycling of most items, whether clothing, building material or furniture, was the norm. One task I had as a youngster was to pull nails from timber and straighten them on a short piece of railway iron for re-use on one of numerous projects underway. For this I was paid one shilling per large tin. To this day I am still using various building items such as nails and bolts accumulated by Dad well over thirty-five years ago. Our father also maintained a large vegetable garden and orchard. By necessity much of our food came from this source. Surplus food was given away to neighbours.

Dad did not tell his four children much about his camp experiences. Like most ex-POWs his stories were generally about humorous incidents. Only occasionally did they take on a more serious tone. He did, however, talk to his older brother, a World War I veteran with two years' front-line service in France. I have strong memories of listening to the two men talk, seated around the open fire on the farm at Watchem in Victoria during the early 1960s. Stories moved between the battlefields of France to Dad's struggles in the jungle of Burma-Thailand. These occasions seemed special to my father as it was perhaps one of few opportunities for him to talk with someone who had undergone similar, prolonged contact with 'an enemy'. They were not morbid discussions as neither of the men dwelt on the past.

Other POW influences permeated our young lives. At an early age I was exposed to the works of Rohan Rivett, Betty Jeffrey and the powerful influences of Lord Liverpool's account of Japanese atrocities. Our father was very disappointed when the film, *Bridge on the River Kwai*, was released. He felt the scriptwriters lost a valuable opportunity to show the cultural and historical aspects of Japanese contempt for prisoners. The manner by which the film portrayed the 'heroics' of defying the Japanese appalled Dad. He said simply that the bashing or worse was not worth the risk. The guards, both Japanese and Korean, were volatile on a good day, without provoking them to mayhem. The manner in which the Australian character 'aka Chips Rafferty style' was portrayed did not appeal to him. It was too forced. More importantly, he felt that the 'gung-ho' antics in blowing up the bridge sadly detracted from the real story, that of building the railway, the real heroics of survival, the huge losses and the single-mindedness of their captors in completing the task at all costs. To him, the films about ex-POWs' Europe were presented far more positively.

Rice was a regular part of our diet. My father never seemed to grow tired of this staple, whether as main course or as dessert. As to how other families in our community, other than those from the Dutch East Indies, regarded rice I am unsure. I suspect it was more common in our household than in many others.

Essentially Dad thought military matters and war were 'a mug's game'. His captivity seemed to harden him to the posturing of politicians and vocal individuals. His post-war experience appeared to reinforce this view. He was not blind to world affairs; he read keenly, particularly historical material, and listened to the world news with interest. At the age of thirteen I sought permission to join the local air cadet unit. My father discouraged such notions. He believed that the nature of modern conflict would ensure that air personnel would be the first to be involved. To this was added the advice that the military were often inexpediently used and therefore it was best to be well out of the way.

In the late 1960s I became involved in draft resistance as the Vietnam War and the issue of conscription came to the fore in Australian social and political life. Dad was concerned about the stance I took. The prospect of his son in jail was not encouraging. More importantly, he felt that it would most likely damage my future prospects for employment, particularly with government bodies. I believe he supported the view I took on Vietnam and was sceptical of the value of conscription in relation to the Army.

The conflict in Vietnam did trigger many memories of his time as a prisoner. Dad was working on the airfield at Bien Hoa in Vietnam early in 1945. He was impressed by the colonial beauty of Saigon. The elegant boulevards and public buildings stayed in his memory for a long time. The Vietnamese people treated the newly released POWs with kindness and humility. Perhaps the most treasured item he returned home with was a small sketch of a Vietnamese woman purchased in the markets of Saigon. The sketch remained in our parents' living room for the rest of his life and has been passed on to my eldest sister.

In 1973 I announced that I was planning to visit Japan for six weeks. Dad was initially taken aback by the proposal. He was not vindictive or bitter towards the Japanese, however, he did still fear them as an economic threat to Australia. He believed the Japanese who lectured them in the camps when they said the war was of long duration, well beyond the current campaigns. On my return from Japan we spoke at length about many aspects of Japanese society. Dad was interested and surprised by many of the topics we discussed. Like many other ex-POWs, my father did not hate the Japanese. On a number of occasions he said that such feelings and energy could not be wasted. At some stage he had realised that hatred deflected from survival and so he chose to win this particular struggle and return home.

At the end, my father suffered a massive heart attack. For the family this was really the first indication of any heart trouble that Dad had displayed. His captivity had finally caught up with him. True to his character, Dad endured four to five hours of extreme pain rather than wake his wife, who had not been sleeping well and needed a rest, and call for medical assistance.

Postscript

In 1982 I was employed as an archivist at the War Memorial in Canberra working with Private Papers. Over the next thirteen and a half years I had the great fortune to work closely with ex-POWs from various theatres of war. The work was often of a very personal nature, intensely intimate and moving. I attended a number of national reunions as part of my work and this encouraged further contact and close friendships. Our task was to develop the national collection and to display the material. To this end we were ably supported by the ex-POWs and their families. Significantly, I worked for twelve of those years alongside a War Memorial volunteer who was an ex-POW of the Japanese. This man's knowledge and care undoubtedly enhanced the work of the national collection.[1]

The vital strength of the former prisoners of the Japanese is their strong sense of belonging to a large family and the depth of their care for one another. Working at the Memorial over this time seemed in part a natural extension of my earlier life. Our immediate family simply became part of the larger POW family.

A Loving, Caring Father

PAULINE MORGAN

Signalman Hilton 'Tod' George Morgan (NX35367)
8th Division Signals, AIF
POW: Changi; Fukuoka No. 26

Hilton's army mates knew him as 'Tod' but to his family he was always Hilton, something that, according to Pauline, has caused some confusion on the occasions when the two groups have been together.

Hilton George Morgan was born on a small farm and orchard at Boorowa, in south-western New South Wales, in 1918. He left school at fifteen and worked as a carpenter's apprentice before being employed on the land. He enlisted in the 2nd AIF on 19 June 1940. Coincidentally Pauline's father had enlisted at

Boorowa just eighteen days before his future son-in-law. But Hilton was twenty-three years old and unmarried when he went to Malaya with J Section, 8th Division Signals, in February 1941. In Malaya, his section was attached to 22nd Brigade Headquarters at Port Dickson, and later in Mersing on the east coast. When the Allied forces were forced back to Singapore Island at the end of January 1942, Tod's section was based in the north-west of the island. Early in the morning of 11 February a Japanese force attacked 22nd Brigade Headquarters on Reformatory Road:

> *It was touch and go for the HQ, but a counter-attack hastily organised by the Brigade Major and carried out by members of 22nd Brigade H.Q. and our J Section saved the situation. L/Cpl 'Bobbie' [sic] Hook and L/Sgt Geoff Bingham were both severely wounded when they, with a handful of signalmen, attacked and destroyed a Jap machine-gun post which was firing right in the H.Q. area. Hook subsequently died of wounds. Geoff Bingham was later awarded the MM (Military Medal).[1]*

And according to J Section veteran, Signalman Harry Fletcher, Tod Morgan should have been awarded a Victoria Cross for his bravery in rescuing the two severely wounded men in that action.[2] Neither Bobby nor Geoff could be rescued immediately but Tod returned to them as soon as he could, despite the continuing fire from the Japanese on the ridge. Unable to move Geoff on his own, Tod brought others to help and Geoff was rescued and taken to hospital. Then, while he was constantly under fire from Japanese bullets and protected only by the table drain, Tod crawled to his other wounded friend. Bobby was able to climb on to Tod's back and they began the return trip. According to Harry, Tod found it so difficult to crawl that he stood up with Bobby on his back and ran to safety.[3]

Bobby was put into a vehicle and driven away to the Alexandra Hospital but the two friends never met again. Bobby was apparently among the patients attacked by Japanese soldiers when they pursued Indian troops through the hospital grounds and entered the hospital on 14 February. Incensed that the Indians were firing at them, the Japanese bayoneted some of the staff and patients, including a patient on the operating table. Tod's other friend Geoff Bingham was more fortunate. He was admitted to the improvised Gillman Barracks Hospital a few hundred yards away from the Alexandra Barracks Hospital and avoided the massacre.

In March 1999, fifty-seven years after he was rescued, Geoff heard that Tod had died. He wrote a letter to Russ Ewin, editor of *Vic Eddy*, the official journal of the 8th Division Signals Association:

Tod was always my idea of a quiet and very strong person. He had a chin which told you so. It seemed to me he had no time for nonsense although he had tons of fun in him. One of the first short stories I had published in The Bulletin *was when we returned to Australia and I called one of the characters 'Morgan Tods'.*

I have never met Tod since we parted in Changi in the early days and he went north... Tod was an intrepid soldier... he had come back into Japanese territory to pick me up after I had received a burst of machine gunfire so that I was helpless.

He brought some other men with him and... they carried me to a vehicle, which was apparently an ambulance. It had four Indians badly wounded and screaming with pain, and I had more or less to be placed on top of them... But for him I would have died on Reformatory Road. I had lost enough blood to certify me medically dead. Being alive at 80 is certainly because Tod rescued me.[4]

But Tod believed that his life too had been saved during the last frenetic days of the fighting in Singapore. He believed that he owed his life to Fred Howe, Di and Pauline's father. According to Di, he was in the communication lines giving instructions about where to move next when her father, the signal sergeant of the 2/19th Battalion, heard his instructions and ordered him not to proceed, saying that they had just seen the Japanese massing there in force. Tod claimed that this saved his life and so, when both men returned home in 1945, they became good friends. They became even closer when Fred gave his blessing to his daughter's engagement to his friend.

In her story of her father, Di Elliott has mentioned her brother-in-law's initial antagonism to her request for information about her father's POW experiences. Pauline has no recollection of that; her only memory is that after Di started to research their father's wartime experiences Hilton started to speak, for the first time, about some of his own experiences. Pauline also remembers how proud he was of all that Di achieved in her research and that he thought she should receive some recognition for all the families that she had helped.[5]

Although this is a story about Pauline's husband, it is very much linked with her story of her father. Pauline is the only person I have met during my research, who was both daughter and wife of a former POW.

My parents, in particular my dad, had no objections to me marrying an ex-POW in 1950. When he returned to Australia in 1945, Hilton had no inclination to resume his former lifestyle, even though he was returning to his mother, brothers and sisters. From then until we married at the end of 1950, he tried his hand at several occupations but found it very hard to stay with them for any length of time. Maybe it was because he was now free from incarceration and could come and go as he pleased. He spent a lot of time in the company of his fellow ex-POWs and even worked with some of them. He resented being ordered about and preferred to work for himself or where he could be left to his own devices. This must have resulted from the standover tactics of the Japanese and the humiliation of that.

On the night of the surrender of Singapore, Hilton had heard a rumour that there was talk of capitulation, so he approached a sergeant and asked him. The sergeant denied it. The next morning when the capitulation

PAULINE AND HILTON'S WEDDING DAY, DECEMBER 1950

was announced, his blind rage was uncontrollable: he had no intention of becoming a POW. Had he been told the truth the night before, his intention was to escape and fight his way out. Before he was killed, he would take a few of the enemy with him. In Australia he had made a promise to his father that he would never be taken prisoner. His father died in August 1944 so Hilton never got the chance to see him again.

When he returned to Australia he made a vow, as the plane crossed the coastline at Townsville, that he would never leave Australia again.[6] A few years ago he was very tempted to go on a pilgrimage to Changi but his health was not good and he decided against it.

From the time we were married until he died, Hilton suffered from nightmares, which always involved the Japanese. He also suffered from a lung condition, a legacy of his time in Japan. It meant a lot of hospitalisation and a lot of time lost from work. When he was fifty-nine he had a coronary and he had to retire, but he tried to enjoy retirement as best he could.

It took many years before he would talk freely about all the atrocities he had witnessed. He told me that when POWs first came home they wouldn't talk very much because they were sure people wouldn't believe them anyway. Not long before Hilton died, he told me that for years he had carried a dreadful guilt about giving a wrong map reading. He thought he had been responsible for shells falling short on his own lines. He eventually discovered that it wasn't true, but it had been an awful burden for him. So who knows what goes on in the minds of ex-servicemen and women? Perhaps even guilt because they survived and their mates didn't?

Hilton was very opposed to Australia being drawn into the Korean and Vietnam wars. He maintained they were civil wars and other countries should not be involved. He threatened to shoot whichever government minister was responsible if our son was called up to fight in Vietnam. Fortunately the Australian troops were withdrawn before our son was eligible for conscription.

We hadn't realised our town was so pro-Japanese when we moved here. At one stage, there was talk of a 'sound and light' show depicting the Japanese breakout. It was going to cost a lot of money and my husband became very irate about this. He even wrote a letter to one of the proponents and suggested they should show a film on the Sandakan death marches as well. Luckily the show didn't eventuate. 'Forgive and forget' was never on Hilton's agenda. Although some POWs were able to do this, I don't think the majority did.

Anzac Days were special for Hilton, particularly the dawn service. He had such admiration for World War I servicemen, even from a young age. He attended other memorial services but they were not as important to him. He used to explain that the dawn hours were specific in most battles. He was always very quiet if he watched Anzac Day services on television. He also loved the pomp and ceremony of Army parades. We attended the Beating of the Retreat ceremony at Duntroon Military College in 1998 and he enjoyed every minute of that.

In the early years of our marriage, the death of a friend did not seem to upset him and he seemed to be able to control his feelings but, as he grew older, he became more and more emotional. Our youngest daughter had an unsuccessful heart/lung transplant at the age of thirty-eight and we knew we were going to lose her. Hilton visited her in Sydney until the week before her death but couldn't stay any longer and returned home. He said he'd seen many men die when POWs, but one of his own family was more than he could handle. He knew both her husband and I would be with her. He was totally devastated afterwards, and probably felt guilty as well. I'd often find him sitting outside just staring into space.

Hilton was a fiercely patriotic man and he very much admired people who battled all sorts of adversities and came up smiling. He hated to see anything happen to hurt a child. He was a loving, caring father and had a great relationship with our three children.

His favourite relaxation was fishing in the western rivers of New South Wales where he could get away from the cares of the world and his health always seemed to improve in the warm, dry areas.

Hilton lost his battle for life on 10 February 1999 after a seven-week struggle in hospital: he had developed all sorts of problems after a routine operation. He was buried on 15 February, the fifty-seventh anniversary of the fall of Singapore. One of his friends sent flowers with a message: 'On the loss of our mate'. Those few words conveyed what the whole family felt.

Eulogy for John Arthur Waterford (18.2.20–13.9.95)

JACK WATERFORD

NAA B883 NX40436

Private John Arthur Waterford (NX40436)
2/18th Battalion, AIF
POW: Changi; Blakang Mati; Burma-Thailand Railway

John Waterford turned twenty-two the day the Allied POWs were marched into confinement in Selarang Barracks at Changi. During his imprisonment he was sent first in work parties on Singapore Island and in Johore province in Malaya and then in May 1943, he went with H Force to the Burma-Thai Railway. On the railway John and eleven others were separated from the main party and put to work clearing an area for huts for the Japanese headquarters of H Force. Although they all succumbed to either acute malaria or dengue fever, his group was fortunate to miss the horrors of the Konyu camp where most of H Force had been sent and nearly 40 per cent of the men died. In November 1943 the survivors of H Force were returned to Singapore.

Thirty years after the end of World War II, John Waterford wrote and published an account of his POW experiences, *Footprints: A Member of the 8th Division AIF Recalls His Years as a Prisoner-of-War and Examines the Issues of Australian–Japanese Relations Today*. His book was translated into Japanese, and begins with the phrase 'I never fired a shot at the enemy'.

Like many POW accounts, John's book dwelt mainly on ordinary camp life, the songs they sang and the mateship that flourished in adversity. He was particularly admiring of two men he encountered: an Australian doctor, Kevin Fagan, and Lionel Marsden, a priest who went to work in Japan after the end of the war.

I had very little personal experience of real brutality and if I had, I would not want to highlight it, or revive old hatreds. In Australia we have a Statute of Limitations, which says that no person can be taken before the courts for debts incurred more than seven years before.[1]

And for the Korean guards who were renowned for their cruelty?

Their country had been overrun and ruled by the Japanese some years before and they had been conscripted into the Japanese Army, although with no rank and very little status.[2]

In his description of the conditions he and eleven others suffered during their work building huts for the Japanese headquarters of H Force, he notes rather wryly that they all slept under old tarpaulins and that the Japanese guards also had only a tarpaulin — albeit a better one than the POWs.[3]

John's son Jack observed that, like so many returned POWs, his father didn't talk about his experiences.

We all knew he'd been a POW, of course, but he didn't talk about it when we were kids. He was a grazier (left school at twelve) though he was well read. But in his forties he began having back problems and knocking up quickly; he was eventually diagnosed as having multiple sclerosis. I was away at boarding school at the time, but the family moved to Sydney (there were eight of us, then aged fifteen [me] to about four). I kept going back to the property etc and was in any event well established in what I was; but most of my sibs came quickly to regard themselves as city kids and the younger ones have scarcely a recollection either of growing up in the far west or of my father as a strong and active man, in control of his life.

But the illness, if physically debilitating, was in many respects a godsend. My mother, who had had a brilliant matriculation pass (2H4A) but had not been able to go to university, went to uni. The family was in Glebe and quickly met up with a wide array of Push, Sydney uni, lefty arty types, and our house was always full of them or rellies from the country and good conversation. The family's politics went from very conservative to left; my father became very involved with a host of activist movements on third-world development etc etc. And as he became somewhat more physically dependent, he devised various forms of therapy for himself, not least in becoming a dedicated family historian (which involved innumerable correspondences with hundreds of rellies from all over) and wrote his own reminiscences about the war — really the first I had heard of it in any personal detail though I knew it as history, and knew quite a few of my dad's old mates — some of whom, as it happened were in Canberra, where I then was. The platoon in which my father had been, kept in touch; its sergeant, Frank Adams, was chief House of Reps attendant, and two other brothers, Bruce and Neil Davis, had come to live in Canberra. (My dad's brother, Bill, who became a grazier out at Lightning Ridge, was also in the platoon: indeed three of my father's brothers and one sister served overseas, although only Dad and Bill were in the Eighth Div and became POWs. All got back.)

So far as experience as kids is concerned, there's a question in my mind about how much things were affected by my father's experiences as a child, and as a POW, and how much it was by his illness. By the time of his illness, his personality was well formed, of course. By then, I had in any event more or less left home. But my sibs, I think, suffered, if rather more from the frustrations of his disabilities than from his nature.[4]

Jack's father had also approached the question of the possible effects of war service:

In the army we often heard fellows say 'The war made me a thief' or 'a drunk' or something else but the general consensus of opinion seems to be that the war brought out the best or the worst in men but it did not make them what they are.[5]

Jack wrote the following eulogy for his father's funeral in Sydney on 18 September 1995.

I would like to thank you all, on behalf of the immediate Waterford family, for coming here today to say with us farewell to, and to celebrate the life of a good and a gentle man.

I could paint you a picture — indeed I will sketch in a few of its elements in a minute — of a man who faced much tragedy and bad luck in his life. I could say his personality and history were purely responses to those troubles and end up, in effect, arguing his life as one of fighting fate and triumphing over adversity. It would be a false picture. In most respects my father took life as he found it, and even if he was not always passive and resigned, he did not waste his time cursing his luck or trying to change it. He was always himself in spite of any misfortune — indeed some misfortune strengthened him — and if there is some triumph in his life it is not of his overcoming fate but of accepting it yet remaining in charge of his life and his affairs to the end of his days.

There are some strong features of him to which I wish to point. He had a deep and abiding faith, a strong and very personal spiritual life and a very firm belief that the exercise of that faith was something which should be shown practically with charity in the world. He showed it himself with many things, including active involvement in church affairs and the St Vincent de Paul Society, while he was practically able. Long after he was not physically able he remained closely involved in and interested in the community and the world and how it might be made a better place.

That commitment was learnt from his childhood and growing up with his family. With his father Will, his mother Gwen, his stepmother Ivy, and his brothers and sisters, Hugh, Marie, Len, Bill, Evelyn, Gwen, Bede and Paula, in the wider families and cousinages in which he grew up and into which he married, and, of course, the family he had with my mother Nan.

Family was very important to him too. He took great pride in all of its achievements. With his own children his visions were not of being notable or important but of achieving our potential, helping people and being happy; and that was true in the wider clan too. He drew enormous pleasure and satisfaction from the practical success which others made of their lives.

With Marie, he was to become an important chronicler and recorder of the clan, at the most mundane level of its births and deaths and marriages, at a level far more important to him of the stories of their lives, their triumphs and their disappointments. It was no exercise in snobbery, designed to prove us former Kings of Ireland or something but a belief in every person's 'worthwhileness', whoever they were or whatever they were doing, an effort to keep strong ties based on common histories, and a desire that we knew and respected who we were and where we came from.

It was an interest he took up, in particular, after it became more difficult to move about and see his wider family at gatherings such as this, our funerals, or weddings and our baptisms — the times these days when the remoter branches are most in touch. The correspondences and the visitors it brought him, of course, meant that he was not left out; indeed that he was often better linked than those of us much more mobile.

The third point which I would underline is his engagement with the wider world. As a young man, living in the country and not terribly well educated in any formal sense — it is only now at seventy-five that he is going to university[6] — the interest had been nurtured by people such as his father, who was closely interested in Catholic social philosophy and had views on most things. It was widened by the university of life at Changi and on the Burma Railroad where one cannot help thinking of good and evil and how things might be better, and it was further strengthened by his marriage to my mother and her own interest in the world, and by reading and by involvement with groups, such as Action for World Development and others, which worked hard to improve understanding between different people.

There was also, always, a large movement of interesting people through our house and opportunities for discussion and honing one's arguments with them, and, of course, as he became more constrained by his body, it could still be nurtured by the excellence of current affairs and other programs on radio and television. All of his children are, in quite different ways, in active engagement with the world, and he was keenly interested in and proud of what they were doing. He used all of his children too as eyes on the world, even when, sometimes, he did not always agree, certainly in my case, entirely with our prognoses. In my case, if there was disagreement, it was because he always had a far more optimistic and idealistic view of the perfectibility of man and was less inclined to be cynical.

My last letter from him which arrived on Friday, two days after his death, was entirely typical; he was arguing that I, and my newspaper, should take a far closer interest in what BHP was doing at Ok Tedi in Papua New Guinea, in both people and environmental terms. He had written me of this earlier and, when last I saw him, I had pooh poohed a part of what he said, but here he was returning to the same point with some fresh evidence. Scores of letters over the years tell not only of family affairs but his views and reflections on Aboriginal matters, on Japan, on Africa, on foreign trade and a hundred other things.

He was, as I say, a good man, and all of his instincts were decent ones. He scarcely said a condemnatory word of anyone in his life. He had a great belief in the human spirit and in the essential goodness of others. He lived, for nearly half his life, inside a body, which increasingly enchained and restricted him, but with good humour and with a free spirit which, if anything, mostly prospered from adversity.

My father influenced a good many people, though he was not by nature or by disposition a leader, and he was not always self-confident or assertive in public. But he was no mere follower. And he had independence of mind, guts and determination, and hope.

John Waterford was only a small and not always well child when his mother died suddenly when he was about five — a quite devastating blow for him. He grew up in a large and loving family with a strong and dominant father, a man of high ideals, deep religion and wisdom, which he impressed upon his children. The family had music and song — how well I remember my father's singing, if not a patch on Bill's, when I was a young child. I must say that any capacity at this proved not to be genetic.

But it was also a hard, and in many respects, a lonely childhood, one which built his self-reliance and which made him private and close too. This was not only because of his frailty and his mother's death, but because the Depression, and its effect on the family's income, robbed him of anything other than the most basic education before he was taken from school and put to work on a farm where he was mostly by himself.

The farm was owned by a businessman friend of his father's who left the property each day to go to work in the town, about 10 miles away. Dad lived on the farm, working the sheep and the cattle, and also clearing and cropping the land in days before the tractor, with a team of horses and a plough. It was hard, often very physical work, with a lot of time by himself, during which he was consciously learning the habits and skills of work on the land and thinking of how he might do things better if it were his place and he had any money. Each weekend, he would saddle a horse and ride back to his family house in Quirindi.

He was, by his own account, a fairly immature twenty-year-old when the war in Europe suddenly got hot and he felt compelled to enlist. So did two of his older brothers, Bill and Len. They began in the same unit until Len, on getting married, found himself posted to another group on his return from leave. At age twenty-one, Dad was on the *Queen Mary* with Bill on the way to Malaya, and impressing some with an ability both to take photographs and to develop them; he soon had a little sideline business on this account. On his twenty-second birthday, he was marching into Changi Jail in Singapore, a part of the Singapore capitulation that saw nearly 90,000 men go into captivity. More than 30,000, including 8000 of the Australians, were not alive to walk out three and a half years later. Those who did survive had a very high mortality later; my father was in the last 10 per cent of survivors.

Dad had a slight wound from a bullet after getting caught in an ambush just before the surrender. As a POW, he was first at Changi, then was sent in a work party to Blakang Mati from which he was evacuated with appendicitis — he told once of hearing the orderlies discuss operations at Changi sheerly in terms of races with each other. Then he was sent to Thailand to work on the infamous Burma Railroad. There were heroic tales told, including by my father, of those times, but he did not see himself to be particularly heroic.

His book about it describes the grace of men under pressure and a struggle for survival that was very real, perhaps the more so when the real enemy of life was not the vile working conditions including a diet that reduced his weight by about half, or the brutality and indifference to suffering of the Japanese guards, but disease such as cholera, dysentery, beri-beri, dengue fever and tropical ulcers and, sometimes, diseases of apathy and exhaustion which simply wore men's spirit away.

To survive was by itself some triumph. Many of his comrades did not. Few of those who died had the relatively clean death that some find in action so much as the wearing away of the body and the corrosion of the spirit from inadequate food, appalling conditions and brutality and tropical disease. Dad survived, in major part, he would say, because he had good mates and because he had faith. For a long time he spoke very little, at least to us as children, of what had happened. It was not for nearly thirty years that he put pen to paper to talk about it.

His book is a good one, simply told, and very much in his own words, most quite self-effacing. It shows a frank admiration for his comrades and for the guts and leadership of a few individuals, and brought into the story something others who had told their stories missed, such as the songs the prisoners sang, and some of the good humour in the most appalling conditions. But what is most striking of it is a complete lack of hatred or malice towards those who were responsible for the deaths and the misery, the brutality and the disease and the malnutrition, and the sheer bloody indifference to the suffering.

And in that too was much faith and forgiveness — and all of his life, he spoke of men such as Lionel Marsden and Tony Glynn, who were inspired by what happened not to anger or revenge but to change the circumstances which had made what happened possible. In his book, he tells of Lionel Marsden, the chaplain, telling the men of his decision to go to Japan as a missionary after the war:

> While trudging to the next camp after his own, carrying his mass gear, he had been stopped by a Japanese officer. This officer had stood him to attention at the top of a deep cutting, even after viewing his pass in Japanese that said he was a Catholic priest. He then kicked Father Marsden roughly down the cutting and walked away without bothering to see if he was hurt. Father Marsden came out of the cutting shaken and bruised but otherwise unhurt, with a

deep burning anger against the officer and all that he stood for. This
continued, he said, for some hours and he felt the anger burning
him up. He then felt ashamed of himself. He had always preached
love and tolerance but now he was feeling like this. He sank down
to his knees, he said, and begged God's forgiveness, and vowed that
if he got back to Australia, he would lead a mission to Japan.

That story tells something of my father's own response to adversity
and of how his own faith and hope were strengthened by it.

After the war, he came back to Australia, to a new community,
because his family had moved during the war. He and his brothers —
another brother Hugh along with his sister Marie had seen war service —
drew a soldier settlement block on Mimosa, on the Coonamble–Quambone
Road. He met and wooed my mother, Nan, and they built a house on their
portion, Wombalano. My older sister, Claire was born, then me, then Sally,
Mary, Chanel, Gerard, Paul and Michele, eight children in all, in what were
on the whole, goodish days on the land, if somewhat circumscribed by the
size of the property, something which led Mum and Dad, in 1963, to sell up
and go for a bigger block at Goodooga.

Those goodish times were, however, percolated by another great
tragedy, the death by drowning, in 1956, of my sister Claire. That shocked
and grieved him more than he could ever tell: by personality or his history
my father was tight with his emotions.

But there were happy times too. For me, perhaps, the 1950s and the
early 1960s at Quambone are the ones I remember best with my family, for
afterwards I went off to boarding school and did not live so intensely in the
family. At Quambone there was ready wider family and we shared and
enjoyed their pleasures too, linked not only by blood and soil but also by the
church.

I remember fortnightly masses at the Quambone Church. In those
days of fasts, people brought sandwiches and billies, and we spent hours
after church breakfasting and making tea, talking about everything under
the sun including of course most of the intelligence interchange about the
business of grazing sheep. My father would flog the *Catholic Weekly* and
take about the plate, and sometimes, later, would go up to the Aboriginal
mission where, in a way I did not then know much about, he was fussed
about the water supply.

I remember well as a young boy planting with my father the trees

Back: CLAIRE, JOHN AND JACK *Front:* MARY, CHANEL AND SALLY, c. 1955

that are still about the church, and for a period, coming into Quambone every other day with him to water the trees with buckets. Many years later when I was at Quambone, at least a dozen people pointed them out to me as his trees. And I remember his simple pleasure when I told him about it. He would be quite comfortable at those being one of his monuments, the way that people remember him and one of the ways they draw him to mind.

In fact, he was very keen on trees. He grew trees — particularly kurrajongs — from seeds and planted them about his paddocks. He had an eye for contours and watercourses, and he sought to protect them. He raised a fine orchard and we grew many of our own vegetables, and he was a careful and a good breeder of cattle.

I remember times of going mustering with him. I think suddenly of the day we saw some emu eggs, and, having lost our wheat bag saddle blankets with a just broken-in tetchy horse, my father stowing about five of the eggs in his shirt. The horse reared while he was bending forward to open a gate, and the eggs, as we soon became aware, were rotten. I remember his steady work burr-cutting, and lamb-marking, and delving bore drains, and of us children being gathered up, usually on the trailer of the tractor to go down to the yards to draft sheep. I remember his pattern of getting up in the morning, of his cutting firewood and building a fire and of the kids rising to huddle in front of it, of going with him to milk the cows, and of the rituals, involving the younger children of making the porridge. I remember too how, apart from the porridge, he was a bloody awful cook and how insulted he was when I told him once, while mother was away in hospital having a baby, how he did not know how to cook rice.

Some of my younger siblings do not have the strong and developed memories I have of him as an active and healthy man. No paragon of strength, perhaps, but someone who could build a fence, work sheep all day, who could, or would sing, who liked an argument and who was more than conscientious in his attention to his religion, his family and his community.

With some of his brothers he played an important local role in very early days in trying to break down prejudice against Aborigines. I read only recently proofs of a book which pays tribute to him and to Bede for their role in a very tense struggle involving not a little courage and which attracted national publicity, in getting housing for Aborigines inside the township of Coonamble — a part of a process by which, to this day, that town now has a far better record of achievement and reconciliation than many of the neighbouring towns.

Dad played his roles in local political groups — in those days on the conservative side of politics though he always had an open mind — and he was a good neighbour and friend to many people.

In 1963 he and my mother decided to strike out for bigger country and we bought a property at Goodooga. There are no regrets about this, but they proved to be tough times, particularly with the elements.

Goodooga was harder country and with much more to do, not the least of which, virtually from the start, was husbanding the country through a very severe drought. And this was when he began to become visibly affected by the disease which he carried for half of his life. In fact there had been indications of it up to a decade before, and at first the debilitation was not obvious; progressively it became more so, and the family moved to Sydney.

In one respect his body was now holding him down; in another, it was for him, and I think for my mother too, a time of new energy. The culture of the family and the bush — though very much a part of us — was in many respects far more circumscribed. In Sydney my father met new ideas, new people and new friends. He welcomed them as eagerly as his old ones. Many of his ideas and not a few of his passions flowered. Progressively, his politics became of the left, sometimes, I must say, well to the left of me. From a stream of people through his house, and from the close attention that he paid, particularly as he became more frail and slowly lost close control over his limbs, to politics and current affairs from television and the radio, those ideas became ones he wanted to see achieved. He wrote letters to politicians. His letters to me are full of comment about the news of the world, particularly about conditions in Third World countries, and about Aboriginal affairs. They show a steady idealism and belief in progress, and not a little bullying or challenge of others to do their bit. He also began to write, in part, I think, as a form of therapy devised with his sister Marie — family history, of his father and his mother, and of their ancestors — a task which involved him in some considerable correspondence, his reminiscences of the war, much of the drafts of which were pecked away on a device some of you may remember called a typewriter; he confined himself to capital letters, but also, as much for himself, spiritual and devotional reflections. One could track the deterioration of his body in letters over a period until a time when he could not even type any more, but that same timescale shows no deterioration in his energy or his mind. Much later he had close friends, such as Marie and his cousin Sheilah, who helped him with his correspondence and I thank them for their help and their kindnesses.

About fifteen years ago his physical condition was such that he was a logical candidate for a nursing home. But he had no interest in dying in one and ample confidence in his capacity to organise affairs to let him carry on. He arranged home-care nursing and a household of people who shared with him on the basis of helping him out. He was helped by a procession of visitors, family and friends who helped him with things he could not do and whose warmth and generosity were at the basis of his dignity, his sunny spirit and general good humour.

We thank all of our family and friends, and the community nurses and others, who helped him, not as I say, to overcome his disease but to live a life as he pleased in spite of it.

And that struggle was, of course, a success. Not only did he succeed in dying in his own home, but also his release when it came was swift and without pain. We thank too the Sydney Casino, which marked, virtually to the moment, his spirit going soaring with a tremendous display of sky-rockets and laser lights.

Dad had dignity, ideas, ideals and values and he had a warm humanity, which brought joy, friendship and charity into the world. We ask you all after this service which celebrates his life, rather than mourns his death, to join with us at Balmain to raise a glass and exchange a story to honour his life and his contribution to the world.

The Traces Left

CLAIRE WOODS

Captain Stanley Stuart Woods, MC (VX63973)
Officer Commanding 2/10th Ordnance Field Park, AIF
POW: Changi; Sandakan/Kuching

On 4/10/17 at ZONNEBEKE, this young officer found himself in Command of 'C' Company, all his senior officers having become casualties.

Single handed he led his Company throughout the operations from 4th to 9th October, and by his skill and determination, inspired the men with confidence.

His leadership was of a high order, and his cheerfulness and courage was beyond all praise.[1]

Second Lieutenant Stanley Stuart Woods, 27th Battalion, 1st AIF, was twenty-four when he won his Military Cross (MC) during World War I. He had fought first at Gallipoli and then on the Western Front.

Stan remained in the Citizen Military Forces (CMF) on the Reserve Officers list after he returned to Australia in 1918 and was called up for full-time duty at the beginning of World War II. He manoeuvred to get himself a transfer and an active command in the AIF. Although already over the age when he could be sent overseas, he was transferred to the AIF and seconded to the Australian Army Ordnance Corps (AAOC) in November 1941.

While he was at Broadmeadows army camp in 1941, Stan (by now forty-seven) met his wife-to-be, Belinda Skeat, a member of the Australian Army Nursing Service (AANS) with the 2/13th AGH. They were both posted to Singapore but Belinda (who was twenty-seven) was evacuated with the other Army nurses just three days before the Allied surrender at Singapore. On 12 February 1942, she and twenty-nine other Australian (together with sixty British) Army nurses boarded the *Empire Star*[2] and returned to Australia.

In July 1942 Stan Woods went to Sandakan with B Force, remaining there until October 1943, when, with most of the officers, he was moved to Kuching after the underground network was betrayed. In October 1945 Stan returned to Australia on the *Wanganella* with the other officers from Kuching. He and Belinda were married in January 1947 in Melbourne.

At home in Adelaide Stan returned to his job in the South Australian State Audit Department and later moved into the Hospitals Department. He continued to look after the Kuching B Force and E Force Officers Nominal Roll until his death in 1982. His eldest daughter Claire remembers the many hours he spent consulting the roll to help his ex-POW colleagues substantiate their medical claims. Claire is planning to organise a published edition of the 'Kuching Officers Nominal Roll' and is keen to pursue research she has begun on other aspects of the Kuching POW experience. In 2003 she visited Gallipoli and

the Western Front to see where her father had fought during
World War I.

Poems for My Father

1
My Father
had the habit
of jangling his spare change
like worry beads in his pockets
as if, despite his still presence,
there was within
an impatience with an ordinary life
concealed.

After
his slow dying,
I wanted to capture his voice but
I couldn't
Yet, I hear the sound of coins,
a tinny jangle
touching memory ...

2
(considering his youth spent on the battlefields of World War I,
Gallipoli and the Western Front, France and Flanders)

Poppies
being fragile dancers on the wind's breath
fall
face down
in French fields;
and make
each year,

immensely sad meditations
in memory
of mud, duckboards, lice,
splinters of lives, khaki scraps
of young men
and the essential loneliness
of each death.

Two poems open this story about Stanley Stuart Woods.[3] They seem, on re-reading, to capture something that seems important to me as a child, a daughter, of a man called to be a soldier in two world wars. In these poems I attempted to say something of the stillness, the calm that accompanied my father as he went about his daily life. There was a dignity, a quiet certainty and authority in the way he held himself and related to others. The poems reflect not only my sense of my father but also my contemplation of how it was he lived an ordinary life: as father, husband, friend to many, colleague and for such a long time the mainstay of the returned soldiers of his original battalion and a key link for many of the POWs with whom he shared so many years in Changi, Sandakan and Kuching. He had experienced war at its most horrific in three theatres of conflict. Four, if you consider that being a POW in a Japanese prison camp was also a theatre of war. He had endured, in 1914–18, first Gallipoli, and then the sodden fields, stench and horror of bombardment on the Western Front. And, in 1939–45 the Malayan campaign, the final days of fighting and the surrender in Singapore, and then POW servitude.

The World War I experience clearly formed Stan as a person, as a man and as a leader. How could it not? Indeed, he claimed that in the final days in Singapore as he showed untrained recruits, newly disembarked, how to load and fire their rifles, he had not lost a man in the close fighting as he dug in 'around the Toorak of Singapore' because his experience in the trenches in World War I had stood him in good stead. While I write here about life with a man who had been a POW, it is impossible to ignore World War I. He had been under fire in appalling conditions at Anzac Cove in 1915, where he was eventually invalided off and nearly died from para-enteric typhoid. He had been so ill that he was shipped home instead of being sent on to France with the rest of the battalion. He would not have been expected to return to the Army. Yet, within five weeks, he signed on again with the 12th reinforcements 27th Battalion, eventually seeing slaughter and despair on the Somme, in battles such as Bullecourt and Villers Bretonneux, and in Flanders, the third battle of Ypres, at Polygon Wood, Zonnebeke and Broodseinde. Here, he won a Military Cross. Then this young–old man of twenty-four came home to civilian life in the country towns of South Australia, to life as a clerk who educated himself at night school to become an accountant, working as an audit inspector for the State government. These were the peaceful years, despite the Depression, between the wars.

Come World War II, he was called up, as since his discharge in 1919 he had been on the Reserve of Officers in the CMF. He sought overseas and active service despite his age. I can only consider this as evidence of his sense of duty, his sense of responsibility as an Australian. He was forty-seven when he arrived in Singapore in November 1941. When he returned home in October 1945, he was described in the local press as 'the oldest combat officer in the camp', the camp being Lintang Barracks in Kuching, west Borneo (now Sarawak). He was fifty-one.

The woman who had waited for him, my mother Belinda, was twenty years younger. She too had known the full horror of the war as an Army

'THE WOMAN WHO WAITED' — BELINDA SKEAT (AANS)

nurse evacuated from Singapore two days before it fell. She was one of the handful of nurses who arrived home safely after being bombed and strafed in Singapore and on the way through to Batavia (now Jakarta) in the *Empire Star*. She knew war and its effects, its traumas and brutality at first hand. Her closest friends, the nursing sisters, had been drowned, massacred at Bangka Island and had suffered in the Palembang POW camp in Sumatra. Her twenties, those years when we find out who we are and really create our adult selves, had been spent as a nurse in the slums of Melbourne in the Depression, in rural Australia and then in Malaya and Singapore, under fire.

Two years after the end of the war, I entered their lives as a post-war child. The detail I have offered is necessary as the backdrop to life for the child of the war. For this is what I, and many of my friends, are: children of the war, because the war shaped our parents in ways unspoken, and thus our lives. My parents did not speak often of this time, even between themselves, in our hearing. But these wars were a presence, an indefinable trace in the lives of my sister and brothers. How could they not be since our parents had spent their young lives (and Father his middle years also) at war? They understood each other's experience. Both had grown up as young adults thrust into the maw of combat and all its horror, although twenty years apart. Both had been in Singapore and shared the Malayan campaign. More than this, the POW experience was the defining time in their relationship. Not knowing where the other was, or whether he or she were alive; not having any means of communication and wondering over almost four years whether they would ever see each other again, yet being sustained by the heartfelt sense of the presence of the other, gave them an intangible force as a couple.

Thus, they started life as returned service people, in suburbia, first in a single room at his sister's house, and then in the early 1950s in a newly built house on a block of land in the middle of just-cleared wheat fields in what was then a new housing area, east of Adelaide. Here they worked hard to establish the block, with fruit trees and roses, and the chook yard under the fig tree in the backyard — my father's prison camp dreams made real at last. For the children it was a simple uncluttered life in 1950s and 1960s Australia, as Stan and Belinda just 'got on' with life. The door of the war, to outward appearances, was closed behind them. They did not need to speak of it, but the war and their experience was simply *there*.

We grew up with Anzac Day as the most important day in the year.

I can count for each of my birthdays after age six, the Anzac Days when I was roused before light, shivered in the dark in my Brownie uniform with my knees shuddering at the dawn service, watched and waved at the Anzac March, and stood silent for the Last Post. I do so today and it would be impossible for me not to. I am moved by the hymns at the dawn service, the music of the bands during the parade, the silence and stillness of the final moments of the service at the Cross of Sacrifice.

My parents shared the world of the POWs. They understood each other. They understood their friends. When Mother's nursing friends visited, we knew who among them had been POWs. We knew how important the POW reunions were; the meetings of the Old Sandakians; the contact with Legacy and the widows and their children. We knew their importance, not because they were spoken about, but because the activities that surrounded them were threads in their and thus our lives.

When I turned thirteen my mother gave me a copy of *While History Passed* by Elizabeth Simons, her close friend. Elizabeth Simons and Betty Jeffrey (*White Coolies*) wrote their accounts of the torpedoing of the *Vyner Brooke*, the Bangka Island massacre, and the Palembang POW camp, from which only twenty-four nurses returned. I read Elizabeth's book many times, and the names of the sisters are as familiar to me as any, so that when Mother referred to Ashton or Oram, I had an image of who these women were. I count Elizabeth's book as one of my treasures. It gave me an insight into my mother's life as a nurse, into her war experience in Singapore, but also into the world of the POW.

I had a greater sense of my father's life as a POW, not because he spoke of it, but because there was an increasing number of books published about the POWs. I read Rohan Rivett's *Beyond Bamboo*, and many other books by civilian and Army POWs, particularly the recollections of men on the Burma-Thai Railway, though never one specifically about the Australian officers in Lintang Camp, Kuching. I read with intensity and emotion, all the autobiographies, the diaries, the reports of POW life I can find. I seem constantly to be searching for what it was that he had to survive, for what he did not speak of except in brief comments, uttered rarely and without rancour. But he did not ever forget, and nor could we, his children, because the POW world impinged on ours. *Barbed Wire and Bamboo*, the journal of the ex-Prisoners of War Association of Australia, arrived regularly in the post. Stan and Belinda joined the Old Sandakians at POW reunions. Of course, as I grew older I read about the Sandakan and Ranau death marches, trying to comprehend such an atrocity. My father commented that if not for the end of the war, after Hiroshima, he and the other officers would have shared the same tragic and inhuman fate as the more than 2000 men at Sandakan.

When not organising or attending some function for the RSL or his beloved 27th Battalion, my father was doing paperwork for the POWs. He had maintained the nominal roll of B and E Force officers from Sandakan in Kuching camp, and carried it home with him; a tattered schoolbook carefully kept, though water-stained and brown with tropical damp and heat. This record of work done on the airfield or elsewhere, and of other activities, but particularly of medical matters, meant that POWs often asked him to verify that they had had dengue, malaria, or tropical ulcers or scabies as they sought war service pensions or TPI (totally and permanently inca-pacitated) entitlements. As children, we were accustomed to the sight of Stan at the dining table, with his brown suitcase and his carefully set stack of cards, papers, envelopes and lists, as he methodically worked at matters to do with his wartime mates. Later, as many of them aged, we would see him suited formally as he set out to attend a funeral or memorial service.

What we knew was that people, friends of our parents, had suffered in what seemed impossible, inhuman ways and under unimaginable condi-tions. We knew that they had been brave, courageous, unflinching in the face of death, disease, starvation, brutality, privation and pain. We knew that our parents were with us — survivors — calm, steady, seemingly un-complicated people who fed us, bathed us, dressed us, took us to the library, to the beach, to Sunday School and church, played cards with us in front of the fire on Sunday afternoons, worked in the garden, and tended the chick-ens and the fruit trees in the backyard as we played nearby. Shielding us from all that they had suffered, they went about daily life and created the normality of suburban safety and peace. But the traces remained and remain with their children still.

I cannot speak for my siblings, apart from knowing of their intense interest in aspects of the events of the war and of course of Stan and Belinda's experience. For me, the trace is ever present. Not only in the writing and research in which I am currently engaged, but also in the way I view the world and set about my daily life — such a mundane one in comparison with theirs.

As I write, the newspapers of the day have published obituaries for the late Keith Miller, ex-fighter pilot and then cricketer and member of

Don Bradman's 1948 Invincibles. Miller was asked once about the pressure of playing cricket and he responded to the effect that it was nothing compared to having a Messerschmitt bearing down on you guns blazing. (I think he might have said 'with a Messerschmitt up your arse'.) Such a seemingly flippant, even lighthearted, response is telling in its comment on sport, civilian pursuits and ordinary activities in light of the extremes of war. In the same way, when as children do, we would whine 'I'm hungry Dad', my father, after offering various suggestions, which in the manner of children we would decline, would say very gently, 'If you don't know what you want, then you are not hungry'. Sometimes he might add, 'You don't know what hunger is. If you were hungry you would eat it'. And of course he knew what it was to be starving, and to be obsessed with thoughts of food. But his words were neither lecture, nor admonition, simply a wry comment to his well-cared-for children.

More than this, however, there is not a day that passes when I do not in my mind refer to the hardship that my parents, particularly Stan and the other POWs, endured. I use the memory of this as a way of setting myself to rights when a moment of tension, fatigue, anger, and personal anxiety or some other physical or emotional difficulty or challenge befalls me. If this seems either a grandiose claim, or a melodramatic position to take, then I plead guilty as charged, for there is nothing in my life that comes close to the trauma that they experienced and which they survived with their humour, compassion and humanity intact. One can talk of 'putting things in perspective', a cliché indeed. Yet, a conflict at work, a physical pain, a temporary setback, the pressure of professional life, means nothing when I think of finding the mental, emotional and physical fortitude to exist as a soldier, nurse or POW. And then to return to ordinary civilian life.

I cannot walk into their shoes. I cannot imagine with any sense of reality what such existence might have been. Only they who have been there can understand. Yet, that they were there and survived and could build their lives and ours has meant something. And this is what I believe should be remembered. For this reason, Belinda spent many of her later years speaking at local community clubs about the experience of the war. She felt it was her duty to keep the POWs' memory alive.

Stan died in 1982, Belinda in 2000. They left behind their letters and cards. And Stan left the tattered documents he had somehow hidden from the prison guards, and a short typed autobiography, written when he was in his eighties. It was more than two years after Belinda's death before I could bring myself to intrude by reading these shards of their lives. The 1941 sepia photograph of them, both in uniform, striding down a Singapore street, arms linked, Stan upright, Belinda slightly turned to smile at him, greets me every day. They did not know then what was to befall them in the years that Stan wrote of as 'The Silence'; they were content with each other, happy to be alive, newly in love. They survived, never giving up hope that the other was somewhere in the world and alive.

My inheritance is their story. My commitment is to do what Belinda set out to do; to keep the story of the POWs alive. If I have learnt anything as a child of the war, a daughter of a POW, it is to have burning in me the desire to write about their story and to have a core of empathy for those who found the personal fortitude to endure when so much must have seemed lost. Stan worked all his life to support his mates, the returned soldiers and their families. Belinda recounted the POWs' story to her community, firmly believing that we have a duty to remember and to help our children understand what it means to be human, and to endure with courage and to care for others. I am embarked on a project to tell their story. The traces left cannot be denied.

THE CAMPS

1 Any POWs still alive at Ranau in August 1945 were executed by the Japanese.
2 Fran de Groen and Helen Masterman-Smith, 'Prisoners on Parade: Japan Party "B"'. Australian War Memorial 2002 History Conference — Remembering 1942.
3 ibid.
4 Hank Nelson, *Prisoners of War: Australians under Nippon*, Australian Broadcasting Commission, Sydney, 1985, p. 77.

MY FATHER'S DIARY: CAROL COOPER

1 The differing survival rates between the British and Australians in F Force are reflected in the statistics. Sixty-one per cent of the British POWs died. Lloyd Cahill, an Australian doctor who worked at Sonkurai, described the British working on the Burma-Thailand Railway:

> ... many of them had come on the last division to reach Singapore. They were Londoners who'd never been out in the bush or anywhere at all ... They had no idea how to set up a kitchen or set up latrines. Even when they were cremating people they had no idea what to do. There was certainly not the communication between the officers and the men as there was with the Australians ... I think that the officers had no idea. [Nelson, *Prisoners of War*, p. 66.]

2 Church envoy Terry Waite travelled to Beirut in January 1987 to negotiate the release of some hostages held there and became a hostage himself. He was not released until 18 November 1991.
3 Approximately 2000 British (mainly RAF) and Dutch POWs were taken to a camp on Haruku, an island east of Ambon. Around 20 per cent of the POWs died on the island.

CAESAR'S GHOST: ROBYN ARVIER

1 Although the Kuching POWs were continually malnourished and the post-surrender food drops saved many lives, the camp had one of the lowest death rates in Asia.
2 Kang kong has a very high iron content and is a bit like a nasturtium. Chekur Manis is a sweet-tasting, green, leafy vegetable with high levels of vitamins and minerals.
3 A number of the POWs at Kuching were university graduates and all the men were encouraged to study to relieve the boredom. An educational group report describing the diverse courses studied in the camp is in the

AWM collection [AWM 54 52/6/2].

4   Information supplied by Robyn Arvier.

IF ONLY I HAD UNDERSTOOD: DI ELLIOTT

1   The articles appeared in the *Boorowa News*, December 1948–May 1949.

2   Di's brother-in-law was Hilton Morgan, better known to his mates in 8th Division Signals as 'Tod' Morgan. Like Di's father, at the time of his enlistment he came from Boroowa. Hilton believed that Fred Howe had saved his life during the final battles on Singapore Island and, when they returned home, he was good friends with Fred. Their bond became even closer when Di's sister Pauline Howe married Hilton in December 1950.

THE BURDEN AT THE OTHER END: PAULINE MORGAN

1   He later named their house after the *Tamaroa*.

A BLESSING AND A BURDEN: MARGARET GEE

1   The 3000 Australians shipped from Singapore to Burma in A Force also began work on the railway in October 1942.

2   Margaret Gee, *A Long Way from Silver Creek: A family memoir*, Margaret Gee, Double Bay, NSW, 2000, p. 241.

3   op. cit., p. 256.

EVERYONE WAS ON THEIR OWN: ELIZABETH MOORE

1   His biography, *Borneo Surgeon: A reluctant hero*, by Peter Firkins was published by Hesperian Press in 1995.

2   op. cit., p. 66.

3   Japanese military police, infamous for their cruel interrogation techniques.

4   Lionel Matthews and eight other men accused of being involved in the network were sentenced to death.

5   Letter, dated 27 March 2001, from Josephine Metcalf, (nee Lentaigne) to Elizabeth.

6   ibid.

7   Letter, dated 26 July 1941, from Mother Macrae to Mrs Taylor.

8   Letter, dated 20 May 1945, from Elizabeth to her mother.

9   Letter, dated 2 October 1945, from her mother in Labuan to Elizabeth.

10   Letter, dated 22 November 1945, from Elizabeth to her parents.

A SPECIAL CONTRIBUTION: PETER SINFIELD

1   Charles Wagner, the 2/18th intelligence officer, was sent to Sandakan with E Force, but escaped and operated with Filipino guerillas until he was killed in action at Liangan (Mindanao) on 21 December 1943. He is commemorated in the Sai Wan War Cemetery, Hong Kong.

THE OTHER YEARS BETWEEN: SUZETTE BODDINGTON

1 With Peg's permission, a transcript of Alex Johnstone's diary has been placed in the War Memorial [AWM PRO1044].
2 de Groen & Masterman-Smith, 'Prisoners on Parade'.
3 Item NX20572, Series B883 2002, National Archives of Australia, Canberra.
4 Dr Kevin Fagan was one of the medical officers in H Force in Thailand, the same force as John Waterford.
5 At this time, Hayman Island was not yet a popular holiday resort.
6 The nickname for the commuter train which runs between the Blue Mountains and Sydney.
7 Ironically, during the mid-1950s Alex underwent a partial spinal sympathectomy at Concord Repatriation Hospital to lessen the pain in his ruined legs. After the operation he could never walk barefoot again.

IN THE FOOTSTEPS OF A HERO: DAVID MATTHEWS

1 Stan Woods was a young lieutenant fighting on the Western Front during World War I when he was awarded a Military Cross for his actions. Both men subsequently went to Borneo with B Force in July 1942.
2 Meeting with David Matthews, July 2004.
3 'In the footsteps of a hero, my dad', *The Advertiser*, 13 March 1999. With permission.
4 'After 58 years, a goodbye to the dad I never knew', *The Advertiser*, 3 April 1999. With permission.

REFLECTIONS: ANGELA GUNN

1 John Moremon, *Australians on the Burma-Thailand Railway 1942–1943*, Department of Veterans' Affairs, Canberra, 2003, p. 70.
2 Nelson, *Prisoners of War*, p. 66. (The British figures were worse: 61 per cent of the 3300 men in F Force died.)

MY HERO: PETER O'DONNELL

1 Jack O'Donnell diary, 8 April 1942.
2 'Happy feet' were very sensitive, burning feet which caused extreme discomfort. It was one of the conditions caused by vitamin deficiencies.
3 O'Donnell, op. cit., 12 May 1943.
4 op. cit., 18 August 1945.
5 An auto-immune condition causing burn-like blistering of the skin and mucous membranes which might have been caused by a staphyloccocal infection.
6 O'Donnell, op. cit., 30 August 1945.
7 Corporal Stella Mary Blood, NF443334.
8 Unfortunately, neither Stella nor Peter have any information about the broom that Jack's diary was reportedly hidden inside.
9 Australia's War 1939-1945 website: <http://www.ww2australia.gov.au>.

HUGH WARING: MY FATHER: DIANA VALLANCE

1   See Joan Kwek's story.

HONTO NI HONTO NI SETSUNAI NE: JOAN KWEK

1   More recently I have read that the ginkgo tree is seen as the 'bearer of hope' by the citizens of Hiroshima. Apparently four of the trees survived the 'A' bomb blast despite being close to the epicentre of the impact.

2   Hayashi Miki, *Senepan ni torawareta shokuminchihei no sakebi*, Miyasaki-gun Sadohara-machi, 1988.

3   Lieutenant E.J. Esler, 8th Division Signals, sailed with B Force on the *Ube Maru* to Sandakan from Changi on 8 July 1942. He was removed from Sandakan with the group of AIF officers who were transferred to Kuching in October 1943 after the discovery of the underground movement at the camp. Post-war, he renewed his language studies in Japanese (and Ancient Greek) at the University of Queensland.

4   *Australian Military Forces — Trial by Military Court — HQ 9 Australian Division 3/2/46. Case 35 — Guard Okabayashi Takemitsu* [AWM 54 101/6/1]

LETTER TO MY FATHER: FRAN DE GROEN

1   de Groen & Masterman-Smith, 'Prisoners on Parade'.

'A BONZA BLOKE ... FOR AN OFFICER': KERIN MOSIERE

1   It was at the end of 1945, nearly five years after Ken Mosher sailed. The tablecloth was 'christened' during their first meal together at their new home in Kogarah in Sydney.

2   Ken loved to fiddle with food colourings and often surprised the family with his colourful recipes.

3   A wok.

4   Named after Colonel Suga, the Japanese officer in charge of POW camps in Borneo. He committed suicide during the War Crimes trials.

5   Lynette Silver, a Sydney author with a great interest in Australian war history, carries the shirt and clogs to speaking engagements.

WHO IS THIS MAN? JOHN 'PADDY' O'BRIEN

1   Communication from John Paddy O'Brien, February 2005.

2   Telephone conversation with Ethnee Brooks, February 2005.

3   Blakang Mati camp held approximately 1000 POWS, including about 600 Australians. From all accounts, conditions there were superior to most of the other camps, with better accommodation, better and more plentiful food, and more generous working conditions. (A.J. Sweeting in Lionel Wigmore, *Australia in the War of 1939–1945: Volume IV, The Japanese Thrust*, Australian War Memorial, Canberra, 1957, p. 519.)

4   Charlie O'Brien's letter, dated 15 October 1945, to his brother Jack.

HUNTER VALLEY HERO: ETHNEE BROOKS

1 'Farewell Captain George McLoughlin', *Scone Advocate*, c. 10 March 1994.
2 *Commonwealth of Australia Gazette*, 6 March 1947, Canberra, p. 760, position 67.
3 Communication with Ethnee Brooks, November 2004.
4 Ethnee's father's ex-POW friends had laid many bets as to which of them would be the first to produce a child after the war. Everyone thought they would be sterile after their years of harsh treatment and starvation, but fortunately most of the men were fine.

LIFE IS FOR GETTING ON WITH: JACQUI HICKSON

1 Russ Ewin's letter is quoted in Robyn Arvier (ed.). *Don't Worry About Me: Wartime Letters of the 8th Division AIF*, R. Arvier, Launceston, Tas., 2004, p. 192.
2 Russ Ewin's letter to his wife Joyce, 28 September 1945, Arvier, op. cit., p. 193.
3 Les sailed for Malaya with 2/10th Ordnance Workshops reinforcements in late January 1942. He was sent to Burma with A Force in May 1942 and was lost at sea in September 1944, when his Japanese transport ship *Rakuyo Maru* was sunk by the American submarine, USS *Sealion*, in the China Sea.
4 When signalling in morse code, V and E (Vic and Eddy) combined are used when first making contact, to indicate 'I have a message for you'. The other party then responds.
5 *Vic Eddy*, vol. 66, June 1996, p. 24.

NO COMPLAINTS: CAROLYN NEWMAN

1 E.K. Fisk, *Hardly Ever a Dull Moment*, Australian National University, Canberra, 1995, p. 46.
2 ibid.
3 J.W. Jacobs, and R.J. Bridgland, (eds). *Through: The Story of Signals 8 Australian Division and Signals AIF Malaya*, 8 Division Signals Association, 1995, p. 48.
4 op. cit., p.156.
5 Australian War Crimes Commission statement by Captain W.D. Fawcett NX70392, 28 August 1946 [AWM 54/101/50].
6 Entry in Richard Phillip's diary, 14 September 1944.
7 War Crimes statement, op. cit.
8 Nelson, *Prisoners of War*, p. 213.
9 Letter, dated 26 December 1945, from Wilf Fawcett to his brother.

PART OF THE LARGER POW FAMILY: RON GILCHRIST

1 Ex-POW Tom Morris (2/19th Battalion) worked as a volunteer at the War Memorial in Canberra until his death in 2004. He thought that he had met

Ron's father at the 55 Kilo camp 'hospital' around 1943. It was Tom Morris that Di Elliott first went to visit to learn more about her father.

A LOVING, CARING FATHER: PAULINE MORGAN

1   J.W. Jacobs and R.J. Bridgeland (eds), *Through: The Story of Signals 8 Australian Division and Signals AIF Malaya*, 8 Division Signals Association, 1995, pp. 120–1.
2   Conversation with Signalman Harry Fletcher, J Section, 8th Division Signals, March 2002.
3   ibid.
4   Letter by Geoff Bingham, *Vic Eddy*, vol. 77, March 1999, p. 15.
5   Telephone conversation with Pauline Morgan, February 2005.
6   According to Pauline, Hilton was too impatient to wait for the official POW recovery team and transport and he 'hitched' a lift from Japan back to Australia in September 1945. He flew first in an American aircraft to New Guinea and then with a New Zealand aircraft to Townsville.

EULOGY FOR JOHN ARTHUR WATERFORD (18.2.20–13.9.95): JACK WATERFORD

1   J.A. Waterford, *Footprints: A Member of the 8th Division AIF Recalls his Years as a Prisoner-of-War and Examines the Issues of Australian-Japanese Relations Today*, J.A. Waterford, Glebe, NSW, 1980, p. 52.
2   op. cit., p. 36.
3   op. cit., p. 37.
4   Communication with Jack Waterford, 23 August 2002.
5   Waterford, op. cit., p. 50.
6   John Waterford willed his body for research purposes to the University of Sydney.

THE TRACES LEFT: CLAIRE WOODS

1   AWM Honours and Awards (Recommendations: First World War) database. File: 1/95P2 — 2nd Australian Division — 1/10/1917 to 10/10/1917, p. 107. [AWM 28 1/95P2].
2   Members of the AANS were evacuated on three ships: the *Empire Star*, the *Wah Sui* and the *Vyner Brook*. The Japanese constantly attacked the *Empire Star*, which took three direct hits, as it sailed south from Singapore, but despite almost 50 male casualties, the *Empire Star* reached Australia. The *Wah Sui* made the trip safely but the Japanese sank the ill-fated *Vyner Brook*, which carried 65 of the Army nurses.
3   'Poems for my Father' were published in *Vintage '99*, a collection of poems and short stories produced by the Penola Festival Committee, Penola, SA, 1999.

References

BOOKS

Arvier, Robyn. *'Caesar's Ghost!': Maurie Arvier's Story of War, Captivity and Survival*, R. Arvier, Launceston, Tas., 2001.

Arvier, Robyn (ed.) *Don't Worry About Me: Wartime Letters of the 8th Division AIF*, R. Arvier, Launceston, Tas., 2004.

Clarke, Hugh V. *A Life for Every Sleeper*, Allen & Unwin, Sydney, 1986.

Firkins, Peter. *Borneo Surgeon: A Reluctant Hero*, Hesperian Press, Carlisle, WA, 1995.

Fisk, E.K. *Hardly Ever a Dull Moment*, Australian National University, Canberra, 1995.

Garton, Stephen. *The Cost of War: Australians Return*, Oxford University Press, South Melbourne, 1996.

Gee, Margaret. *A Long Way from Silver Creek: A Family Memoir*, Margaret Gee, Double Bay, NSW, 2000.

Hayashi Miki, *Senepan ni torawareta shokuminchihei no sakebi*, Miyasaki-gun Sadohara-machi, 1988.

Jacobs, J.W. and Bridgland, R.J. (eds). *Through: The Story of Signals 8 Australian Division and Signals AIF Malaya*, 8 Division Signals Association, 1995.

Jeffrey, Betty. *White Coolies*, Angus & Robertson, Sydney, 1954.

Johnston, Don (with story by George Forbes). *Borneo Burlesque: Comic Tragedy, Tragic Comedy*, Sydney, 1947.

Keith, Agnes. *Three Came Home*, Michael Joseph, London, 1948.

McKernan, Michael. *This War Never Ends*, University of Queensland Press, St Lucia, Qld, 2001.

Milne, David. *POWs in Japanese Camps*, The Jungle Room, East Melbourne, 2002.

Moffitt, Athol. *Project Kingfisher*, Angus & Robertson, Sydney, 1989.

Moremon, John. *Australians on the Burma-Thailand Railway 1942–1943*, Department of Veterans' Affairs, Canberra, 2003.

Nelson, Hank. *Prisoners of War: Australians under Nippon*, Australian Broadcasting Corporation, Sydney, 1985.

Ramsay Silver, Lynette. *Sandakan: A Conspiracy of Silence*, Sally Milner Publishing, Burra Creek, NSW, 1998.

Richardson, Hal. *One-Man War: Story of Jock McLaren*, Angus & Robertson, Sydney, 1957.

Rivett, Rohan. *Behind Bamboo*, Angus & Robertson, Sydney, 1946.

Ross, Sheila. *And Tomorrow Freedom: Australian Guerrillas in the Philippines*, Allen & Unwin, Sydney, 1989.

Russell of Liverpool, Lord. *The Knights of Bushido*, Cassell, London, 1958.

Simons, Jessie Elizabeth. *While History Passed*, Heinemann, Melbourne, 1954.

Smith, Kevin. *Borneo, Australia's Proud but Tragic Heritage*, K.R. Smith, Armidale, NSW, 1999.

Sweeting, A.J. 'Prisoners of the Japanese', in Lionel Wigmore, *Australia in the War of 1939–1945: Volume IV, The Japanese Thrust*, Australian War Memorial, Canberra, 1957.

Uhr, Janet. *Against the Sun: The AIF in Malaya 1941–42*, Allen & Unwin, Sydney, 1998.

Wall, Don. Sandakan *Under Nippon: The Last March*, D. Wall, Mona Vale, NSW, 1988.

Waterford, J.A. *Footprints: A Member of the 8th Division AIF Recalls his Years as a Prisoner-of-War and Examines the Issues of Australian-Japanese Relations Today*, J.A. Waterford, Glebe, NSW, 1980.

JOURNALS AND PAPERS

Barbed Wire and Bamboo, official journal of the Ex-Prisoners of War Association of Australia.

de Groen, Fran and Masterman-Smith, Helen, 'Prisoners on Parade: Japan Party "B"', Australian War Memorial 2002 History Conference — Remembering 1942.

Peters, Betty. 'The Life Experience of Partners of ex-POWs of the Japanese', *Journal of the Australian War Memorial*, Issue 28, April 1996.

Sabretache, Journal of the Military Historical Society of Australia.

Vic Eddy, official journal of the 8th Division Signals Association (NSW).

Contributors

ROBYN ARVIER grew up in Brisbane and graduated as an occupational therapist from the University of Queensland. She has worked in both Australia and the UK but since 1990 has lived and worked in Launceston in Tasmania, where she is completing postgraduate studies in Applied Linguistics. In December 2004 she self-published a collection of wartime letters, *Don't Worry About Me: Wartime Letters of the 8th Division AIF*. If she's not reading or writing about military history, you will usually find her in the garden.

SUZETTE BODDINGTON and her husband John live at Dalton, in the Southern Tablelands of New South Wales. Both are avid readers who love gardening, music, theatre and travelling. After thirty years as an English/Visual Arts teacher, Suzette is now endeavouring to be an artist in her own right and, since coming to Dalton, has had work shown in five exhibitions at the Goulburn Regional Art Gallery. She still does some casual teaching, both at the art gallery and at some of the regional primary schools.

ETHNEE BROOKS is a happily married mother of two wonderful young people, Kate and Matt. She is a trained nurse and midwife and has worked in the health profession for the past forty years. She loves people and social interaction. Her hobbies include acting, horse riding, bushwalking and dancing.

SUE BYRNE, as the only surviving child of Henry Sweet and Maureen Devereaux, was always showered with love. The death of her brother when she was four, which so profoundly changed her family's dynamics, also influenced her career choice to become a registered nurse specialising in paediatrics and obstetrics. Her husband Chris died in 2002. They were very lucky to have two wonderful children Bregitta and Andrew who are now young adults. As Sue's dad would say: 'C'est la vie'.

CAROL COOPER is very involved with Children and Families of the Far East Prisoners of War (COFEPOW); she believes it is essential work, meaningful and very rewarding. But her husband and family always come first, and time with her three grandchildren is even more precious. Travelling, writing and time in the garden complete her life.

FRAN DE GROEN is an associate professor in the Humanities Department of the University of Western Sydney. Her publications include *Xavier Herbert:*

A Biography (1998), and *Xavier Herbert Letters* (2002), co-edited with Laurie Hergenhan. She is currently preparing a book about the experiences of Australian prisoners of war confined in Korea and Manchuria during World War II. Fran has two sons, loves reading, gardening and theatre-going, and plays competition squash. In her spare time she enjoys socialising with friends over a meal and a glass or two of red wine.

DI ELLIOTT married her husband Paul in 1970 and together they have lived in Sydney (she still remembers the embarkation parties when she worked at P&O Cruises), Goulburn, Wagga, Leeton, Coleambally, Wollongong and Hillston. They settled in Canberra with their son and daughter in 1984. Since then, Di has spent every spare moment undertaking voluntary research for innumerable people and organisations.

MARGARET GEE commenced her working life as a journalist with the Melbourne *Age* and then embarked on a career as a book publisher for twenty-three years. For the last six years she has acted as a literary agent for many well-known Australian authors. Margaret is fifty and lives in Sydney with her husband.

RON GILCHRIST was born and educated in Gippsland, Victoria. A keen bushwalker, traveller and archivist, his outdoor pursuits and lifelong interest in history have taken him on extended working holidays overseas. Between 1982 and 1996, Ron was a curator at the Australian War Memorial in Canberra. Now he is pursuing another passion, farming. He and his New Zealand wife Deborah are running a mixed sheep and cropping property in the eastern Riverina area of New South Wales.

ANGELA GUNN completed her BA at Adelaide University and a DipEd at the University of Melbourne, before spending some years teaching in both Australia and the UK. For the last thirty-one years she has lived happily in Melbourne where she and her husband Ben have three adult children. Her passion is voluntary guiding at the National Gallery of Victoria, which she's been doing since 1989.

JACQUI HICKSON graduated with a BA and DipEd, taught for three years, then travelled through Europe for six months with her husband Tony. On their return to Australia, they produced two delightful girls. She became interested in computers and undertook several university and TAFE computing subjects, and now works from home as a volunteer web master for two environmental organisations. When not sitting at the computer she can be found playing tennis, gardening, bushwalking or having lunch with her parents.

JOAN KWEK saw the essence of life in its details. She loved her family, the study of art, design and linguistics and the languages and cultures of China and Japan. She used these skills to research and study her father's POW experiences. Joan died of cancer in 1998, aged forty-six.

DAVID MATTHEWS was educated at King's College (now Pembroke School) in Adelaide and joined *The Advertiser* newspaper as a copy boy in 1956. He remained with the company as a journalist, working in newspapers, radio and television until he retired in 2003. A keen sportsman, he played amateur league football until he was thirty-four; he also played hockey and represented the Army in athletics as a national serviceman. He married in 1961, and has three children. He's since remarried and is thoroughly enjoying retirement in the foothills of Adelaide.

ELIZABETH MOORE met Keith when she was nursing at St Vincent's Hospital in Sydney and he was a resident medical officer. They married in 1954 and during the next eighteen years Keith had practices in the country town of Inverell in northern New South Wales and in Redfern in Sydney. Together they produced six wonderful children. Following Keith's death in 1972, Elizabeth returned to nursing part-time. She is now retired and enjoying her five grandchildren, doing some charity work, playing bridge and researching family history.

PAULINE MORGAN married her husband Hilton in 1950. Together they moved around New South Wales, living in Dubbo, Windsor, Boorowa, Sydney, and finally, Cowra. They had three children — Roberta 'Bobbie', Phillip and Carolyn (deceased). Since Hilton's death in 1999, Pauline has spent a lot of her time researching family and military history.

KERIN MOSIERE has been a music teacher for more than thirty years and has recently qualified as an interior decorator. She has two adult children and a four-year-old Siberian husky. Her hobbies are french polishing, picture framing, op shopping and bargain hunting.

CAROLYN NEWMAN was born in Adelaide and studied at the Australian National University (BA), the University of Sydney (DipEd) and the University of New South Wales (MDefStud). She has a particular interest in the plight of Allied POWs and civilian internees captured by the Japanese and the broader effects of their imprisonment and for the past four years has been contracted to research and write for the Department of Veterans' Affairs website, 'Australia's War 1939–1945'. After years of navy postings, both interstate and overseas, Carolyn and her husband have finally settled in Sydney.

JOHN 'PADDY' O'BRIEN pursued various 'careers', including banana farming and timber felling, before joining the Royal Australian Navy in 1960. His son and daughter were both born while he was working as assistant to the naval attaché in Jakarta. Paddy retired from the RAN with the rank of warrant officer and joined the Department of Defence in Canberra as a civilian until his retirement in 1996. He was widowed in 1998 and remarried in 2003. He and his wife now spend six months each year caravanning around Australia.

PETER O'DONNELL would, if he could, spend every day out on his boat just sitting, fishing and watching the birds and wildlife. He has been teaching for thirty-one years and is one of the few male primary teachers in the New South Wales education system, which he says makes him an 'endangered species'. Like his father, he is a keen sportsman who loves the outdoors but he also finds time for his art, working with pencils and watercolours.

PETER SINFIELD joined the Royal Australian Navy when he was fifteen and a half and saw service in HMA ships *Anzac* and *Sydney* during the Vietnam War. In 1989 he retired from the Navy as a lieutenant commander and is now a public servant. He is married with two children and has lived in Canberra for more than twenty years.

DIANA VALLANCE, like her father, enjoys reading and writing, family life and the environment, travel and existential discourse. She now lives in Rockhampton in Queensland and works as a guidance officer for Education Queensland.

JACK WATERFORD is editor-in-chief of *The Canberra Times*. He has a degree in law from the Australian National University and has been a journalist for thirty-three years. His manias are reading (particularly 17th-century British history, war, colonial government, and colonial Australia) and children (he has four daughters and two grandchildren).

CLAIRE WOODS is currently professor, Communication and Writing, at the University of South Australia, and Director of International Programs, in the School of Communication, Information and Media. She teaches in Singapore, Malaysia and Hong Kong, as well as in Adelaide, but still manages to squeeze in as many kilometres as she can, walking and running to keep fit, in the Adelaide Hills. Of course there is also her husband and family, her writing, her research and her interests in music, theatre and art.

Index